D0340771

# NIGHTSHIFT NYC

# NIGHTSHIFT NYC

RUSSELL LEIGH SHARMAN &
CHERYL HARRIS SHARMAN

PHOTOGRAPHS BY COREY HAYES

UNIVERSITY OF CALIFORNIA PRESS
BERKELEY LOS ANGELES LONDON

University of California Press, one of the most distinguished university presses in the United States, enriches lives around the world by advancing scholarship in the humanities, social sciences, and natural sciences. Its activities are supported by the UC Press Foundation and by philanthropic contributions from individuals and institutions. For more information, visit www.ucpress.edu.

University of California Press
Berkeley and Los Angeles, California

University of California Press, Ltd.
London, England

Library of Congress Cataloging-in-Publication Data

Sharman, Russell Leigh, 1972–
    Nightshift NYC / Russell Leigh Sharman, Cheryl Harris Sharman ; photographs by Corey Hayes.
        p.  cm.
    Includes index.
    ISBN 978-0-520-25271-4 (cloth : alk. paper)
    1. Night work—New York (State)—New York.   2. Night people—New York (State)—New York.   I. Sharman, Cheryl Harris.   II. Title.   III. Title: Nightshift New York City.

HD5113.2.U6S53 2008
331.25'74—dc22

                                        2008014160

Manufactured in the United States of America

17  16  15  14  13  12  11  10  09  08
10  9  8  7  6  5  4  3  2  1

FOR MARION "MAMO" MARYE
"NIGHTY-NIGHT"

This is the face of New York when it's asleep, or as nearly asleep as any city ever is. . . . Do the machines in a factory ever need rest? Does a ship ever feel tired? Or is it only people who are so weary at night? There is a pulse to a city, and it never stops beating.

**THE NAKED CITY, 1948**

I'll take my chances on the nightshift.

**CLIFF, NYC TAXI DRIVER**

# CONTENTS

# PROLOGUE: NIGHTFALL

The most familiar story of New York is of the city as celebrity. From its rough-and-tumble beginnings and early rise to fame to its midlife crises of fiscal failure and recent renaissance, New York City is an archipelago of public fascination. From the soaring heights of the Empire State Building and the Statue of Liberty to the still-gaping wound of the World Trade Center, New York is the city that America consumes as greedily as any public figure, rejoicing in its triumphs, mourning with its losses, and gloating over its failures.

But there is another New York.

After the tour buses disgorge their tourists into the sleek hotels of midtown Manhattan, and after the day-dwellers lock themselves in against an accumulated fear of the night, the city slowly slouches into its own skin, revealing a vulnerability and an occasional mean streak to those who brave its darker side. This is the "other" New York, the city as bleary-eyed insomniac that replaces the manicured tourism of daylight.

At night, the city teems with sympathetic insomniacs scuttling toward islands of light in a diffuse but still living cityscape. By day, the city is populated by citizen tourists who marvel at the occasional native grumbling at the hordes of slow-footed interlopers. But by night, the city is left to those who know it best. They relish the empty sidewalks and streets, relax into the slower pace, and—gasp—talk to one another like old friends in a small town.

There are those who work the nightshift and those who live in the night. Submerging the natural rhythm of human life, workers on the nightshift live in service to the city that refuses to sleep. These are the fry cooks and coffee jockeys, train conductors and cab hacks, the cops, the docs, and the fishmongers selling cod by the crate. These are also most often the immigrant newcomers, the underemployed, and the economically marginalized.

And then there are those who live in the night. These are the tired, the homeless, and the tempest-tossed seeking refuge at Colossus's most vulnerable hour. They are the sleepless patrons, passengers, and patients. They move about under the lamps of bare fluorescence and neon—keeping the restless city company.

New York has been called the city that never sleeps by filmmakers, songwriters, and at least a century's worth of news stories. In 1930, a journalist for the *New York Times* wrote: "By night, New York is a changed city, as different from the New York of daylight as two worlds may be. This nocturnal city never wakes until the lights of Broadway rouse it into activity. Then its denizens and its workers rub sleepy eyes to begin their day's occupations by asking, 'What is the news this evening?' as other men say 'this morning.'"

Edward Hopper captured a version of this nightshift city with startling clarity in his 1942 painting *Nighthawks*. Three patrons sit on stools in an all-night diner while a white-haired, white-jacketed man goes about his nightly labors. Evoking the now familiar noir feeling of this other New York, Hopper captures the alienation of modern urban life through his signature depiction of light and shadow. The fluorescent glow from inside the diner is as harsh as it is welcoming, and the people spaced around the angular counter are isolated, from one another and themselves. They're also trapped, with no visible door to exit the diner. Outside, the city lies in darkness.

More than a half century later, *Nighthawks* still evokes a familiar side of the nightshift, but there is more to the story. What follows is an ethnography of the night. Night passes, marking time between days, but it is not where most of us live. For those who do, the nightshift is more than simply out of phase with the diurnal waking life; it is out of place as well, another social space altogether. The borders of that space are fluid and shifting, in part because of the expansion and contraction of night across the year, in part because of the overlapping shift work required by the global incessant economy. More than simply the study of a particular place, New York City, during a particular number of hours, nightfall to daybreak, this book examines the specific social space of the night: a social space that is highly structured and inherently subversive, as transnational as it is transgressive, and shot through with inequalities of power.

Welcome to a place and people that live only a few hours and a world away.

———————

It's Memorial Day, 2006. Or it was, on Monday. Now it's technically 2 AM on Tuesday, but it's hard to keep track of the days. We're on the corner of 110th Street and Lexington Avenue in East Harlem, just a few blocks from our apartment, watching as a dozen or so Department of Sanitation workers take a break. Though we've been sticking close to a nightshift schedule for a few weeks now, we have not adjusted. We don't know it yet, but in the year to come it will not get any easier. The unnatural hues of artificial light in delis, diners, train stations, and hospitals will sap whatever energy we get from unhealthy doses of caffeine. Eating meals after midnight will leave us sluggish and soft. We won't see many of our friends for weeks at a time, unable to accommodate their dayshift schedules. For now, we are simply tired, but we manage to strike up a conversation.

One of the sanitation workers stands near the Plexiglas night window of Dunkin' Donuts waiting for his hot chocolate. He works midnight to 8, a pretty typical nightshift schedule, but he doesn't drink coffee to stay awake. "This has more caffeine than coffee," he says, pointing to his steaming hot chocolate. He's been "a garbologist," he says, for three years, and still lacks seniority. He's retired, actually, from a day job; he rolled his pension into the Department of Sanitation. "It's a challenge," he admits, "to go from a shirt and tie to manual labor." He could work in a Department of Sanitation garage, he says, "but you make more money collecting."

We stand chatting for a few more minutes while the rest of the sanitation workers gather in loose clusters around the idling trucks across the street. We explain our project, a book on nightshift workers in New York City. Since moving to New York in 1999, we've noticed the hum of life after dark, even in our neighborhood. There's the laundromat down the street that stays open twenty-four hours, mostly so that a small crew of undocumented Mexican women can wash and dry towels from a downtown sports club. And there's an all-night auto repair shop on the next block, run by a tight-knit group of West Africans who service the gypsy cabs driven by their countrymen. There's even a nearby deli, or bodega as they're known in these parts, that leaves a recent Yemeni immigrant locked inside each night to transact business through a small window until dawn.

As newcomers to the city, we experienced these as curiosities, fascinating bits of the New York night. But we were writers and social scientists, and our individual work brought us into contact, quite incidentally, with more and more of those who worked the nightshift. We began to see the contours of a joint project. We would immerse ourselves in the nightshift, participate in and observe a diverse cross section of "after hours" employment. We would explore the motivations and implications of an inverted schedule, and try to experience it firsthand.

A few weeks in, and 2 AM was still a brick wall of fatigue.

The garbologist smiles. He assures us we'll get used to the hours, then hurries back to his truck. His break is over. As the trucks rumble into gear, we descend into the subway and out into the city.

Fifteen million people in the United States work "alternative shifts" in the evenings or nights. In 2004, this accounted for 14.8 percent of the labor force. The majority of these alternative-shift workers work "evening shifts," which the Bureau of Labor Statistics (BLS) delineates as working between the hours of 2 PM and midnight. The BLS classifies nightshift employees as those whose shifts fit somewhere between 9 PM and 8 AM. In 1997, those who regularly worked the nightshift accounted for 3.5 percent of full-time employees. In 2004, 3.2 percent, or four million people, regularly worked overnight. More than half of them work in "protective services" and, depending on the year, about 41 percent work in food services. They tend to be men. They tend to be single. They tend to work alternative shifts because of "the nature of the job." About one-fifth, however, choose these shifts for "personal preferences." Nationally, they tend to be black or African American, followed by Asian, Hispanic or Latino, and then white.

In New York City, according to 2005 American Community Survey data from the U.S. Bureau of the Census, 245,163 workers went to work between 4 PM and 4:59 AM. That's about 7 percent of the city's 3.3 million workers. Reflecting national trends, more men than women worked these alternative shifts, especially shifts beginning after midnight. Since New York is a city of immigrants, and immigrants tend to be overrepresented in low-paying, low-prestige jobs, it is no surprise that many of those found working through the night were born on foreign soil.

What is surprising is how little has been written about nightshift labor. One of the first and most comprehensive works was *Night as Frontier* by the sociologist Murray Melbin, published in 1987. Since then, a few writers have taken up the theme, but by and large social scientists have allowed Melbin to have the last word. Much has changed in the two decades since Melbin's admirable, and prescient, work. The global incessant economy has deepened in complexity, implicating immigrants and native-born alike. Communication technologies have connected that global world in ways never imagined just twenty years ago. Urban crime statistics, at least in New York City, have plummeted, creating a very different nighttime world than that of the 1980s.

In short, Melbin's "frontier" has become a more settled territory lately. As the historical analogy suggests, when frontiers become territories, inequalities and hardships do not simply disappear. There are new hardships to endure and new challenges to overcome, not least because most assume the problems have all been solved.

This may be particularly true of New York City. From the earliest Dutch settlement, New York has had an intimate relationship with the night. Chronicled in the historian Mark Caldwell's *New York Night*, the city's character was forged as much under the cover of darkness as it was in the light of day. When electric lights finally made their appearance at the end of the nineteenth century, there was no stopping the incessance of New York City. And the public's fascination with the New York night is perennial: in the same year as our research there was a retrospective of Hopper's paintings at the Whitney Museum and an exhibit, Transformed by Light, about the effect of lighting technology on the twenty-four-hour city at the Museum of the City of New York.

To explore this prime example of twenty-four-hour commerce, we spent more than a year on the nightshift in New York City, interviewing and shadowing more than a hundred workers at dozens of sites. To get a handle on the variety and scale of nightshift labor, and to gain a sense of how shifts overlap and sometimes compete, we limited potential sites to those that stayed open twenty-four hours. Within each site, we focused exclusively on the nightshift worker, though night tourists, as the journalist Kevin Coyne calls them, passed through frequently enough. We further narrowed our focus to those who worked shifts that straddled two days and to those who have maintained a consistent nightshift schedule. Much of the data on shift work focuses on rotating shifts, where workers may rotate through day and evening shifts, but little research has been conducted on those who, after initial adjustments, stay on the nightshift for years if not decades.

Most of the sites were welcoming, though some of the larger agencies proved inaccessible. The New York Police Department, the Metropolitan Transit Authority, and the Port Authority all refused to cooperate. Where individuals' participation exposed them to reprisals from their employers, or their residency status exposed them to deportation, we used pseudonyms and/or disguised some descriptors to protect them.

Not surprisingly, most of the interviews took place at night. Finding it difficult to interview nightshift workers during the day, we flipped our schedules to match theirs—working nights and sleeping days. Our working together as a married couple seemed to put people at ease at 2 AM; even formal interviews proceeded more like fluid conversations as we were able to play off each other. And with no children, we had little to slow us down in our all-night ramblings. Working together also meant that if one of us was losing steam, the other could get us through to the next site and on to the next interview.

But the key to making the project work was taking our time. With the slower pace of night, we could sit at a diner counter or in a train station for hours, sometimes from dusk to dawn, and then come back again the next night. This consistency allowed us to see the variety of nightshift experience, especially across the span of a year as the night hours expanded and contracted, but it also built rapport with those working the shifts. We quickly found that the nightshift breeds a kind of familiarity among strangers. We rarely came across anyone unwilling to chat about his or her experiences, and almost all those we encountered were willing to sit down for a formal, recorded interview, sometimes for multiple sessions. The slower pace meant that interviews could be gathered on the spot, during a break or after a shift.

For all the advantages, our method had many disadvantages: we overslept for doctor's appointments and were charged anyway; we still had daytime meetings and classes and had to learn how to operate on very little sleep; our cognitive functioning seemed to decrease; we did not know whether to eat at night or only during the day, or when to exercise, and soon gained weight; we saw our friends less often since they worked days, we worked nights, and there was little overlap in our leisure time; and we became ruthless about saying no to extracurricular activities, constantly feeling that any unallocated time was best spent catching up on our sleep.

As any seasoned journalist or ethnographer knows, there are good days and bad days. The fact that we were conducting interviews at night exaggerated both. There were nights we set up dozens of interviews at several sites just to make sure we got one interview, and none of them panned out. And it was snowing. And the trains took us from Manhattan to Brooklyn just to get back to Manhattan. Then there were the nights that a chance meeting led to a long, rambling, gold mine of an interview. One such night, we called a cab driver we'd met months before and found him dropping off a fare right outside on our street.

The net result of all of this labor is presented in the stories that follow. There are some familiar sites, such as diners, delis, and taxicabs, but there are some unexpected corners of the nightshift as well, such as a walking tour of homelessness in Manhattan after dark and the *Brooklyn VI*, a night fishing boat out of Brooklyn. But all of them offer some surprises for those unaccustomed to the nightshift. The chapters are organized around occupation, though some range over several workers while others offer a more intimate portrait of one individual. But like life on the nightshift, there are often only tenuous connections from one occupation or one story to the next. As we moved through the city at night, we passed through distinct nightshift worlds, each one disconnected from the others, insulated by the surrounding darkness. To evoke this often isolating experience of working and moving through the nightshift, we've ordered the chapters so that at times there is an easy flow, and at others there is a jarring change of setting and pace. To complete the effect of recreating our year on the nightshift, we begin and end with two different diners, one block apart in Manhattan, bringing the narrative back to a familiar resting place with a new perspective.

Likewise, there are times when we pull back from the narrative, placing an individual's experience within a broader historical or sociological context. But more often than not, we obey the writer's cardinal rule of "show, don't tell." In these pages there is a palpable sense of urban life, time passing, night presenting an alternative reality to day, simultaneously mediating and reflecting life in a changing city. Sometimes there is an argument to be made; other times the analysis is implied, allowing readers to draw their own conclusions. Like a Hopper painting, there are intentions underlying every aspect of the composition, but we hope readers will immerse themselves here until it makes sense with their own lived experience—to sit with the stories until they feel as though they've been there.

We trust that the text bears witness to how well we work together; we did not divide the labor of analysis or description in the writing because our styles are so strikingly similar. We simply traded drafts back and forth until we agreed that they captured the feel of the people and places we experienced in the research. And although we struggled with whether or not to include ourselves in the narrative, we ultimately decided that ours was merely a taste of life on the nightshift; the men and women who do this night after night deserve the spotlight. This book is not about us; it is about the nightshift workers from Senegal, Burkina Faso, Côte d'Ivoire, Guinea, Greece, Turkey, the West Bank, Yemen, Egypt, Bangladesh, Pakistan, India, Indonesia, Jamaica, Mexico, the Dominican Republic, and, yes, even New York City. Experiencing this brief immersion in the nightshift inspired an immense respect for those who work the other nine-to-five. They get too little sleep, too little time with friends and family, and too little respect for their often demeaning jobs.

In these pages you will find the stories of these most generous of souls who sleep too little and work too much. And in those stories you will find the soul of a city hidden in the graveyard shift of twenty-four-hour commerce, when the sun goes down and the lights come up.

11:09 FILM SET

11:11 EAST RIVER RESCUE TUG

11:21 ALL-NIGHT LAUNDROMAT

12:24 TAXIS ON TENTH AVENUE

# ONE: ONE BIG FAMILY

**S**teve, 27, the night manager at the Skylight Diner, stands behind the counter eyeing a disheveled, middle-aged man smiling into his coffee. It's 3:30 AM on a Thursday and the man has been there since 5 the previous evening.

"Need something?" Steve asks him.

The man giggles and replies, "First, a psychiatrist; second thing, a girl; third thing, a job." The man launches into a story about massage school, and then offers a free massage to Steve. Steve rolls his eyes and turns the channel on the television overhead to a rerun of *Fresh Prince of Bel Air*.

"This is funny," says Steve, pointing up at a young Will Smith. "Watch this."

Steve moves his considerable frame down the length of the counter, putting some distance between himself and his would-be masseur.

The Skylight is almost always busy. That's partly because of its location on 34th Street, a two-way thoroughfare that conveniently links the Copacabana nightclub to Penn Station with the Skylight in between. It also happens to be around the corner from the 35th Precinct of the New York Police Department (NYPD), attracting a steady stream of hungry nightshift police officers. But mostly it's the blue-and-red neon sign framed in stainless steel that beckons patrons at all hours of the night: Open 24 Hrs.

Inside, the Skylight is all gleam and polish. Its Art Deco stylings give it that classic diner aesthetic: black and white tile, stainless steel fixtures, and a menu designed to feel oversized and intimidating in your hands. There is a counter to the left that curves seductively from the entrance to the kitchen, with swivel stools on one side, coffeemaker, shake machine, and pie case on the other. To the right, there are booths for the more leisurely, two rows of black vinyl that extend back to a mirrored wall, creating the comforting illusion that the diner could go on forever.

Large black-and-white photos of New York City in the 1930s and 1940s suggest some connection to the legacy of prewar diners, but something is amiss. The food is satisfyingly familiar—overstuffed sandwiches, burgers, breakfast anytime—but there is a sheen to everything that suggests the Skylight is an overbright redux of the original. In short, it is clean. Too clean.

Steve holds court behind the aquamarine Formica counter. He is an imposing figure, dressed entirely in black, but he moves from customer to customer with surprising grace for a man his size. "I eat once a day, believe it or not," he explains. "One big meal, and then I go to sleep. That's why I'm so big." Steve has managed the Skylight for only a few months, but he's worked in diners as a busboy, waiter, or manager since junior high, almost always on the nightshift.

Two cops push through the front door and Steve gives them a nod. "How ya' been?" he asks them.

"We're really busy out there," one of them says. He settles onto a stool and smiles at the man who is still trying to give Steve a massage. "There's drunk people everywhere."

Steve can relate. As a manager on the nightshift, he has seen a fair number of intoxicated and otherwise rowdy customers. At night, inhibitions are lowered and a wider range of behavior is tolerated. But there is always a limit. He shares a story from his "old diner," where he worked for nine years. It still makes him laugh. "One night," he begins, delivering his lines with the rhythm of a practiced comedian, "I was managing and the busboy comes to me and says, 'You know what, Steve, there's two people in the bathroom having sex.' So I go to the bathroom, I knock on the door, because it was the women's, you know, and I opened up and the guy was with the girl in the stall. You know, they had the door closed. So I said, 'Hey!' and they didn't answer. And you know, you could see the movements. So I kicked the door in, and he was like, 'Whoa, what are you doin'!' 'What am I doing?' I says, 'What are you doing?' He goes to me, 'It's okay, I know John,' he says. He's the manager. I was like, 'I don't give a fuck who you know, pull your fucking pants up.' He was like, 'Come on, I've been coming here for years.' Unbelievable sometimes." Sure enough, tonight, four hours after he says this, Steve finds a teenage couple having sex in the men's room in the Skylight's dank basement.

Steve says that drunk people sometimes tip less, sometimes more. "Depends on the people." He places a paper cup upside down on one of the coffee machine spigots. This is diner code for don't-use-that-spigot, as they have to be cleaned out between batches. "The best," he continues, "are the Irish. They order a cheeseburger and I give them eggs, they eat it, and they leave a five-dollar tip. Greeks too, but they make you work for it, they'll send it back five times. I say that and I'm Greek."

But not all those who come to the Skylight after dark are looking to refuel after the last call at local bars and clubs. Steve knows the rhythm of the nightshift from experience, watching the evening rush spill into the late-night stillness and then back into the hurried pace of early morning. Customers who come in after dark are just as likely to be shift workers on break as late-night revelers. "Night is young people," Steve explains. "Occasionally, you get elderly. But they don't come out too late, like after 2. But then you start getting the morning people, who are going to work."

Diners have long served the overlapping and variable schedules of shift workers—and they have always been associated with the night. Richard J. S. Gutman explains in *American Diner* that the first in New York City opened in 1893. It was a horse-drawn "night lunch wagon" operated by the Church Temperance Society in hopes of drawing business away from bars and their ten-cent meals. For thousands of old-world immigrants, mostly young men, the night lunch wagon was a surrogate for home and a moment's rest. They were so successful they became the charitable beneficiaries of wealthy New Yorkers such as Cornelius Vanderbilt, who endowed a night lunch wagon in Union Square.

By the 1920s, public lighting opened up the city streets to regular late-night commerce and the old night lunch wagons conveniently forgot their altruistic roots. There was too much money to be made. The eateries put down foundations and were dubbed "dining cars," alluding to the railway experience and retaining the idea of meals on the move. Their manufacture and aesthetic became standardized—tethered to the streamlining of American industry throughout the first half of the last century.

Within twenty years, the shortened "diner" would be permanently fixed in the popular romantic imagination. First Edward Hopper and then Hollywood cast the diner as the model setting for urban social interaction, or lack thereof. Both contributed to the image of the diner as the one place where those whose consciences would not let them sleep could be alone, together. What began as a philanthropic outreach to new immigrants became part of a manufactured image of immigrant cities such as New York—dark, dangerous, overcrowded, and yet strangely alienating and lonely.

Today, the diner remains an archetype of urban social space, though it has undergone a series of transformations since the postwar period. Suffering a steep decline in the 1960s with the rise of fast-food chains, the diner was resurrected by Greek immigrants in the 1970s. The Greek influence not only contributed moussaka to the standard menu, it kept the image alive long enough for restaurateurs to see the market for diner nostalgia. By the late 1980s diners like the Skylight were being built to look exactly like the "dining cars" of the 1930s and 1940s.

As a result, New York is home to a varied collection of all-night eateries that fall roughly into the category of "diner." A veritable museum of dinerdom, the city has the early mass-produced "dining car" models, such as the Cheyenne around the corner from the Skylight on Ninth Avenue; the Greek reinterpretations, such as the North Shore Diner in Queens; and the nostalgic recreations such as the Skylight. Together they manifest the continuity of the city feeding its sleepless at all hours, and the collective nostalgia for that "other" New York, historical or imaginary, that was less alienating than today.

"The king is here," Steve mutters under his breath. It's after 4 AM and a guy has just walked in wearing a red and gold crown. His date wears a glimmering tiara. They are quickly followed by a group who say casually that they need seating for twenty-two people. Their waitress, already at work for eight hours, sighs audibly and leads them to the back.

Most weekends in May and June, just about every twenty-four-hour eatery in the area is full of high school students from Long Island and New Jersey partying after the prom. It is not uncommon for groups of prom-goers to rent limousines for the night and come into the "city" for nightclubs like the Copacabana. After 3 AM, the Skylight fills up with boisterous teenagers in wrinkled tuxedos and tight-fitting dresses.

Inevitably, limo drivers follow their charges into the diner and settle down at the counter to wait for the drive back to the suburbs. One such prom night, Louie sits at the counter. He's a retired NYPD officer who now owns a fleet of limousines on Long Island. Though an owner, he says he still likes to drive the cars himself. He does, however, delegate the dayshift to his employees. "I love working at night," he says with a thick Long Island accent. "I do all the nighttime jobs." Louie says this is because it's "quieter at night," meaning less traffic. "And plus," he says, "I get to see my kids during the day. When I get home my kids will be just getting up for school. I make breakfast, see them off to the school bus, go back and lay down until about 3 in the afternoon, and my day starts again. I love the nighttime. I love it."

Louie is an exception to the typical labor arrangement of what Murray Melbin, in *Night as Frontier*, describes as "incessant organizations." Outlining three historical schedules for labor and commerce, Melbin writes that the first, tied to agriculture, had a clear delineation between night and day. The second blurred the lines of morning and evening by requiring some activity before dawn or past sunset. Finally, the third schedule, where industries keep going all the time, is that of "incessance."

Incessant organizations require special solutions to unique problems. This is particularly true in regard to staffing: they must have teams equipped with the right skills for specific functions and they must be replaceable due to high turnover. Thus the need for round-the-clock shift work. This is complicated, however, by status hierarchy and authority. Melbin suggests that since managers want to keep their elite status position without sacrificing their sleep, they assign the nightshift to lower-level employees. One result of this is that if anything goes wrong at night, those with the power to make decisions are often not on site to handle the problem.

Though he owns the business, Louie prefers to work nights. He enjoys the flexibility nightshifts provide, and the time with his family during the day. But his status as the owner is intact: he has the power to choose his shift.

As an employee, Steve also prefers the nightshift, though for different reasons. The lack of oversight provides a certain amount of freedom and just enough responsibility without the burden of actually running the business. His experience is not uncommon; nights often afford opportunities to people who lack education, language skills, or other forms of social capital. This is especially attractive to those who may be socially or politically invisible, by choice or circumstance. These can be immigrants, other minorities, women, or anyone without seniority.

This invisibility creates a bond among those who work nights. Social status markers recede with the daylight. People move more slowly, respond more kindly to strangers. On the nightshift, even in New York City, a man who owns a limo company will take the time to chat with a man who manages a diner. They both seek lucid conversation and both have time to spare.

Louie runs out to the twenty-four-hour florist to buy roses for his wife and returns saying that this is one of his last trips. He is selling most of his fleet and leaving New York, moving to North Carolina next month. He explains how some of his Long Island neighbors discovered a planned community near Charlotte, North Carolina. He figures that he can make twice what he earns in New York and live at half the cost there. After forty years in New York, Louie is selling out: "Really," he says, "I mean, yeah, it's a beautiful city, it never sleeps, it's wonderful. But between the crime, the taxes," he trails off. "If you have any real estate in New York," he says simply, "sell it."

Louie ends his pitch as Steve walks over. "You don't know me, right?" Steve asks Louie. "I could tell you a story right now, and you're gonna call me a moron." Steve tells Louie about his father's cousin, who owns a diner in Maryland but wants to retire in Greece. "Listen," Steve begins, impersonating his father's Greek cousin, "I had a son your age, he died in a car accident a couple of years ago. I've got a daughter, she lives in Atlanta and she doesn't want to bother with a diner. I'll make a deal with you. I'm 72 years old. You come down here, you send me $3,000 a month, and I go to Greece. And the place is yours." Steve waits, leans over the counter for effect, and adds, "But I'm still here."

Louie hesitates a moment, and then obediently cries, "You're a moron!"

Steve smiles and says, "What did I tell you?"

---

It's after midnight at the North Shore Diner in Queens, and Steve is on his second Corona with lime. It's June, and it's hot. It's also baseball season, so Steve wears his Yankees pinstripes tonight—number 25, Giambi—with a pair of baggy jeans. His oversized frame is wedged into a small seat at a four-top table in the center of the pastel dining room, but he could not look more comfortable. Completely at ease, Steve's is a commanding presence in the room.

Dominating the intersection of Northern and Francis Lewis boulevards in Queens, the North Shore is one of only a handful of twenty-four-hour diners in the borough. But it is aptly named: Gutman points out that Long Island was once known as "diner island" for the countless all-night eateries that lined its northern and southern shores. But as with many regions of the Northeast, the old diners could not compete with the fast-food chains that came with increasing urban sprawl. When Greek immigrants breathed new life into the industry in the 1970s, the diner reappeared with a distinctly Mediterranean aesthetic. With its pastel accents and decorative arches, the North Shore is a monument to that influence.

"Greeks do two things," Steve explains. "It's either diners or construction."

A waiter brings Steve another beer. He is short, stocky, Latino. Steve smiles and says, "Thanks, *mi amor.*" He says he picked up Spanish in the diner business. It's his life. He explains, "80 percent of the diners, I know somebody. Even in the city."

The "city" is Manhattan, more than an hour away by bus and subway. And at this time of night, the bus passes only every hour or so. This is Steve's night off from the Skylight, and he is spending it here with old friends. He comes back to visit every now and again, maintaining his connections to the various diners throughout the city.

"It's like a big fraternity," Steve continues. "One person knows the other, and when one person leaves from here they could end up in Manhattan or somewhere else. It's really good money, if you know what you're doing. That's what gets you stuck in this business. That's what got me stuck. I planned on doing this like a year or two."

Steve has worked in a diner since he was 12 years old. His mother, who first emigrated from Greece in the late 1970s, got him started as a busboy at the Lantern Diner in Hempstead on Long Island, where she was a waitress. Five years later, in 1996, he got a job as a waiter at the North Shore. For the next nine years he would wait tables and manage the North Shore Diner, almost always on the nightshift.

"You do this for a year, you'll get used to it," he explains. "When I was working days, I couldn't sleep at night because it was too quiet. I couldn't sleep. I was used to the trucks passing by and my mother talking on the phone, that's what puts me to sleep. Sometimes, when I worked days, I used to sleep with the TV, because I couldn't go to sleep without any noise. I know it sounds crazy, but I guess I got used to it."

At 27, Steve finds it easier to work the nightshift and still have something of a social life, including a girlfriend he met at the North Shore. She is ten years his junior and worked as a hostess on the dayshift. "We've been doing this for two years, so we're used to it. She does her things, I do my things, and we see each other. We talk on the phone all the time. Sometimes I'll go the whole day without sleeping because I spent the day with her." When he was younger, he could string out several days and nights in a row. "I would get off work at 7 in the morning and go have beers until 1 or 2 with guys from here. Go home, shower, and back to work at 5. But I was 17 at the time. If I do that now, I would pass out. When I was 17, though, I could do that for five or six days in a row."

But even Steve admits he has few social connections beyond the diner. "I don't hang out in my neighborhood," he says after he returns from a cigarette break. "I've lived there for seventeen years and the only time I'm there is when I'm sleeping." Not long ago, a coworker from the North Shore passed away. He was 42 years old. "I cried harder at his funeral than I did for my grandmother, my grandfather," explains Steve. "I used to spend sixty hours a week with this guy, and ten hours with my girlfriend. That's why it hit us so hard when he passed away. We're one big family."

That family lives exclusively on the nightshift. Steve makes a clear distinction between those who work during the day and his coworkers at night. "People who work the nights are more easygoing. People who work in the day usually have kids, they're serious." As a night manager at the North Shore, Steve worked a fourteen-hour shift that overlapped with the dayshift for four hours during the dinner rush. For those four hours, Steve says he would hardly speak to his dayshift coworkers. He knew his girlfriend for a year and a half before they even spoke. "She was one of the daytime people," he says with some disdain.

Diners are not the only place where tension exists between dayshift and nightshift employees. Nurses, train conductors, deli owners, and numerous other nightshift workers draw sharp distinctions between dayshift workers and themselves. As Steve says, "This is a secret that nobody talks about, the daytime people don't like the nighttime people, and the nighttime people don't like the daytime people. Any diner you go to, there's like a feud going on. If something goes wrong, and it's daytime, the daytime will automatically blame the nighttime people. Every diner you go to, it's the same way."

Beyond the tensions between dayshift and nightshift workers in the same job, there is also the tension between the dayshift city and those who work at night. From seemingly benign city ordinances about noise levels after dark to more concerted efforts to remove sex workers from the streets, the night has not shaken its image as dark and dangerous, as a place where anything can happen.

Steve's "old diner" is one such place where violence tends to break out at night. They were in the newspaper six times, Steve says, for fights that turned violent. "Manhattan is not as rowdy as they are out here. Out here, I've had fights break out with people who came together." Then he gets on a roll, telling stories about all the fights he's witnessed—and often had to break up—in the diner. "That's why they liked me as a night manager," he says, "because I'm big."

Steve says that the fights are why so many diners have security cameras. "If you're twenty-four hours, you gotta have them." The cameras are there, he explains, "not because of robberies, this place has been robbed once in twenty-five years." The cameras are there for the fights. Steve elaborates: "One night we had a fight with like thirty people. And they broke so many fucking dishes we had to get them on camera to know who they were." It turns out that they were regulars. "Next time they came in, they wound up paying like $800 for all the damage."

Late-night brawls aside, Steve actually prefers dealing with people on the nightshift. "Because in the daytime you got people who are not drunk, but they're old and pains in the ass. They'll send you back ten times if one thing is wrong. Drunks don't give a fuck, whatever you serve them, they'll eat it." Steve has learned a lot about handling the various customers who come to a diner after midnight. This extends, apparently, to an easy generalization of ethnic groups and the individual customers who represent them. "You've gotta have a different way to talk to the blacks, a different way to talk to the Greeks, different way to talk to the Irish, to the Spanish. You learn from experience. I just picked it up along the way."

Steve finishes his beer just as John, the night manager, stops by the table to say hello. He is middle-aged with thinning jet black hair combed straight back. He is slight of frame, dwarfed by Steve, though he carries a compact potbelly. The two chat in Greek for a while as John shows off some photographs of a Greek soccer team that came into the diner not long ago after a local game. John smiles and musters a few words in English, but he is obviously more comfortable in Greek, even after twenty years in New York.

Working the nightshift for the past decade, Steve has fewer opportunities to chat with coworkers in Greek. "Ten years ago it was 90 percent Greek," he explains, "now it's all Spanish. I have no idea where the Greeks went." According to Steve, when his mother started in the business, there were no Latinos working the diners as waiters or cooks. Even as late as 1996, when Steve started at the North Shore, there were four nightshift waiters, all Greek. "Now, there's five waiters at night," says Steve. Then, pointing at a middle-aged waiter who could be John's twin, same slight frame, same thinning, jet black hair combed straight back, "This guy Jimmy, he's the only Greek. And he's the guy that took my spot. So before that, I was the only Greek at night."

On the dayshift, the distinct evolution from Greek to Latino is not as clear. "In the daytime, the cooks are Mexicans, but not the waiters. The waiters are all different. There are some people from Europe." Steve takes another swig from his Corona. "I don't know why, but the last two years there are a lot of Polish girls starting to work in diners." But on the nightshift, Steve witnessed the transformation firsthand and even helped it along. "In this place," he explains, "I taught two Mexicans and a Salvadoran how to be waiters. They were busboys."

According to Steve, most of the nightshift laborers in the kitchens are undocumented Mexican immigrants. And he has witnessed the transience of undocumented migrants as they move back and forth across the border, maintaining economic and social ties in Mexico and New York. Like the economy, the twenty-four-hour diner workforce is in constant flux, requiring a constant supply of labor to keep the doors open. Since the nightshift is often an entry-level job for low-wage workers, it is increasingly staffed by immigrant workers in much the same way unskilled jobs were a century ago. For recent immigrants from Latin America working the nightshift, this is literally another *frontera*, or border, they have to cross. Once they have left behind wives and husbands, fathers and mothers, daughters and sons, and all other reminders of home, it is not much of a stretch to leave behind the familiar schedule of working days and sleeping nights.

Over the years, Steve has picked up a functional amount of Spanish language to manage the influx of immigrant labor, along with a self-conscious racism that older immigrants often feel toward newcomers. Typically, these ideas begin with some variation on "I'm not racist, but . . ." As Steve says, "I'm not racist, because I love Mexicans and blacks just as much as whites, but Mexicans are stupid. Because they'll make $100 and go drink it. Or they'll blow it." Interestingly, Steve himself suggests this stereotype may be less about ethnicity or nationality and more about nightshift labor in diners, Greek or Mexican. Steve confesses, "I'm the same way, though, but Greeks are not like that. Typical Greeks. They save their money. They do not spend money. I'm like a mix of Mexican and Greek. Because I live the Mexican kind of life, but I'm Greek."

John gathers up his photos, pointing at one of him and the Greek soccer team with pride. Before he heads back to the small counter by the front door, he says in halting English, "Twenty years at night. The daytime, I don't like. I want a good life with my kids." He smiles and adds, "The boss wants someone to trust at night."

Billy, John's brother, owns the North Shore along with two other diners in Queens, and will not have anyone but family overseeing his business. "Billy, the owner, he's never here at nights," Steve says. "This place makes a lot of money, and you can't trust anybody. I'm the only person he used to trust in this place that's not family." That didn't stop Steve from quitting three times to work other diners, one in East New York, Brooklyn, and one just down the street in Queens. Now, as night manager of the Skylight in Manhattan, he is making good money and is less inclined to return. Billy, however, still wants him back. "He says to me, 'Forget about the *malakias* and come back.' That's what the Greeks say, the *malakias*, the bullshit."

Steve would sooner take up his father's cousin's offer to run the diner in Maryland than come back to the North Shore. But as he told Louie back at the Skylight, "I'm still here." When asked why, Steve says, "Honestly, I'm afraid to leave New York. I grew up here. I know where I can get anything at 4 in the morning. Out there, my cousin was telling me, at 9 everything is closed. Everything. You can't even get cigarettes after 9, which is, like, nuts. It reminds me of my father's island in Greece. You have to drive a half hour just to get cigarettes."

Steve leans in close and adds, "I mean, I know there is crime here and all that, but still I grew up here. I've been here twenty years. It's not easy to leave. Even though I've got a gold mine waiting there for me, which sounds crazy, but . . ."

———————

It's just after midnight at the Skylight and Steve has taken his second delivery order in a row for matzo ball soup. "It's normal people now," he
says. "After 1 it's all drunk people."

Baseball season ended last month, and the first cold blasts of winter
are moving across Manhattan. Steve has settled into his position at the
Skylight after a few more months and is less and less likely to return to
the North Shore Diner in Queens. He recently broke up with his
dayshift girlfriend and, improbably, seems to have put on a few more
pounds.

Two women in their midtwenties prance into the diner. Steve takes
notice. They giggle as they walk, wobbling a bit on their high heels, but
there is a world-weariness about them suggesting they have not just
come from the Copacabana. The hostess seats them at a table by the
window.

"Why doesn't anyone sit at my counter?" he asks no one in particular.
"I got two seats right here."

As if on cue, a mother and daughter push through the front door. The
girl, no more than 8 years old, is wide-eyed and a little giddy. The mother
directs her to the two seats at the counter, and coaches her through the
enormous menu. Apparently it is the girl's first diner.

"The great thing about a diner," the mother explains, "is that you can
get anything in the world."

The phone rings.

"Skylight," Steve says, a bit wearily. He jots a few items on a pad, then
turns to a waitress.

"What do you charge for a banana?"

"75 cents," she replies, robotically.

"75 cents?" Steve says, dismayed. "What is this, a deli? Charge two
dollars."

Steve hangs up the phone and calls the order in to the kitchen. He un-
corks a bottle of Chardonnay and pours it into a paper cup for the delivery order. He takes in the low hum of the diner, the smattering of customers in the booths, and the mother and daughter still deciding on a
midnight snack. He remembers why he likes the nightshift.

"The boss isn't here, standing over you, watching what you're doing," he says. Then he turns to the waitress. "We should just leave. We'll lock the door and go home."

He laughs quietly, mostly to himself, and asks, "Where is the key to the door?"

She answers, deadpan, "I don't think they have one."

# TWO: I'LL TAKE MY CHANCES ON THE NIGHTSHIFT

**N**ight cab driving," says Malik, "the first three hours is important."

Malik, 46, is at ease in the driver's seat of his yellow cab cruising over the Triborough Bridge. He drives with one hand on the wheel, one hand on the gearshift, and talks about life as a taxi driver. As he talks, he glances up in the rearview mirror, a practiced cab driver routine that enables him to see what's on the road as well as who's in his cab. His large molasses brown eyes look kind, rather like the eyes a child might draw if asked to make a picture of friendly eyes. He wears a gray hat, a button-down shirt, and loose-fitting pants.

Manhattan sparkles in the night across the river. "It is a beautiful city," he says.

Malik explains how the first three hours of the nightshift, from 5 to 8 PM, make or break a cab driver. If you find enough passengers then, Malik says, you've made enough to break even and the rest of the night is profit. You might even have what he describes as "good money": "Good money means you get passengers. You drop one off and you get another." But perhaps "good money" connotes something grander than the small sum a cab driver takes home at the end of a shift. "The first three hours is important," he reiterates. "If you could not make money in those three hours, you have to struggle to make money."

The city's 24,000 active yellow cab drivers earn their living through a very complicated system. The New York City Taxi and Limousine Commission (TLC) requires every yellow cab to have a license, also known as a medallion. First issued in 1937, medallions are private property and thus transferable, creating a market that has inflated their value to well over $300,000. At such prices, individual drivers rarely have the capital to invest in their own medallions. Instead, they lease the right to use one from a "broker" who may own as many as fifty of the 13,028 medallions in circulation.

Drivers, who must also be licensed by the TLC, enter into a number of different types of agreements with these brokers for the right to use their medallion. The most common arrangement is for a driver to lease both the medallion and the car by the week on either the dayshift or the nightshift at rates ranging from $500 to $800. Another common arrangement is a daily lease, which varies in price but is more expensive per day than the weekly rate. A third option, and where many drivers lose a lot of money, is to lease the medallion but purchase the cab from the broker through a high-interest loan. The pitfall of this last arrangement is that maintenance costs are borne by the driver and can be quite considerable. Moreover, each lease arrangement carries a night differential that penalizes the driver: the nightshift lease is $100 more per week than the dayshift because brokers argue that the earning potential is higher. At night, every fare earns an extra 50 cents; between 4 and 8 PM, an extra $1.

The net result of this complicated system is that drivers begin their shift in debt. Whether leasing weekly, daily, or as owners of their own cabs, the cost of the medallion means at minimum a $100 deficit before their first fare. Add in the cost of fuel (at least $30 a shift), and most drivers spend the first several hours of their twelve-hour shift just breaking even.

By 11:30 PM on this Monday night in late January, Malik knows it is not a good money night. "The weekend is okay, but regular days nobody's out. At 11 o'clock everybody goes home." He says some drivers may leave Manhattan and head to JFK International Airport to try to find a good fare there. "Sometimes in the city there is no business," Malik explains, "so the cab drivers go to JFK, get some rest, and when they get a passenger at least they have $45." He heads there now.

Originally from Pakistan, Malik has been driving a New York City taxi for more than twenty years. "I started with the taxi. That's all I've ever done," he says softly. He speaks in almost a whisper, drawing listeners physically nearer in an attempt to catch every word. It's the combination of the intonations of his native tongue, Urdu, and the timidity he feels speaking English. "My English is not too good," he says, though it's fine.

Malik says he left Pakistan when he was "20 or 21" years old. "It was a long journey," he says, "to come from there to here." Malik traveled first to Mexico, then paid a *coyote* to help him cross the border into the United States. "It was very expensive," he says. But for him there was no alternative. "It's very hard to get a visa," Malik says softly. "If you are poor, you don't have a bank balance, you don't have the background. All the students, the parents are rich and they can afford to have their kids here. Like me, cab drivers, everyone is from poor families."

His first job was on a farm near Los Angeles. "We didn't go out," he says. "They said, 'Don't go out. The police will catch you and send you back.' That's why people like to go to agriculture areas because there are no cops. You do your work and make money." Malik pauses a moment. "But that life is very hard."

Malik applied for amnesty in the 1980s, received his legal status as a farmworker, and came to New York City. Though he spends his life driving, he has one answer for why he left L.A. for New York: "Here you can find everything traveling by subway, buses. In L.A. it's very hard; you must have a car."

From the start, Malik says he loved New Yorkers. He tells the story about the first day he drove a cab, laughing heartily, almost loudly. He was driving days then, leasing his cab from a large Manhattan garage on Canal Street and First Avenue. He had no idea how to navigate the city. "I still remember," Malik admits quietly, "I didn't know where to go. One gentleman, my first fare, said, 'Don't worry, I will teach you how to go.' He gave me directions and he was so polite." At the end of his shift, Malik remembers, he could not find the garage. With twenty years of experience and a compass on his dashboard, Malik no longer gets lost.

But he does grow animated, if still barely audible, describing the city's controversial plans to outfit yellow cabs with global positioning system (GPS) devices.

"I drove two years in the daytime," Malik says, changing lanes, "then I started the nighttime. Night is okay. There is less traffic. Daytime, traffic is crazy. When you're driving in Manhattan, traffic is crazy, you have to watch everything."

Generally, Malik can make more money on the nightshift than during the day. But it is still risky. "In the nighttime you don't know. If the roads are clear and you have a long fare, you make good money. And sometimes you are just burning gas." Also, he says, you have to drive weekends. "Friday night and Saturday night," he says, "are very tough. When they pass, you relax. If you cannot make money on those two nights, then the week money is not good. We depend on those two nights." By contrast, dayshift drivers, "don't have any problem. Every day is the same."

Malik glides past La Guardia Airport, heading east, then follows the signs for JFK airport. "I will tell you one thing about the taxi business," he says. "You will make money, but you will lose a lot of relationships, friends. Sometimes I feel like I'm human, but sometimes I'm greedy. Like my friend will call me up, and say, 'Come out,' but I think, 'It's Saturday night.' Sometimes my body is not good, but sometimes I'm greedy to make money and I go. Sometimes I feel like money is okay, but you lose friends."

--------

"It's not normal, because your body is not made to work at night."

It's a crisp night in November and Cliff the Cabbie, as he likes to be called, has just put his yellow cab in gear. He continues, "You're supposed to be sleeping at night and working in the daytime. It's not normal." After a sigh, he adds, "Well, it's how I make my living."

Cliff, 46, is a largish man with a quick laugh and the gift of gab. A Jamaican immigrant, Cliff speaks with the lilting English of the Anglophone Caribbean. "You always say you're gonna get out of the business," he confesses. "And you get out for a month or two, but then you go right back. You fall into a rut. You can't get out." He references a story from Jamaica to make sense of his dilemma. "You ever hear the story about the bucket of crabs?" he asks. "You get a bucket and you put a dozen crabs in it, you're not gonna make it out of that bucket, unless you're going into a pot or something. The other crabs are gonna be dragging you back into it."

Cliff idles at a red light heading north on Third Avenue. He used to drive the dayshift, but as he says, "It's too much stress. I can't do it anymore." The traffic lights all along Third Avenue turn from red to green, like an ascending chain reaction, giving Cliff a clear shot north. He has no traffic, nothing to slow him down. He smiles into the rearview mirror and says, "I'll take my chances on the nightshift."

Two months later, Cliff is flying down an empty avenue on a freezing January night. Tonight he wears a black leather jacket, jeans, and a light shirt. "I came straight from Jamaica with $50 in my pocket," he says. That was twenty-one years ago. Soon after his arrival in New York, he went to work in Westchester County cleaning houses. "If you don't have a green card," he says, "whatever job you can get you just go do it."

His patience paid off and under U.S. amnesty laws he became a legal resident. In 1992, he started driving a cab on the dayshift but, after a few years, switched to nights. "I can't do the dayshift anymore," he says. Leaning back into the seat of one of his garage's new hybrid vehicles, Cliff continues: "There's more stress than in the nighttime. There's a lot more traffic and a lot more people." For taxi drivers, driving the nightshift means the 5 PM rush through to the creeping daylight of 5 AM. In between, the traffic wanes and the streets belong to the yellow sedans trolling for the infrequent fare after midnight.

In fifteen years behind the wheel of a yellow cab, Cliff has seen his share of curiosities on the nightshift.

"One night I picked up two Indian people at the Marriott Hotel in downtown Manhattan," he begins. The middle-aged couple asked to go to 68th Street between Second and Third Avenues. Not long into the ride, the husband demanded that Cliff stop the cab. "He said, 'Stop here, stop here!' We were right near the World Trade Center. And I said to him, 'Listen, man, I can't stop here, this is the highway.' So I made a turn on Murray Street and they got out. And they had this book and a bottle of water, and he started sprinkling the water outside the cab." Cliff pauses for effect, then explains, "What they were doing was moon worship. I thought I'd seen it all. They were there for a good ten minutes, bowing and talking. They took out two candles, lit the candles. And I'm thinking, 'Come on, man, let's go.' The meter was running but I didn't want to spend ten, twenty minutes doing your worshiping." He laughs his full-throated laugh and exclaims, "*That* wouldn't happen on the dayshift."

As is occasionally true for diners, sex is also part of the nightshift experience for taxi drivers. "A lot of strange things happen on the nightshift," he says, "but most of them are sexual encounters." He remembers a night at 72nd and West End Avenue when a young couple hailed his cab to go to Hoboken in New Jersey. "So I'm driving down West End Avenue and I don't know whose it was, but I saw a leg pop out through the little window in the partition. I said, 'Oh, Jesus.' I just kept driving. I didn't say anything to them because I thought, 'These people are not gonna stop, if they can do that in that little space.' And it's a little space, it's not a big space. I thought, 'Man, these people are contortionists.'" Once in Hoboken, the couple asked him to keep driving. Cliff refused, laughing now at the memory, "I said, 'No, this is it, man. Get out. This is over. You need to go inside or get a hotel room or something. I have work to do.' This was 2 or 3 in the morning. They paid, a good tip, but I should have charged them for the room." Cliff says it happens often at night. "That was the first time I actually saw somebody do something like that. But it happens a lot. After awhile it becomes disgusting to you. You're not supposed to be doing that in a cab. They just want to do it out in public so everybody can see what they are doing."

Not every fare is good for a laugh. Cliff has had his share of thieves and has had to learn how to finesse dangerous situations with the right amount of friendly interaction with his customers. He recounts an example from another driver. "This thief," Cliff begins, growing animated, "would go to JFK airport, then walk out of the terminal with a bag, like he's coming off a plane, join the line, and get into the cab. Then he'll take you to Brooklyn and he'll rob you." Cliff's friend had the man in his cab, and as Cliff says, "I guess sometimes you can just sense things. He started looking at him while he was driving and he thought, 'Oh man, I'm in trouble.' So he just started talking to him, having a nice conversation, 'Where you from, where you going, family,' all that kind of stuff. Just nice talk. And when he got to his destination, the guy in the back said to him, 'Man, I was going to rob you, but you're such a nice guy, I can't rob you.' And he paid him!" Cliff says, laughing hysterically now. "He paid his fare!"

Still, says Cliff, you have to be careful. "It can be scary, depending on who you encounter. That's why I try to be nice with people. You find that if you're nice with people, they won't bother you."

Cliff's niceness policy means he often finds himself picking up the passengers that other drivers turn away. As he turns right onto another Manhattan street of brownstones, the streets dusted white with fresh snow, he gives an example. "Last week, I was on Fifth Avenue and 28th Street," he begins, always remembering exactly where he was, "and two black guys got out of one cab and got into my cab. They were very angry and very upset." They told Cliff how they had been in the other taxi on their way to Brooklyn. "They told me that the driver slammed on the brake hard, swung the car over, then told them that his transmission was gone." Cliff shakes his head and says, "This guy didn't want to take them to Brooklyn. They knew what he was doing. They told me where they were going and I took them." They repaid Cliff for his kindness. "It was $25 on the meter," he says, "and the guy gave me $40."

Cliff says he sees discrimination all the time. After a moment's hesitation, he says, "I don't want to pick on any race of people, but the Arabs, they do it a lot." He pauses again. "But you have to look at it the other way too. Sometimes you have problems with black people or minorities. You do get problems with them, and I guess some of these guys don't want to go through the headache."

Discrimination has been a much-publicized problem among New York City cab drivers. In 1999, the actor Danny Glover tried and failed to hail a cab on multiple occasions. In his outrage and with his celebrity status, he raised awareness about this practice of African Americans being passed over for white passengers. In response, the TLC initiated Operation Refusal in which TLC officers posed as prospective passengers, often one black and one white. If the driver passed the black passenger in favor of the white one, they gave the driver a ticket or suspended the driver's license on the spot.

A member of the organizing committee of the New York Taxi Workers Alliance, Biju Mathew, suggests in his book *Taxi!* that Operation Refusal was a failure. In his view, TLC did not reach out to drivers but instead enacted a sting operation aimed at shoring up its public image. Whether the word was out or taxi drivers did not engage in this practice as much as people thought, they did not catch many drivers. Mathew argues that drivers themselves met with Danny Glover and his lawyers to address the very real issue of racial profiling among nonblack taxi drivers. Their argument was simple economics. Drivers begin their shifts in debt, and therefore prefer a high volume of short trips during peak hours rather than fewer long trips out of Manhattan that inevitably become bogged down in traffic. Even recent immigrants behind the wheels of yellow cabs learn quickly that white customers are more likely to live in Manhattan than nonwhite customers. Nonwhites, even those of the same ethnicity as the driver, tend to live further from the center and are therefore more costly over the course of a driver's shift. Drivers' response to Operation Refusal was to demand a more equitable arrangement with the TLC and brokers to make their livelihoods less dependent on shorter trips.

Cliff eases his cab around the northwest corner of Central Park. The sidewalks are deserted, and in this part of Manhattan there are few restaurants or bars to troll for that one big fare that will put him over the top for the night. He's thinking of heading back to the garage early.

————

"Night driving is dangerous," says Malik.

He is cruising along the parkway across Queens. The lanes are empty, but he keeps to the speed limit. "Before," says Malik, "every week a cab driver was killed. Everybody knows they have the cash." Now, he claims, times are better, but "before" and "now" become conflated as he describes the persistent fear of particular passengers. "People, especially the black guys," says Malik, "they like to go to Brooklyn or the Bronx." Corroborating Cliff's commentary on discrimination among some cab drivers, Malik neglects to add that he too lives in Brooklyn. "We cannot refuse to anyone. This is the law. So we are afraid," he says. "Most drivers, they don't like to work in the night. It can be very dangerous driving in the nighttime." He explains that drivers frequently think, "Maybe they're going to show a gun or something. Maybe they are going to rob me."

Though nothing violent ever happened to Malik, his views on the possibility are informed by the experiences of taxi driver friends who have been robbed. One driver had three men in his car, one of whom showed a knife and demanded the driver's money. "He took the money," says, Malik, "and stabbed him with the knife." Another driver had two passengers in his cab and one of them pulled a gun. Malik relates how the two men had the driver stop the car, get out, and then they handcuffed him to a fence. "They took his car. He was two hours crying and nobody would stop." Malik grows even quieter and says, "Now, where he is, I don't know."

Anyone who lived through the slew of murders of New York City gypsy cab drivers in 2000 knows that the job is a dangerous one. In May 2000, the Occupational Safety and Health Administration put a firm number to the violence by reporting that taxi drivers were "60 times more likely than other workers to be murdered on the job." Using Bureau of Labor Statistics data, the report also said that they were more likely to experience violent assaults than any workers other than police officers and security guards. The suggested "protective measures" included the installations of partitions between the front and back seats, surveillance cameras, GPS devices, "cashless fare systems" (credit cards), and several others. The TLC voted to require drivers to install either partitions or cameras by May 18, 2000. Drivers had to cover the cost themselves.

Violence against drivers is especially likely at night. The sociologists Diego Gambetta and Heather Hamill, in their book *Streetwise*, discuss a survey they conducted of *New York Times* articles. Of those that reported the time of the crime, 64 percent of drivers injured or attacked were victimized between 10 PM and 6 AM. But now, says Malik, it's "99.9 percent better." In fact, it's 55 percent better. Violent crimes reported by the New

York Police Department, according to the U.S. Department of Justice, dropped from 174,542 in 1990 to 78,945 in 1999.

With more than twenty years of experience driving a taxi, Malik has seen the city change. "Before," he says, "the meatpacking district . . ." He pauses, then says, "Now, it is a very expensive part of the city." But before the area's gentrification, no one wanted to go there. "There were no clubs, nothing. The homeless were there. And now it's a very expensive place. A lot of restaurants, bars, and everything." He says the same was true of the Lower East Side. "You would never get passengers. Some *not* nice people were living there." But now, says Malik, everyone knows that if you cannot find passengers elsewhere, you can find them on the Lower East Side. "Go there and you will get passengers." Another rule of taxi driving, says Malik, is the direction that passengers want to travel. "Evening time," he says, "everybody goes from downtown to uptown."

Instead of violent passengers, says Malik, he most often has trouble with drunk ones. They are not allowed to wake up passengers who pass out in their taxis, so Malik often tries to rouse them by tapping loudly on the partition. Malik demonstrates his tapping technique: tap tap tap. It's as quiet as he is. He says if that doesn't work he will say, "Please wake up, wake up." But that's hardly loud enough to wake a baby. So on four or five occasions he's had to call the police to wake them. "But New York police," he says, smiling, "they are just like angels. They help us a lot. Right away they help. I love the New York police."

———————

Cliff drives past a number of restaurants and bars on the Upper East Side. It's a Monday night in January, and according to Cliff, it's a slow night. He's hoping for a long ride out of Manhattan. "A nice long ride is $25 or $30," he explains. "What a lot of drivers do is go to restaurants and bars and just hang out. Just park and hope for the best." But that's also when he starts thinking about going home for the night. "As soon as 2:30 comes, I start preparing myself to go home. Tuesday night I'll do the same thing. Wednesday I'll stay a little later. Thursday I don't want to go home until like 5. A lot more people are out, so you make a lot more."

"You make it work for you," Cliff says. "Even though some nights,

Monday nights, Tuesday nights, you get discouraged that you're not making enough. Some nights I make like $6, $7 to go home with. Sounds incredible, but it happens once in a while. Three weeks ago, Monday night, I went home with ten bucks. After I paid gas that's all I had left." Cliff smiles, shrugs, and says, "But then Saturday night, I had $200 to go home with. That's how it is."

Cliff lives in the Bronx but as a yellow cab driver he works mainly in Manhattan. As he explains it, "Most yellow cabs stay in Manhattan. Yellow cabs have the right," he pauses, then adds, "I don't know if it's a privilege, so let's just say the right, to work the five boroughs. The guys in the so-called gypsy cabs out in the boroughs, they cannot come into Manhattan and work. That's how the rules are."

And there are a lot of rules.

One common complaint among cab drivers is the tickets they receive for having a "dirty" cab. The $25 tickets can add up quickly and eat into what little earnings they make in a night. "You can get a ticket," Cliff explains, pointing to the receipt paper hanging on the meter, "for each receipt that you have hanging." If four customers fail to ask for receipts and the driver has not had time to throw them away, the TLC can issue $100 in tickets to the driver. "It sounds ridiculous, right?" He's laughing, a little. "It's the TLC." The reasoning behind this ridiculous practice, says Cliff, is that "some guys used to juice their meter." In other words, the driver would keep lots of receipts wrapped around the meter so the passengers would not be able to see the fare. Then the driver would use a "zapper" to electronically raise the fare as often as he or she cared to instead of the standard four blocks.

Both "TLC cops" and "regular New York City cops," says Cliff, enforce this type of thing these days. "At one time, New York City cops would not bother with yellow cabs. It was not their responsibility. But then they changed the rules. Now, you get it from all sides."

For all of the regulation of the TLC and the struggle to make a living, Cliff's main problem with driving nights is the lack of sleep. "I feel really drowsy when I just start working. It's the weirdest thing. Twilight. When I come out at 5, I wash the car and then come down and sometime between 6 and 8 I'm feeling drowsy. But as the night goes on, I perk up.

My eyes open up. Like now, I don't feel sleepy." It's only midnight, but then again he has been driving for more than six hours. "I try to get my rest," says Cliff, "because I know it's dangerous to not get enough rest."

"Some guys," he says from experience, "live out of their cabs. They'll rent the cab for a week, and some of them don't go home. They live at the airports. If they go home, it's just to take a shower and go right back to the airport." For some people, says Cliff, it works. He says he knew a guy who bought a car, leased a medallion, drove eleven to twenty hours a day, slept at the airport, and eventually made enough money to buy a house in White Plains. Cliff says that though the man had a family he was always either driving or sleeping at the airport. "He would go home just to shower. He said, 'I gotta make the money, man.' It worked for him."

Cliff speaks from experience. In 2003, he bought a used cab and tried to make a go of it himself. By owning his own car and leasing the medallion, Cliff paid roughly $800 per week without the added cost of leasing the car. His plan was that once he paid off the car loan, he would have saved enough money to recover the cost of the car. But without a partner to help him pay for the lease, he soon learned that he needed to work all day to make enough money to cover his costs. He would begin driving at 5 AM and still be on the road at 2 AM. "I would go home, shower or whatever, and then go back to the airport to go to sleep until 5 or 6 in the morning when the first flight comes in." Eventually he recognized that this was not a good way to live. It didn't help that the car itself, with 114,000 miles on it, was unreliable. "The miles on it were hard miles," he says. "I learned that the hard way. The car was fine while I had a one-month guarantee on it, and then it just kept breaking, breaking, and breaking. I literally rebuilt the whole car."

Cliff returned to leasing a cab, saving himself the headache of maintenance. But driving a cab is as hard on the body as it is on the car. "You have to plan some time to go out and exercise when you're off. If you don't do that, you'll gain a lot of weight." Cliff started walking over the summer, two or three days a week. "I did it from June to October and I dropped off a good fifteen or twenty pounds. Just walking at a brisk pace.

Now I've cut back because it got so cold. I know I've gained back some of the weight. I need to get myself a treadmill."

Cliff grips the wheel of his cab, scanning the sidewalks for prospective fares.

"You sit behind the wheel," he says, his eyes on the street ahead, "and it's not healthy."

———————

Malik pulls up next to the chain-link fence that surrounds the Central Taxi Hold at JFK airport. He explains that the holding lot can sometimes be a good bet when you've had a slow night, but he is reluctant to take his place at the end of the line. Before they built Terminal 4, taxis waited in a small lot before they went to the terminal to pick up passengers. Since its inception in 2001 this huge lot off 150th Street in Queens is much more systematic. Everyone has to wait in one of fifty-four lines for a ticket with a terminal number on it. Once he has the ticket, he can go to that terminal and pick up a passenger.

When a taxi driver gets a fare at the airport, or anywhere, it's always an unknown: no driver knows where he'll end up dropping that passenger. "When they sit in their car there," says Malik, "they don't know their destination. This is the nature of the business. We don't know where we will go."

The holding lot has its advantages and disadvantages. The main advantage is that if you wait it out you're guaranteed a passenger and, if they're going to Manhattan, a $45 fare. There's even a shop where you can buy coffee or food. You can sleep, read, get out of your car, sit with another driver and chat in the other driver's car. But with space for seven hundred cabs in the holding lot, drivers can sometimes be in line for hours. This is especially true late at night when the arrivals at JFK are fewer and further between. And then, says Malik, "you're stuck and you cannot make money." You can leave and return to the city, but you're giving up that potential $45 fare. "But in the city," Malik counters softly, "sometimes you make more than that. It's a gamble. You don't know."

It's always a gamble. Some nights, a taxi driver might wait an hour or two at the holding lot, get the ticket and the passenger, and then get only a $10 or $20 fare to someplace near the airport. On the other hand, Malik remembers a night in Manhattan when a passenger asked to go to New Jersey. "There was no traffic, nothing! I took the Holland Tunnel, went to Hoboken, dropped him off and came back. Again, I got a fare for New Jersey! So sometimes, you get lucky and you make good money, and sometimes . . ."

Whether or not Malik will stay in New York long-term, he says, "It depends on the kids." He has a wife and four children who split their time between New York and Karachi in southern Pakistan. He slips into a cab-driving analogy. "Now, I am driving a cab. And when I get a passenger, I don't know where I will go. So, when the child grows up, we don't know where they will go. American culture is different. Our culture is different. Here, the boy or the girl, they have the option to go anywhere." In Pakistan, he says, "We try to stay with the kids. Maybe our son will stay, if he likes, but if not then we have to think about where to go." And Malik has good reason to worry about his children staying in New York. "I remember a guy I picked up in Tribeca. He said maybe this is his last ride in a yellow cab. I asked, 'Where are you going?' He said, 'I'm quitting New York.' I said, 'Why?' He said, 'It's very expensive now. My one-bedroom apartment is $3,500. I cannot afford it.'"

Malik's rent is only $900 a month and if he's working regularly he can pay it. Sometimes he makes enough to send money back to Pakistan. Sometimes not. "There is no fixed money," he says. "Sometimes you feel like, 'Where is the money?' You don't have a fixed idea of how much. Sometimes you are sick. Sometimes two days you make good money and the third day you get sick so all averages go down." This means that Malik cannot budget. "When you start you cannot say, 'I will make $200.'" Every night is different. Tonight he's made $190. Some nights he barely makes enough to cover the cost of the lease and fuel. And there's always the risk that the car will break down.

Trying to capture the ethereal nature of his income, Malik says, "It's air money."

Still idling near the holding lot, Malik pulls out his incongruously hi-tech phone, very shiny and silver. "You can get information," he says in his melodic near-whisper. "If you are close to JFK, you can get information on the phone." He punches a few buttons, and a loud speaker comes on. Instantly, a recording of a man talking in a very thick New York accent bellows, "GOOD MORNING, WELCOME TO JFK CENTRAL TAXI HOLDING HOTLINE." It's a startling contrast from Malik's speaking voice, which never rises above librarian levels. The voice continues: "TODAY, TUESDAY, JANUARY 30TH, 2007, AT 12 O'CLOCK IN THE MORNING. AT 12 O'CLOCK IN THE MORNING, CTH HAS A VERY, VERY SLOW ACTIVITY, HOLDING AT 40 PERCENT."

Malik hangs up and puts away his phone. "It's after 12 o'clock," says Malik staring at the lines of taxis in the lot, "I don't think they're gonna get a fare because after 12:30 there are no planes." His kind eyes close a bit as he allows himself a small smile. He repeats, "I don't think they are going to get a fare."

# THREE: OUR OWN LITTLE CITY

I t's past midnight in Terminal 4 at JFK airport and the flight from West Africa is late. A few dozen West Africans wait impatiently behind a gleaming metal railing for their loved ones to trail out of customs. Some wander off to the few eateries still open in the terminal, but most stand in groups of two or three watching the frosted partition that divides the baggage claim area from the terminal.

Peter, a U.S. customs border protection officer, steps from behind the partition and heads for the café in the middle of the waiting area. He is in his early twenties, with a bright smile and an easy, disarming charm. Customs border protection officers, those uniformed men and women who sit behind Plexiglas booths at passport control, are the ones who ask those seemingly innocuous questions about where you've been and what you've been doing on your international travels. On this Friday night in early October, Peter scans the crowd as he walks, mostly out of habit, noting anyone who might seem out of place at this hour. A recent rise in the threat level means more frequent patrols of heavily armed U.S. National Guard troops. Although this may raise the anxiety level of passengers, for Peter it means that he can relax a bit while in the terminal.

The terminal is cavernous, its soaring white canopy overhead evoking an open tent. Largely empty at this hour, the scale of the place seems even more impressive compared to the relatively few people waiting inside. The acoustics amplify the low murmur of visitors' voices, and every few minutes, the white noise of the murmuring is punctuated by distinct words and the staccato sounds of luggage carts rolling across the polished floor. Above the arrivals area, the JFK AirTrain slinks through the terminal, linking travelers to the E train at Sutphin Boulevard. An enormous question mark draws visitors seeking information, though no one is around to offer any at this hour. Here, there, and everywhere are orange-and-red MasterCard signs that read: "Staying Up in the City That Never Sleeps. Priceless."

"You still mad at me?" Peter asks with a twinkle in his eye. Shirley, the nightshift employee at the twenty-four-hour Au Bon Pain, smiles widely at him in spite of herself. She's making coffee and looks very tired. Working nights, she says, "sucks." He turns back to the crowd.

The overall effect of the terminal architecture blurs the sense of being indoors, especially at the Au Bon Pain. The café is designed to look as though it were on any city sidewalk, complete with fake shrubs dividing several tables from the main concourse. It's an effect so fully realized that a flock of small birds swoops down from the rafters to pick at the crumbs left on the tables.

"I like this," Peter admits from his vantage point at the café facing the crowd, "because I like watching people." He's worked as a customs border protection officer for the past few years, working the nightshift while putting himself through college. JFK is his second home. "I meet celebrities and some of the most interesting people in the world," he says. "And I meet some of the world's dirtiest." As Peter talks, he periodically drops the smile and then resumes it in a way that seems both natural and practiced. He is genuinely warm, but he is professionally obligated to discern the hidden. So he is both charming and intimidating; it all depends on what happens to that smile.

With more than 18 million travelers on the move through JFK each year, Peter has learned how to spot the square peg in the round hole quickly and expertly. The Department of Homeland Security reports that 87 million people fly into U.S. airports each year, and JFK is the busiest. According to Peter, "JFK is probably the size of the island of Manhattan in square mileage."

Peter takes a certain pride in his people skills, growing animated and using his hands to emphasize a point here and there. "You just learn a lot from people." Still, there's no arrogance but instead great humility that he is permitted to have such power over people. "The one thing that I've come away with from here," he says with a unique mixture of modesty and satisfaction, "is sorting through people's lies. These days I can sit and within a matter of three to five sentences that come out of a person's mouth, I can see whether they're sincere or they're trying to deceive you."

Peter marches off into the crowd. "You learn what questions matter," he calls back behind him, moving at a rapid pace, "what things matter, and what things really don't."

He talks a bit more about work. "I've been working, on and off, since I was 10 years old." Peter works what's known as a "hardship shift," but he has not been working since he was 10 out of financial need. "I always loved working and making my own money," he says. "I always felt bad asking my parents for money." As he explains, still walking at a fast clip, "The nightshift, I'm telling you, it's just the interruption in your day to give you the means to do what you really want."

Peter races around the massive terminal. He makes his way out of the waiting area, through a holding pen for confiscated luggage, and up an escalator to the departure level concourse. There are fewer people here, some waiting for the first flight out in the morning, but a couple of the fast food kiosks stay open all night.

As he hikes through the terminal, he elaborates more on his work ethic. "Maybe it's just my own personal feeling, but work should never be the basis of your life." He explains that most of his JFK nightshift colleagues work this hardship shift because they have something else going on in their lives, or because this is a second career for them. Like many who work nights, they may have a spouse who works days, need the extra money, want to spend the days with their children, need to be in school during the day, or all of the above. "Or," Peter says, his eyes a dead stare, "they have another job."

Within minutes, he's talking to a nightshift coworker, an airline representative. As Peter approaches, her tired and grouchy expression turns to mirth. Still, she says without reservation, the nightshift "sucks . . . in a word." To work this shift, she explains, she sleeps only about thirty minutes a day. "And that's a luxury," she says of those thirty minutes. "If a plane comes in late," she begins, shaking her head. Peter laughs. Planes coming in late are a routine part of their jobs, and they have to stay until the planes land and all the passengers have passed through customs. And "late" can mean really late. A recent arrival from Bogotá, Colombia, was not even scheduled to land until 4:50 AM. "If a plane comes in late," she says again, "I'm here till 5, 6 AM and then I go straight to work." That's because "work" is her full-time day job somewhere else. "This job," she says wearily, "is part-time."

Peter and his coworkers often have to deal with a lack of sleep. Overtime is part of the job, and can mean a nightshift extends well into the afternoon of the following day. Giving his coworker a nurturing squeeze of the elbow, he runs off again. He says, "We work a lot of overtime and a lot of mandated overtime." He explains that they can either volunteer to work overtime or stay because they are mandated. And there are a number of reasons why customs border protection officers may be required to stay past quitting time. "If we make an arrest," Peter explains matter-of-factly, "or if we are dealing with a case or a situation where an alert level goes up and they need to staff more people." It's part of the job. "You understand that you're mandated to stay for extra hours beyond your regular shift," he says cheerfully. "They tell you that before you even start the job."

Now that it's autumn, Peter works what they call the "dayshift," from 4 PM to midnight. That still does not mean that he leaves when his shift is scheduled to end. "There are times," he admits, sounding tired for the first time, "when there are snowstorms, or you're here until like 4 or 5 o'clock." He means 4 or 5 in the morning, and in those instances it's easier just to sleep at JFK than go home. Some officers live in the city or on Long Island, Peter explains, but some live in Westchester County, Connecticut, or Pennsylvania, so it often makes more sense for them to stay at the airport until they begin their next shift. Unlike some nightshift workers, they work five days a week. This means that even if a shift scheduled to end at midnight lasts until 5 AM, he has to start work again eleven hours later. "Sometimes it's not by choice," Peter says. "But there's a place in the back, a couple of couches. There's a male side and a female side. They have recliners and couches and you can just fall asleep there."

And if he actually does get home at midnight, he feels life is really good. "I see sunlight," he beams. "If I get home at midnight, I sleep until 8 or 9 in the morning, and I still have a full day until I have to be at work."

Plus, he adds, the overtime money can really add up. He earns a good salary as it is, just over $45,000. "But because we work a lot of overtime and a lot of mandated overtime," he explains, "we can earn up to $35,000 more." There's also the night differential. "Most law enforcement agencies will give you a night differential, and it's an added bonus for working this shift." All told, it's pretty typical for officers to bring home more than $80,000 a year.

Peter's brightness fades a little, however, when he talks about how this job affects his performance as a student. Back in September he admitted, laughing a little, "I've pretty much gotten dumber since I started this shift. Any kind of quick cognitive thing that used to take me less than a minute, I can stare at for a good two minutes now." Tonight, he contends that his GPA does not reflect his actual abilities. One semester, he says, he tried an experiment. "I wanted to see what would happen if I didn't work at night and I just focused on school." Working only days, he made a 3.92.

The job itself, he admits, can also be taxing. "Most of the people coming here," Peter recognizes, "have been sitting in the same spot for eight to twelve hours, maybe more." So the first thing those passengers are dealing with, says Peter, is the anxiety of travel. The second thing they face, says Peter, with characteristic empathy, is "the anxiety of seeing family they haven't seen for a while, or the business they are about to conduct." His sympathy fading, Peter continues, "Everybody seems to be on a time schedule, for some reason. 'I've got to be on a connecting flight.' Or, 'Somebody's outside waiting for me.' This and that. And some people are very relaxed and happy they've gotten here safely, and some people are just very high-strung."

Peter's job is the same, regardless of the hour or origin of the flight. But not every new arrival appreciates that fact. "If I stop somebody who is really in a rush, I'm gonna get the routine grievance. Especially if they're from here. If they're U.S. citizens, you'll get a lot of 'I'm a U.S. citizen.' But you know what, a lot of U.S. citizens are criminals, too. You're not exempt because you're a citizen of this country. You've gotta go through the same formalities as everyone else. Everybody's gotta go through it."

He recognizes that he has a position of authority and that it is largely built on trust. "Trust is an important public good," he says philosophically. "I'm entrusted with a certain position. I've earned the trust of a lot of people." He chooses his words carefully. "Trust takes a long time to build, and it's so quickly taken away," he says, sounding much older than his years. "One event could take it away, but it takes twenty or thirty events to build it. Why ruin years' worth of work for a day's worth of stupidity?"

Working at JFK puts him in contact with people from all over the world, and Peter enjoys the challenge of learning how to deal with different ethnic groups. "Especially in New York," he says, "you have to know what ethnic group you're dealing with." Peter speaks several languages at various levels of fluency and travels widely. He knows which groups to talk to with a more direct approach and which require him to be more creative: "You gotta kind of do like a crab and walk sideways and take it from the side. You have to make inferences." And he has developed some working theories about culture, values, and behavior. "You learn about people's lifestyles in comparison to your own. The majority of people that you meet these days, especially from Third World countries, the biggest emphasis is on family. When you meet people from Westernized countries, the biggest emphasis is on money and travel."

Regardless of these differences, Peter tries to treat everyone exactly the same. "I try to give everybody the same amount of respect," he says, eyes unblinking, smile bright. "No matter where they come from, no matter what they do, I give them the respect they deserve." He pauses, looks away a little, and relaxes his smile. "But," he begins, "when you don't sleep . . ." He stops.

"The one thing that I've noticed that I have lost from working the nightshift," he says, "is my patience." In the summer, after three or four

nights in a row where his shift was supposed to end at 8 AM but he returned home at 2 PM, he noticed his patience lapse. "Somebody would
blow up," he explains, "I'd ask them to calm down once." His face turns
to stone. "After one time," he says sternly, "I would raise my voice back
and let them know, 'Listen, I'm boss and that's it. Let me do what I need
to do and then get the hell out of here. I don't want to talk to you anyway, but let me do what I need to do.'"

The lack of sleep has also affected his health and social life. "I kind of
feel weaker, basically," he admits. He gained ten or twelve pounds on the
midnight to 8 AM shift. He never ate at work, but did eat before his shift
began and then again right before bed. "Go right to sleep, wake up
maybe a half hour before I had to be at work and then rush to work."
That leaves no time to exercise.

And no time to see friends. "You never really feel like you have a social life," Peter says. "I've been blessed with some of the best friends in
the world," he says. But he acknowledges that it's hard to stay connected
to them. "I have to work really hard to have a life," he says. "I have to sacrifice sleep. I have to sacrifice something, to have a life." His friends, who
all work days, understand his life and his need for sleep. They do not
push him to come out with them if he's tired. "And if I say yes, they ask
me, 'Are you sure, have you gotten sleep?' I say, 'Don't worry about it.'
But if I fall asleep in the car, they're not gonna mess with me. They're
like, 'Just let him sleep.'"

Peter also has strong relationships within the nightshift community at
Terminal 4. "If you ask anybody here what they think about working the
nightshift," Peter says honestly, "they'll tell you it sucks. People are rude,
people are nasty. It's not worth the money, not worth what it does to your
body." He pauses. "But," he begins, smiling widely again, "I kind of built
my own little community here." He does admit that it is a community
strictly limited to their time at work; they do not socialize after work.
"But I know Shirley, I know the airline reps, I know the guys in the pizze-
ria, guys at Au Bon Pain. If they haven't seen me in a few days, it's like,
'Where you been? Is everything all right?' So, we're our own little city
in this one terminal. We see each other every day."

Peter thinks that this same level of relationship would not be possible on the dayshift. Because so many more people pass through JFK during the day, Peter says, "I don't think they have the time or the ability to have such strong interpersonal relationships." He has no desire to work days. Also, he adds, there's something different about conversations on the nightshift. "Especially at night," says Peter, "no matter what, you just start somebody on something they like to talk about, and they'll talk to you for hours. And you know what? You might not even say anything, you might ask a question here and there, but they'll come away thinking, 'Wow, they really talked to me.'"

The glass doors slide open and Peter waves goodbye to his coworkers before heading home. He steps out into the early morning hours of another blustery fall day, across the damp pavement toward the parking garage. Pointing to the right, near the garage, he says, "You know how people bring their pets with them everywhere? Well, people bring their cats, and sometimes these cats' cages fall and they open and they scurry off." As he speaks, a half dozen cats dart in and out of the concrete support columns of the parking garage. Some nibble on cat food left in large plastic containers just outside the lair. "A whole community of them developed here," Peter explains. "Somebody who works here actually feeds them."

Behind him, a line of yellow cabs inches forward. A few West Africans load their bulging bags into the trunks of the first few cars. Each driver holds a small paper ticket from the holding lot, each one hopes for that long trip into Manhattan.

12:33 HUNTS POINT FISH MARKET

1:17 CARGO SHIPS PASSING UNDER BROOKLYN BRIDGE

1:17 UPPER WEST SIDE DOORMAN

1:25 LAST BUS TO STATEN ISLAND

# FOUR: A STILLNESS

**B**y 11:30 PM the emergency room waiting area no longer feels chaotic. It's a cold night in early December, though a couple of broken candy canes strewn across a corner table are the only holiday decorations. The place is far from festive. It has that typical nondescript hospital beige feel. Bland-colored linoleum floors jut up against creamy walls with blue accents and generic sets of impressionist watercolors. Everything feels scuffed, worn, and old. The newest, shiniest things around are the Purell hand sanitizer dispensers adhered to the walls.

The only windows in the waiting room look not outside but onto little offices. There's a triage office, a patient representative office, and a security office. Security and surveillance are omnipresent. Staff security guards go in and out of the security office. Two cops linger near the triage window awhile, then handcuff a tall guy when he comes out of the ER and whisk him away into the night. Over the next two hours, other officers will filter in and out of the waiting area. Their pace is practiced, leisurely, and does not reveal whether or not they are dealing with any emergencies. One officer, just before 1 AM, stands inside the triage office. He opens the door to the waiting area, ushers in a gray-haired man, and partially lowers the blinds. A nurse comes to take the man's blood pressure.

Another nurse, Rachel, is being trained in triage tonight. She wears the navy scrubs that designate her as an ER nurse, but they're not the standard-issue, ill-fitting scrubs. Like other medical professionals who value style as much as comfort, Rachel orders her scrubs made to fit. In her midtwenties, with her blondish brown hair, slender face, and slight frame, Rachel looks fit and fashionable.

"It's dead tonight," she says, though the waiting room is crowded with family members. A mandatory suspension of visiting hours in the ER fills the waiting area. They await an announcement notifying them that they can go back inside. When the Letterman show filled the ceiling-mounted television there were less than fifteen people waiting here. By the time Craig Ferguson begins at 12:50 AM, there's about double that.

Everyone seems calm. Most people speak Spanish. One large group talks extensively about Santo Domingo, suggesting a link to the Dominican Republic. Most signs are in both Spanish and English. One sign says "Medicaid Cuts Are The Wrong Medicine for Health Care." It's only in English but it's inside one of the offices. On the table with the candy canes, a flier asks, "Do You Need Financial Assistance for Your Healthcare Needs?" In English on one side and Spanish on the other, the flier details available assistance options.

Rachel takes in the waiting room and says, "In this neighborhood, this ER tends to be used a lot more as a clinic. They don't know how to use primary care, they don't have primary care, or they're illegal and they don't have healthcare, or whatever the case may be."

According to a 2003 report by the Center for Studying Health System Change, insured patients are as likely to cause overcrowding in hospital ERs as uninsured; in fact they accounted for most of the 16 percent rise in emergency room visits between 1996 and 2001. During that same time, however, insured patients were also seeking medical care from their primary care physicians at an increased rate, while the uninsured were visiting private physicians 37 percent less. The result: the uninsured were relying on emergency rooms for 25 percent of their doctor visits in 2001 versus 17 percent in 1996. Perhaps more revealing, less than half of all visits to hospital emergency rooms in 1999–2000 were "emergent," requiring care in fifteen minutes or less, or "urgent," requiring care within an hour.

"It does get frustrating to be used as a primary care clinic," Rachel admits. "A lot of times you think, 'This is such a waste of our resources. It's not how our system is supposed to be used.' But the system is so broken, what are the choices?"

Tonight, despite the full waiting room, the ER is relatively empty. Most of the patients who use the ER for primary care have come and gone by midnight, and the hospital is on diversion, so emergencies are sent elsewhere. This can happen for many reasons. "It seems to happen more on Monday or Sunday night," Rachel explains. "There's a lot of people that they'll hold over the weekend that could really be discharged. So it gets backed up into the ER. There will be some nights that we might have 30 percent of the patients in the ER waiting for a bed. So it really shoots our census way up."

The census is the number of patients in the ER, and here it can be as many as 150, though normal capacity is usually less than 100. With that many patients, the on-site security can come in handy. "We have security in the ER 24/7," says Rachel. "Most of them work for the hospital. Some of them keep an eye on the waiting room, and there's some of them that are always in the Psych Emergency Department."

Rachel nods to a couple of the officers, whispers a few words to another nurse, and slips out through the sliding glass doors to the ambulance bay. Across the street, an all-night deli serves coffee and sandwiches to nightshift nurses, doctors, paramedics, and the occasional waiting family member. Rachel orders her usual large coffee, though the coffee shop next door offers her preferred soy milk. She settles down at one of the two or three tables inside the deli, a recently remodeled section that somewhat pitifully suggests a quaint café. It's late, close to 2 AM, and there is nothing quaint about the place in the overbright fluorescent glow.

As "Rock'n around the Christmas Tree" plays overhead, Rachel explains the difference between working the dayshift and the nightshift in the ER. "On the dayshift," says Rachel, "when your shift begins the census is at the lowest it's going to be for the day." She elaborates, "You come in and it's not too busy. So you kind of have that time to catch up, see what's going on with everyone. Then your day gets progressively busier and busier as it goes on, it gets crazier and crazier." Rachel takes a sip of her coffee and adds, "It's also an older staff because you have more senior nurses because everyone wants to work days."

The nightshift moves in reverse. "If you come in at 8 o'clock at night in the ER," Rachel explains, "that's the busiest time. So you come in and it's absolutely crazy. There's a ton of people. And your night gets calmer as it goes on." Rachel describes the ebbs and flows of the nightshift, the crush of patients treating the ER as a primary care clinic starting around 5 PM, then a lull before patients are transferred upstairs around 2 AM. "Less people are coming in, more people are going up to the floor, and then the people that came in at 5 in the afternoon, who didn't need to be admitted, have been worked up and taken care of and sent home. So it's kind of a nice feeling to come in and have it be crazy and then have it clean up and get better as the night goes on."

As a new nurse, Rachel spent some time on the dayshift during her orientation a few months earlier, so she can compare the two shifts. She's still studying, hoping to become a psychiatric nurse practitioner and, like most new recruits, she was hired for the nightshift.

"You have a younger staff at nights," she explains. "They don't have the seniority so it's younger nurses." It's one reason she prefers the night-shift, and may be why she feels the nightshift nurses work well together compared to those who work the daylight hours. "For the ER at least, I think the night staff just works better as a team than the day staff does," she says. "I really like nights better. And I like coming in and having it be crazy and then having my day get nicer as it goes on instead of crazier."

She takes in the quiet hum of the deli and adds, "And I can come here and sit and drink my coffee for an hour and it's quiet. You don't get that during the day."

Rachel gathers up her paper cup of half-drunk coffee and pushes through the glass door of the deli. It's snowing out, but it's only a few dozen yards to the emergency entrance. She passes the empty bays where ambulances would wait were they not on diversion and steps through the sliding doors of the emergency room.

Before heading back into the maze of beds and whirring machinery, she stops and says, "I think working nights has created a stillness in my life."

———————

On a sunny September morning at 8 AM, a corner diner down the street from another Manhattan hospital bustles with medical professionals—doctors, nurses, emergency medical technicians—some coming, some going. In the hospital that looms overhead, thousands of employees have just gone through the daily shift-change ritual. Two nurses from the pediatric intensive care unit (PICU) slide into a booth. They've both just finished another twelve-hour shift and have come here for the cheap breakfast special before heading home.

Tamar, 29, smiles behind black-framed glasses, her dark hair pulled back from her face. She's on permanent staff with the hospital. Jessica, 25, has long, straight, dark brown hair and a contagious laugh. She works as a traveling nurse, a free agent in the healthcare system. Unlike Rachel, they both wear baggy green scrubs, the kind they get for free from the hospital.

The waitress, a middle-aged, well-rested, but gruff woman, stands by the table, pen and pad in hand. Jessica, surprisingly energetic after her long night, rattles off her usual variation on the breakfast special: eggs, scrambled; juice, orange; toast, cinnamon. Like most on the nightshift, the two nurses' eating habits have conformed to the odd hours.  ·

"I'll usually wake up at 4 PM," says Jessica, "then I take a shower or whatever, and then by 5 I usually eat dinner." She can't eat much before starting work at 7 PM, however. "So at 11 or midnight, that's when I start the grazing." She laughs uproariously.

Tamar, deadpan, adds, "On whatever's available."

They talk over each other and the rattle of diner dishes behind them about the things they've eaten at night on the unit. Jessica muses a minute, then says, "I have a prelunch lunch, lunch, and a postlunch lunch, and then breakfast." The prelunch lunch, or the meal right after she wakes up, says Jessica, is not cereal. "It's like dinner food."

The night staff on the PICU consists of eight or nine nurses on a good night. The perennial nursing shortage can mean as few as six on any given night. But they are a close-knit group, especially on the nightshift. As Tamar confesses, "In my ideal world, I would work the dayshift, but I love the staff at night."

According to Jessica and Tamar, most of the nurses on the nightshift are less than 30 years old, and almost all are women. They recently hired two new male nurses to the PICU staff, but they both wonder how they will fit in. "We are so girly at night," says Tamar.

Having colleagues their own age is one reason neither Jessica nor Tamar would switch to days if given the chance. "The younger, single nightshift girls all live in Manhattan. The married dayshift nurses live in Jersey," explains Jessica. "We have a couple of nurses that are in their late thirties, forties, but they're kind of the exception."

The food arrives. Thick porcelain plates clatter onto the table, forcing both of them to raise their voices.

"We've both had the opportunity to work days," admits Jessica.

Tamar finishes her sentence, "But we have a really nice group on nights."

"Yeah," agrees Jessica. "Everyone is so nice and helpful, and the nightshift is just really laid back. There's less people around. There's not doctors doing rounds all the time."

Tamar smiles mischievously, "I think we're less catty. The dayshift is a real catty group. They've all been there for fifteen-plus years together. If you're new on the dayshift, you've invaded the club. You're on the outside."

Neither of them have worked the PICU for very long. Tamar started two and a half years ago, and Jessica, as a traveling nurse, started only several months ago. But both must interact with the dayshift nurses during the shift change, and as they explain, they get the scoop from overlapping medical staff. Typically, new recruits are hired onto the nightshift, only moving onto days once they've established some seniority. As Tamar and Jessica point out, however, there are some clear advantages to staying on the nightshift.

"I like the challenge of being more autonomous at night," Tamar says. She elaborates with some equivocation, knowing she's treading on hospital hierarchy. "We have so many new residents that you really have to know so much more. The patient is really in your care, not in the doctor's care."

Jessica interjects, "The residents aren't there, permanently. They float in and out."

Growing bolder, Tamar continues, "I mean, we really are the one who's taking care of that patient for that night. The residents are really there for a referral service." She pauses, then adds, "Almost. I think during the day they're much more on top of the patients."

But perhaps most important to both of them is the stillness that Rachel referenced. At night, with doctors at home and the hospital settling down into a dim-lit quiet, they enjoy the simple, unrushed duties of bathing and weighing the children in their care. They also find that stillness can create stronger bonds with parents than would be possible on the dayshift.

"Everything they do on the dayshift is very important," Jessica explains, "but a lot of parents don't understand the importance of all these drips and changing all this stuff. Sometimes at night, the dayshift has done those things, so you have a chance to do other stuff." She laughs, adding, "Also, I think the parents, in their pajamas just hanging out, you just form a bond."

Tamar agrees, saying, "I always get parents who had to go home and they apologize for calling and bothering me. And I'm thinking, 'I work all night, I'm up all night, I'm here for you to call. I should be apologizing to you for laying at home thinking about it, but I'm here, this is my day. This is like 10 AM to me.'"

There is a trade-off for the stillness and the bonding that takes place at night on the unit. Time becomes a slippery concept, both during the shift change and in their personal lives. As Jessica explains, "It's so confusing when I give report, because it's like, 'Well, last night he did this.' But I mean yesterday, but yesterday was your yesterday, not my yesterday."

Both of them work a typical nursing schedule, three twelve-hour shifts a week. Even if they pick up an extra shift, they work only four nights. But, as Jessica says, "All my friends are very jealous. They're like, 'I can't believe you have three days off a week.' And I'm like, 'Yeah, but I work 48 hours. In order to see you sometimes, I don't sleep.'"

And sleep is a constant struggle. They both have roommates, but as Tamar explains, "It's not the roommates that are the problem. It's the light."

Jessica has tried blackout curtains, but her roommate is particular about decorating so she hasn't put them up in their shared bedroom. Instead, she's trying a sleeping mask to block out the light. "I put it on and I had a dream that I was wearing sunglasses and I couldn't get them off."

Tamar laughs, but admits sheepishly, "In the winter I sleep with a hood on my head, over my eyes."

"Why in the winter?"

Tamar replies, "It's too hot in the summer."

Both of them try to return to a "normal" schedule for their time off. They are not always successful.

"A lot of times," says Jessica, "if I don't have anything to do that night, I'm like, 'Forget it, I am sleeping until 5 o'clock or whenever my alarm wakes me up.'" She takes a bite of cinnamon toast, frustrated, "But then I miss the whole day sleeping."

Tamar nods knowingly, "That's the frustrating thing about working nights is that you waste a whole day of your week catching up on your sleep."

Jessica adds, "That's why we work three days because we technically work four, one of them sleeping."

"But it is amazing," continues Tamar, "once you get through that day after your last shift, you bounce back to a normal person's schedule just like that. I can go back and forth now without a problem."

Not that they don't both need a little help heading into another three-night week.

"Caffeine," says Tamar. "It's all about the caffeine."

The surly waitress has already cleared the table and only a few smears of grease remain. Jessica and Tamar climb out of the booth and weave their way to the door. Outside it's early fall, and the morning light is diffuse and calming. They move toward the subway, heading downtown to errands or bed. Jessica mentions a semiregular routine of hopping off the train near Central Park and taking a walk.

"I like walking across the park in the morning because there's not too many people," she says. "It's almost like you get a second wind after you've been up for so long."

# FIVE: STAY AWAKE

**S**he's sleeping now." Angela points to a monitor crowded with digital indicators. "Her waves have changed."

It's nearly midnight on a Wednesday night in February. Angela, a respiratory therapist, and her colleague are settling down to a long night of watching other people sleep in a clinic designed to diagnose and study sleep disorders. Angela, a thirtyish natural blonde, slender and soft-spoken, is originally from the West Coast, where she also worked nights as a respiratory therapist. At the moment, she stares intently at rows of data scrolling across a monitor in the cramped control room. In one corner of the monitor, a small window shows a live feed from an infrared camera aimed at a sleeping woman. Angela points to an undulating line on the monitor and says, "She just had a little arousal here. This is her alpha here, she's awake. Then it starts to slow down a little bit here. Then right here there's like a little bit of sleep. Then the voltage gets really low and then she's in her sleep."

None of this is clear to the untrained eye, but Angela does her best to make it seem obvious. The woman in the next room looks peaceful enough on the monitor, bathed in the green hue of the infrared camera; her low snore seeps out of loudspeakers next to the monitor. Angela describes the various wires and tubes that took her most of the evening to tape and tie onto the woman's body. "She gets a partial EEG because we're looking at sleep stages. Any kind of leg movement that she might have, we look for restless legs, periodic limb movements. Her snore sensors, she gets two of those. And then we have two airflow channels, the cannulas that are in her nose. One measures airflow by temperature changes in exhaling and the other one measures it by pressure changes. And then we have respiratory belts, one around her thorax and one around her abdomen watching the rise and fall of her chest and abdomen. And then her oxygen we always monitor, and then her pulse. And the position that she's in, too."

It is a wonder the woman can sleep at all.

"We call this stage two sleep," explains Angela, referring to the patient. "There are five stages. Stage one and stage three are transition stages, you don't stay in those for very long." She scrolls back through the timeline on the monitor to demonstrate the different stages. "This is stage one, very low frequency and you can see she's only in it maybe for a total of two minutes, and then she goes into stage two. Throughout the night, you probably spend most of your night in stage two. Then there's stage three and four, which are considered slow-wave sleep, delta sleep. Three is kind of a transition, you only stay in it for a very short time and then you go into stage four. Then stage five is REM."

Angela explains how most people move in and out of the various stages through a normal ninety-minute sleep cycle, staying in REM sleep, the deepest sleep, for only 20 to 25 percent of the time. "Now, this is for normal people," she says. "We don't get a lot of normal people here."

The body has a natural clock. That clock, better known as circadian rhythms, regulates more than just the hormones that induce sleep, such as melatonin. They also affect body temperature, heartbeat, respiratory function, blood pressure, urine excretion, hormone secretion, cell division, liver function, amino acid levels, DNA synthesis, and metabolism. In fact, circadian rhythms affect most body functions in one way or another. Circadian rhythms, from the Latin meaning "about a day," regulate these functions in peaks and troughs that come in roughly twenty-four-hour cycles. Nerve cells in the brain's hypothalamus receive information from the eyes, which is why changes in light affect circadian rhythms. It's also why circadian rhythms peak in the late afternoon and drop in the early morning. One way to think of the effect of circadian rhythms on a person's energy level is like a solar-powered light: after several hours of sunlight, the lamp burns brightly, but during the night its energy lags.

Working nights, or even rotating shifts, upsets the body's natural clock. For instance, melatonin is usually produced at night when our eyes are closed, shutting off light to the retina. Nightshift workers who stay awake all night do not produce as much melatonin as dayshift workers, even if they catch up on sleep during the day. But the health effects go far beyond sleep deprivation; decreased melatonin has been linked to higher risk of breast cancer and colorectal cancer. And it is especially true for workers who switch back to a dayshift schedule on days off, because their bodies never fully adjust between the two. Kevin Coyne, in *A Day in the Night of America*, writes that "night workers lose on average a full night's sleep each week, and with it goes some of their concentration, creativity, short-term memory and decision-making ability."

A soft but persistent alarm sounds in the control room of the sleep clinic and Angela turns to look over her colleague's shoulder. The oximeter from one of the patients has come loose and his EEG indictor is bouncing wildly back and forth.

"He's sweating," the colleague complains. She gets up to enter the patient's room and try to open a window. "And he keeps playing with the wires."

Angela is unconcerned. The EEG reading is an artifact of the perspiration, not an accurate reading. There are only two patients tonight, though there is room for four, so there is much less to do. According to Angela, Wednesdays are usually slow.

Except for the fact that Tuesday through Thursday, the clinic hosts a sleep deprivation study. Unlike their typical patients who have trouble sleeping, the sleep deprivation patients are part of a research study looking at the effects of prolonged, well, sleep deprivation. By Wednesday night, Angela explains, "they've been up since Tuesday morning."

The study participant tonight is chatting on her mobile phone in low tones out in the hallway. "It's her second night," says Angela. "She seems okay, but the doctor caught her sleeping this morning." There's not much for Angela to do in regard to the study, except keep the participant awake. "Sometimes they're sitting here on the computer and every two minutes you're saying, 'Stay awake, stay awake, stay awake.' "

By the time the participant leaves the clinic on Thursday morning, she will have been awake for more than fifty hours. "They get paid for it, it's a study," explains Angela. "They take memory tests, they take tests on the computer, they have an MRI. It's mostly young college kids. They find it on Craigslist."

The study participant, a young African American woman, shuffles into the control room. She looks more bored than tired, offering a small smile. She sits down at an empty computer and kills some time online looking at MySpace.com profiles while Angela and her colleague keep an eye on the other monitors.

Sleep deprivation describes a range of conditions related to a lack of sleep over a specific period of time. According to Dr. Clete Kushida, editor of the definitive volume *Sleep Deprivation,* there can never be a complete absence of sleep, but a great enough "sleep debt" can accumulate over time to make continued wakefulness a feat "bordering on the heroic." Numerous studies have found a host of medical problems associated with a lack of normal sleep. Some focus on shift-work sleep disorders, which entail clinical levels of excessive sleepiness at night and insomnia during the day. Others concern the nightshift's significantly increased risk for accidents and errors. Another group of researchers report associations between shift-work-related sleep problems and increased health problems such as coronary heart disease, gastrointestinal disorders, diabetes, and depression. Numerous studies have also pointed to a possible link between shift work and cancer. In December 2007, the World Health Organization's International Agency for Research on Cancer signaled a significant shift in policy by confirming the link and adding night work to its list of probable carcinogens. Still, despite such extensive research, Columbia University sleep expert Dr. Robert Basner argues in the *New England Journal of Medicine,* "It is not yet precisely clear to what extent human cognitive and social performance is affected by acute or chronic sleep deprivation."

The snoring from the loudspeakers has gotten louder, but Angela does not seem to notice. "It's tough sometimes," she admits, referring to the low rumble coming from the speakers. "But actually, she's not very loud. Sometimes I'll call my husband just to tell him goodnight, and he's like, 'What the heck is that in the background?'"

Angela started work at the sleep clinic two years ago, and has worked the nightshift almost the entire time. "I went on maternity leave," she explains, "and when I came back I was working two nights and one day. Now I'm back on three nights, twelve-hour shifts." She pauses, then adds with a laugh, "Or thirteen, or fourteen."

Perhaps surprisingly, the freedom with which Angela moves on and off the nightshift, especially as a young mother, has been hard won. For more than one hundred years, bans on night work for women have been on the books. As early as 1898, the New York State legislature passed a night work law that stated, "No female shall be employed, permitted, or suffered to work in any factory in this state before six o'clock in the morning, or after nine o'clock in the evening of any day." Less than ten years later, the law was overturned as unconstitutional by the New York State Court of Appeals, but a movement against women's nightshift labor was under way. Prominent political figures, such as the Supreme Court justice Louis Brandeis with his tract "The Case against Night Work for Women," helped to create bans against women's nightshift labor in twenty-four states by 1913. By 1919, the movement went global when the International Labor Organization passed Convention no. 4 prohibiting industrial night work by women.

The twentieth century proceeded with greater and greater restrictions on women's labor at night, particularly in Europe. Midcentury social movements against such discriminatory labor practices eventually overturned the bans on night work for women in the United States, but as recently as the last ten years, debates on allowing women to work the nightshift were still taking place in France, Austria, and India. The stark paternalism of such regulation is difficult to discount, but advocates for the bans on women's night work argue that women, especially those with children at home, face greater exploitation from industries dependent on nightshift labor. Where social convention expects women to be primarily responsible for childcare, these advocates argue, forcing them to work nights creates grossly unfair conditions. At the very least, they argue, pregnant women should have the option of switching back to days during and after their pregnancy.

As a new parent, Angela has had to find creative ways of making her schedule work with the demands of an infant. "I work Wednesdays, Thursdays, Fridays," she says, "so he goes to daycare Thursdays and Fridays for about five hours, just so I can go home and get a few hours of sleep before I pick him up. The only thing that I miss is him sleeping, because he goes to bed thirty minutes after I'm out the door. And my husband probably likes the fact that it's just the boys a couple of nights in a row."

While her immediate family has conformed to the off-hour schedule, not everyone understands the peculiar challenges of the nightshift. "Even here sometimes they don't understand that you just got home two hours ago and they're calling you at 11 or 12 o'clock to ask you some trivial question about something that happened the night before. And I'm like, 'Do you realize I just got home at 9:30?'"

Not that she would trade places with the dayshift clinicians. As she explains, "It's black and white here. At night it's nice. During the day it's crazy. You want to stomp on the phone. This is why I didn't resist when they said, 'You gotta go back on three nights.' During the day here it's chaos."

Still, the irony is not lost on her and her colleague that they must stay up all night to watch others sleep. "As we're watching people in this nice sleep, we think, 'That looks nice.'" She claims she is one of those people who can sleep anytime, anywhere, but she knows there must be long-term effects of working nights. "You think that you get used to it," she says. "I think everyone who works the nightshift, no one sleeps well. So whatever amount of sleep that you're getting . . ." Her voice trails off. Then she speaks again in the hushed tones that come from working in a sleep clinic. "I don't think people that have worked the nightshift for thirty years have normal sleep."

---

In another hospital on another night in another borough, a tired second-year resident stands in the cardiac intensive care unit behind the nurses' station. He's in charge for the night. The resident, Dave, is tall, thin, unshaven, and glassy-eyed. He smiles weakly, then stares straight ahead. "I'm very tired," he says, "and sleepy." He explains that his extended shift started at 8 AM. It's just past 10 PM. Fourteen hours down. Thirteen hours to go.

A cheery third-year resident stands nearby. Catherine is the hospital's "house doc" for the night. She too is tall and lean, though bright-eyed and well-rested. "Don't start the countdown," she cautions gently. "You can't really start the countdown until like 2 AM."

The night has been a slow one, so Dave may get to sneak away for a nap in the lounge. "If it's a good night," he says. His tone isn't optimistic. He sounds downright grouchy. He's worked this shift every fourth night for almost a month. After he leaves tomorrow at 11 AM, he will have to do this marathon shift only one more time. When asked why interns and residents work so many hours, Dave thinks for a moment and says, "It makes no sense."

Catherine remembers some recent studies about residents and long shifts but not where they were published. She asks Dave if he knows. He opens his half-closed eyes a little wider in order to concentrate but seems confused by her question. He starts several sentences but cannot complete one. Once they come out as full sentences, a significant amount of time passes between each one. "My friend worked on that study . . . ," he begins. "I forget his name . . ." His words are slow, his eyes unfocused; he could easily be confused with a weary partygoer at night's end. It's unclear whether he cannot recall the name of the study author or of his friend, or if it's one and the same person. "He's like a medicine guy . . . ," he pauses, "who does sleep." In slow motion, Dave says that the study was published in the *New England Journal of Medicine* and that the author works at Brigham and Women's Hospital in Boston. "If I wasn't sleep deprived . . ."

Catherine returns a page about a patient she is "cross-covering" for a colleague and then tries to make an exit to allow Dave to get back to work. "The thing is," he says in something close to a slur, "I forgot what I was doing. I was going to go somewhere . . ." He stands motionless at the nurses' station. His eyes have closed more than halfway and he opens them widely again. He's trying to concentrate on what he was doing, but cannot remember. "It doesn't matter," he finally concludes.

Catherine makes a stealthy exit then admits that being the resident on this unit is a difficult job. "The worst thing," she says conspiratorially, is that if a patient under her care goes into cardiac arrest, "they'll call an overhead 'arrest-stat,' and it's the worst." Even if the resident has managed to get a little sleep, she says, they are the ones on call to run to the scene with the defibrillator. It does not matter if they are asleep, or if the patient is on a different floor, they're in charge. "And then, when you get there, you're responsible for resuscitating the person. You're the boss. And you're so foggy, you can hardly even balance because you have to jump up so fast." That's if you can even get to sleep in the first place. "When you're sleeping you're on edge because, 'what if they call?'" She stops, shakes her head, and adds, "It's just bad."

Dave slips into the bathroom across from where Catherine stands talking. As she winds up her story Dave steps back out and says, "Chrysler. Chesler. Or something. C-H-something. Charles. Czeisler, Charles Czeisler." Then he steps back into the bathroom. Catherine's pager goes off.

The study that Dave eventually remembered is a *New England Journal of Medicine* study by the Harvard Work Hours, Health, and Safety Group; the longtime sleep expert Charles Czeisler is a coauthor along with Christopher Landrigan. Published in October 2004, the groundbreaking study was the first to directly link sleep deprivation and medical errors. They compared interns working a "traditional schedule" (24+ hours every other night) with those on an "intervention schedule" (no extended shifts and no more than 63 hours per week). Interns working the traditional schedule made 35.9 percent more errors, 22 percent more "serious errors," 20.8 percent more "serious medication errors," and 560 percent more serious diagnostic errors. The intervention schedule was designed not only to give interns more sleep but also to minimize "errors due to handoffs of patient care and cross-coverage."

Another 2004 study by Czeisler and Steven Lockley, published in the *New England Journal of Medicine*, sought to investigate sleep-deprived interns' decreased ability to pay attention. "Attentional failures," such as Dave's inability to remember what he was doing, occurred more often at night. They also occurred more than twice as often on a traditional, extended schedule, such as Dave's, than on an intervention schedule with maximum sixteen-hour shifts and eighty-hour weeks. The intervention schedule called for an afternoon nap before the "night call" portion of a shift, and this alone added 5.8 hours of sleep per week to the tired interns' lives. Conversely, each additional hour worked resulted in a loss of 19.2 minutes of sleep per week.

There are more studies, yet a yawning gap exists between research and practice. A 2004 report titled *Keeping Patients Safe*, issued jointly by the Institute of Medicine and the Board of Health Care Services, finds that accident rates increase after 9 hours, double after 12 hours, and triple after 16 hours at work. With only 168 hours in a week, some interns still report working 140 hours. In 1998, the New York State health commissioner Barbara DeBuono found many New York City teaching hospitals in violation of state regulations to limit residents to eighty hours per week, with 20 percent working almost one hundred hours per week. In 2003, the Accreditation Council for Graduate Medical Education threatened to revoke the accreditation of a program at Johns Hopkins Hospital for violating rules about shifts. In 2006, *Chronobiology International* published research in which health care workers were found to be more efficient, more alert, and in a better mood with as little as a forty-minute nap.

Perhaps most staggering of all is another finding from the report *Keeping Patients Safe*. The report finds that "prolonged wakefulness" results in "performance impairments equal to or greater than those due to levels of intoxication deemed unacceptable for driving, working, and/or operating dangerous equipment." As an example of "prolonged wakefulness," when a person has been awake for seventeen hours, his or her performance impairment is equal to a blood alcohol level of 0.05 percent. This is the legal blood alcohol limit for driving in many European countries, although many international alcohol policy experts say that problems often begin at 0.04 percent. Belize, Guatemala, Mexico, Nicaragua, Paraguay, Canada, and the United States set the limit at 0.08 percent.

Surpassing even that, when a person has been awake for twenty-four hours his or her performance impairment is equivalent to a blood alcohol level of 0.10 percent.

As Dave says, fourteen hours into his twenty-seven-hour shift, "It makes no sense."

# SIX: YOU HAVE TO GIVE UP SOMETHING

**T**he first shift they offered me was the nightshift."

Esther, 52, sits erect, arms folded in front of her, at a green-trimmed table in the spacious if rather dreary hospital cafeteria. "I had to take it," she continues, her English tinged with the verbal rhythms of southern India, "because I had to work."

As usual, Esther is early for her shift at the squat outer-borough hospital. Though not yet 6 PM, it's February and night has already fallen. Outside, traces of the last snow still muddy the streets, and freezing rain drizzles from the sky. Inside, Esther is at home in the familiar hallways, waiting rooms, and cafeteria. She's worked here for more than twenty years.

The cafeteria is nearly empty at this hour, closing for the night before Esther's shift even starts. The large dining room feels much smaller than it is, cramped by its low ceiling and dim fluorescent light. The walls are painted a meant-to-soothe-you beige with an accent of mustard yellow to brighten the mood, and the linoleum floor picks up the same color scheme. It is perhaps a blessing that it closes early, forcing Esther to bring food from home to eat during her shift.

Esther managed to cajole some hot tea from the staff before they shut down the kitchen. She is soft-spoken, compact, and energetic—a beguiling combination of demure and assertive. Her black hair, pulled back into a barrette, is streaked with gray and auburn highlights, framing a round, bronze-skinned face. She still has not changed into her hospital scrubs, but you would never know it from her own loose-fitting navy pants and a white top with splashes of color.

"Nightshift is very hard, especially as a nurse," says Esther, shaking her head. She is reluctant to complain, but continues, "It is not easy at all, because you have to be on your feet, maybe all twelve hours." She elaborates, gesticulating a little with her small hands. "Most of the nurses, they don't stay on nightshift. They, after one or two years, go back to days. Because," she pauses, "healthwise." She lets that last point hang in the air, but the SUNY Center for Health Workforce Studies (CHWS) confirms her claim: only 20 percent of hospital registered nurses (RNs) in New York State work nights. Esther adds, laughing, "Well, they want to sleep in their beds. At home!"

Born and raised in Kerala, India, Esther pursued nursing despite her parents' protestations. "My parents didn't want me to go but I decided to go, because it is a noble profession and there is always a job security." Esther adds, "And then I really wanted to go abroad."

Esther's desire to work abroad seemed possible after finishing nursing school because of the perpetual nursing shortage in the United States. In 2002, the New York State Education Department predicted a shortage of 30,500 RNs by 2007. In January 2007, the New York State Nurses Association (NYSNA) reported that although predictions fell short, it is clear "supply will not meet demand" in the years ahead. NYSNA suggests this is largely because new nurses are not staying in the workforce in high enough numbers to compensate for the loss of retiring RNs.

Large numbers of foreign-born nurses in the United States help stave off the shortage. Nationally, 8 percent of RNs are foreign-educated. In New York State, more than 10 percent of RNs working in hospitals are foreign-educated, according to the CHWS. In New York City, a full 35 percent of RNs are foreign-born. Esther's hospital still recruits nurses from the Philippines, the origin of more than 30 percent of foreign-educated nurses in the United States and 5.6 percent in New York State hospitals.

Though trained as a nurse in India, Esther's route to the United States came through traditional social networks rather than nursing recruitment. She explains, "As a nurse I didn't come but as a housewife I came." At the time, in the early 1980s, her husband-to-be, also from south India, already lived in the United States. His sister, Esther explains, came to the United States in 1969 after changes in federal immigration policy permitted more foreign nurses to work here. She sponsored Esther's husband and four other siblings. "All of them are here," says Esther.

Once Esther's husband settled in New York, he returned to India for a wife. "He wanted a nurse," she says. "So they were looking for people, because we always have arranged marriages. So the family arranged the wedding, he married me, and then he petitioned for the visa."

She arrived in late 1983 on an immigrant visa. Like most foreign-educated nurses, Esther took her licensing exams here in the United States. In the year or so that it took to finish her exams, she worked as an LPN (licensed practical nurse) in a nursing home. The first job she got as an RN was at the hospital where she works now.

With no seniority, Esther's first job was on the nightshift. "In the beginning," she admits, "I was kind of sad to do nightshift, kind of jealous of my husband, because he's asleep at home. At that time it was hard for me." Then, her daughter was born, and the nightshift proved invaluable for sharing the childcare duties with her husband. "After she was born, it was so convenient for me. We only care about our children. Once they are born, we only want to take care of them. So it doesn't bother me at all anymore."

As members of the Christian Mar Thoma denomination, Esther and many other South Indian Malayalam-speaking women choose to work nights—usually as nurses—so that someone is always at home with their children. The trend is so pervasive that she can calculate how many years someone has worked nights by the age of her oldest child. In this way she knows that her sister-in-law has worked nights for thirty years. "Well, let's see, her son is what, 30 years old, so thirty years. As soon as the first child is born," says Esther, "we switch to nightshift." Although nursing still runs in the family, with a niece working as a nurse here in New York and a nephew studying nursing back in India, this trend of staying on the nightshift may change. Her niece worked nights for a year but, according to Esther, she did not like it. "Each person views their life in a different way."

Esther has seniority at the hospital now, which means that she could switch to the dayshift. "But I don't want to," she says. "I prefer nightshift." Her daughter is in college now, but Esther still prefers the nightshift because of her other devotion, church. The sociologist Sheba Mariam George studies Christian Keralite nurses in the United States, women like Esther, who demonstrate a consistent commitment to their churches and their families. George identifies three types of marriages within this community: those with equal partnerships, those that involve the husband's "forced-participation" in caring for children, and those in which the wives do everything. Esther's marriage is an equal partnership, but in order to participate fully in the life of her church, she says, "I forgo my sleep."

After her shift ends at 7 AM, she embarks on her one-and-a-half-hour commute by subway, eats breakfast, and goes to sleep. Her daughter has her own apartment and her husband works days, so she has the house to herself. "At home, I have nobody to bother me. I can sleep eight hours maybe. But any slight noise, any form, will wake me up and after that I cannot go back to sleep."

Esther puts that occasional insomnia to good use. She and the other women in her community who work the nightshift spend the day attending church services and helping people who need them. If she has to work that night, she will try to sleep an hour or two before returning to the hospital. Still, the routine can be taxing. As she admits, "We always sacrifice our sleep."

Esther grows animated when she hears that some nightshift workers do not have active social lives. "That is up to you!" she says. "You make your own friends. You keep up your friendships. It doesn't matter that they work nights, days, or which hospital, or where, that's up to you. It's up to me, whether I have friends or not. I want to have a community life. I want to have friends. I want to help them. I want them to help me. So that depends on me, on how I deal with people. If I don't call that person, I don't keep in touch with them, they will stop calling me too."

Esther refuses to allow her relationships to atrophy. "That's my routine," she explains, "I just sit down, grab the phone, sit there, have the cup of coffee, and call each one I want to call and check how they're doing."

This willingness to put relationships above sleep keeps Esther from being disconnected. "Sleep is a problem," she says simply, "but in order to accomplish something you have to give up something."

Esther admits that the nightshift schedule has some drawbacks. "Sometimes I get very irritable," she says, adding, "and I get migraine headaches when I don't sleep very well during the daytime." Mirroring others' comments, she admits she is also affected by the eating schedule. "When I go home, I usually have a breakfast and then go to sleep. That's not good for me," she scolds, "but if I don't eat something then I get headache, you know, hypoglycemic headache." Part of the problem is the lack of services on the nightshift; the cafeteria is closed and her responsibilities make it difficult to take an extended break. As she explains, "At 6 in the morning you really crave some food. Your stomach is empty. The Indian nurses, we all say, 'Now is the time we'd like to have some Indian dishes.' There are special dishes, the hot pancakes, or whatever, that we make. But we cannot get anything at that time. We have to go home and do it."

Her meals include breakfast after work, a meal when she wakes, and another meal before her shift. It's almost a dayshift eating schedule but it can still cause digestive problems for her. On her four days off she stays on a dayshift schedule. "By the time I get adjusted," she says, "then I am back on work. But I cannot complain. It's a long time now I have been working like this. The body adjusts to the routine." Esther smiles; she borders on giddy.

Unlike some people who say they never see their spouses or children when they work nights, Esther has no complaints. Her husband works Monday through Friday 8 AM to 4 PM and has weekends off. She works only alternate weekends, so they have every other weekend together and the weeknights that she does not work. Moreover, she does not take any extra shifts that would take time away from her family. Single nurses, says Esther, often pick up such extra shifts. "That's what everybody does. All nurses do that. But I don't do it. You need money, but it's not the first thing in my life."

According to Esther, the nursing profession is very well paid. CHWS numbers indicate that more than 50 percent of full-time New York State hospital RNs earn at least $60,000 per year, and nearly 24 percent earn between $60,000 and $69,999. Of course, the cost of living is high in New York City, but it is still a lot of money, especially when compared to other nightshift workers in the city who work far more than three nights a week for far less than $60,000 a year.

Money is not what keeps Esther loyal to her profession or her hospital. Not only did she have her one and only daughter at this hospital, as well as a hysterectomy and other surgeries, but her unit has always accommodated her schedule, she says. At one point, things were so difficult in her personal life that she carried around a resignation letter. She was ready to turn it in if she could not have the flexibility she needed. If she needed to work double shifts, or whatever shift she needed, the hospital made it work. "So I am really grateful to this place," says Esther. "I could go to Long Island somewhere but I am always grateful for how they treated me when I was in need."

It's 6:45 and she still needs to change into scrubs in the nurse's lounge on her unit. Like a gazelle, she swiftly rises and glides across the floor toward the elevator. Esther works in the Neonatal Intensive Care Unit (NICU), and has since her second year at the hospital. Hers is a Level III NICU, which means they care not only for newborn babies but for those that are especially critical. The NICU is an especially difficult place to work nights, she says, because the babies require such acute care. "It's not like other patients, where they call you, pressing the light. We have to be at their side all the time." This is because the babies, who can weigh as little as 500 grams, do not have fully developed organs. They are in danger of respiratory failure, brain damage, and a host of other life-threatening ailments. "We cannot sleep," Esther says emphatically. "You have to be mentally alert all the time. Any change in their heart rate, or respiration, or whatever, you have to call the doctor, we have to attend them. Every minute we have something to do."

She does not wear a watch or any other jewelry. In the NICU they are not allowed to wear any jewelry except a wedding band, no nail polish, and no long nails. "The babies are really tiny babies and they catch infection right away so we have to be very careful," she explains. She takes this seriously and does not even wear a wedding band. "We have clocks everywhere," she says, "so we count the heart rate and everything by looking at the clock."

The elevator stops and Esther steps off on the NICU floor. She carries with her two paper cups, one half-full of tea and the other full of milk for "night coffee" on the unit. Since the cafeteria is closed and they cannot leave the babies' sides, they can eat or drink only what they remember to bring with them. Whereas most people on the nightshift sing the praises of caffeine in all its many forms, Esther has "maybe one cup of coffee" during the twelve hours of her shift.

At once speedy and graceful, Esther breezes by the pediatric intensive care unit and swipes her security card at the double doors to the NICU. The unit decor is the usual hospital beige with bits of accent colors. Esther waves hello to a nurse in the small reception area and marches past the first two rooms on her way to the back of the unit. Though the South Indian nurses primarily work nights, her unit also has nurses and doctors who are Korean, Filipino, Haitian, and Russian. "We have a really diverse community," she says. "It's really nice."

The room nearest the reception area has incubators arranged in a U-shape, most of them unoccupied. A man sits in a chair holding his premature baby. The baby's mother stands beside him in a hospital gown. The lone nurse, who Esther points out is from Korea, wears a face of complete calm. The father hands off the baby to its mother, and the nurse begins to teach him how to do CPR on a doll. "You're taking too long," the nurse says. Her tone is both serious and joking. The mood is light, casual. "It's been sixty seconds," she says. "Hurry up. One, two, your baby's dead now."

Farther up, farther in, the next room is busier, but nevertheless calm. A couple of nurses move about, but they are unhurried. The back room seems smaller; each room seems to get smaller as you go back into the unit. Another mother dressed in a hospital gown prepares to hold her baby. All of the babies are black. There are three females working in this part of the unit. In fact the father learning CPR is the only man in the NICU.

"This is our set-up here," says Esther proudly. The babies are in small incubators that look like spaceship pods. Myriad monitors, cords, and cables attach to the walls and feed into the incubators. Physiologic, or cardiorespiratory, monitors check respiratory and heart rates. Scales measure weight in the smallest of increments.

There is so much equipment, so many vulnerable infants, such constant beeping from so many different machines. Like most units in a hospital, it is an overwhelming sensory experience to the uninitiated. And yet those who work on these units are relaxed, at home. Another NICU nurse stands near an incubator monitoring a baby. Describing this unit where the smallest people get a chance to live, she says, "This is where we hang out." They are all so calm. "We have to be," she says, "otherwise we'd be AHAHAHA."

Esther walks up to an incubator where a very tiny baby lies sleeping. "This is our smallest baby," she says. "In earlier days," Esther says quietly, "their parents were on drugs and things like that, and we used to get very bad babies . . . very critical ones. Now it is less. Because of the education, the maternal education and care, it is less than before. Before, we used to get a baby, a child has a baby, she's only thirteen and she has a baby, but now it is less like that. It's better now."

Since the 1980s, Esther has witnessed changes not only in the increasing health of the premature babies in her care but outside the hospital as well. Though she now lives on Long Island, she once lived across the street from the hospital. "We used to get mugged," she says simply. "My husband has a gunshot wound here," she says, pointing just below her eye. "The scar is still here. That scar is still here! They hit him with the gun, because he didn't give the wallet, because he was practically new to the place. But now, the hospital, the surrounding is changed. Every day it's changing, new buildings are coming up." She nods again and says, "Before, it was so scary, but not anymore."

Esther turns back to the tiny infant encased in plastic. "She was born very premature," she explains.

But, Esther adds proudly, she is getting bigger every day.

1:26 COUNTER SEATS

1:37 BODEGA OWNER POLAROID

1:40  STATEN ISLAND FERRY

1:42 CLOCKS NEAR TIMES SQUARE

# SEVEN: FULFILLING MY DREAMS

**H**ow much do you think he's selling this for?"

The bleary-eyed woman sways ever so slightly, holding up a large spool of green ribbon. It's 1 AM on a January Tuesday at the Lucky Stop Deli, a tiny island of light on the Avenue of the Immigrant on the Lower East Side of Manhattan. Hassan is busy with another customer, and the ribbon woman waits her turn.

"How much you selling this for?"

Hassan, 21, looks at her, and then the ribbon in her hand. His head of curly black hair and thin goatee frame a confused stare. He scans the items in the small store, cases of soda and beer on one side, chips, crackers, and other dry goods on the other. He looks back at the woman.

"What is that?" he asks.

The woman laughs. "You're so funny, man." She shuffles back toward the refrigerator cases with the mysterious ribbon. "This is the best store."

Hassan watches her go and laughs. It's a clear, enunciated laugh—ha-ha-ha—that proves infectious. Between customers he bounces to the music pouring from a portable stereo below a display of potato chips. It might be anything from Led Zeppelin to Lambada, but tonight it's the Middle Eastern dance-fusion music of the late Ofra Haza, a Yemenite Jewish pop icon.

Originally from Yemen, Hassan moved to New York six months ago, and has worked the nightshift at the Lucky Stop Deli for the last five. On slow nights, he passes the time joking around with Santiago, his coworker from Mexico who makes sandwiches and works the small grill. Tonight is a slow night. "On the weekends people come in drunk and very hungry," he explains. "Sometimes girls come in here just messing around and don't order anything."

Corner convenience stores like the Lucky Stop are a mainstay of the block-based economy of New York City neighborhoods, though there is entrenched disagreement on what these stores are actually called. To many they are delis, descendants of delicatessens opened by Jewish immigrants more than a century ago. To many others, especially in Latino or formerly Latino neighborhoods, they are bodegas, descendants of the small grocery stores established at midcentury to serve communities that seldom received attention from larger national franchises. Whether it was Jewish immigrant entrepreneurs at the beginning of the twentieth century, or Latino *bodegueros* in the second half of the century, delis, bodegas, and corner stores have always been part of the immigrant history of New York City. Hassan is now one small part of that history.

The ribbon woman shuffles back to the counter with two forty-ounce bottles of Ballantine malt liquor. "This is a great store," she says again. She pays and turns toward the door as a Domino's pizza delivery man enters. The ribbon woman pauses and says, "I mean, if the Domino's man comes to this store, then . . ." She resumes her exit, adding, "They know the value of a . . . whatever." And she shuffles out of the store.

Like the nurses and cab drivers, Hassan works a twelve-hour shift. But he works seven nights a week. His shift is from 11 PM to 11 AM, a grueling schedule that pays $500 a week and a free place to live in Brooklyn. But Hassan is not complaining. "I like the nightshift," he says. "I don't like the sun, the daytime. I like to sleep in the daytime and stay up all night." His sister, who is studying medicine in Belarus, is not so enthusiastic about Hassan's nightshift work. "She told me it is not good," he says. "Because in the body there are hormones that are very active in the day, not in the night. So she does not recommend it."

To pass the long hours of the night, Hassan tries to keep it interesting. "Some nights are very, very boring," he says. "But some nights are funny. A lot of customers are like my friends now, they come every day. They stay with me, like dancing. I have all my CDs and we dance. If there is a beautiful lady there, I just put a good CD on and she will start dancing. Sometimes I dance by myself, me and Santiago." For Hassan, watching the clock just makes the night longer. "But as long as I do my job, do all the things that I have to do, time goes by so fast. Very fast. Especially these days, because I have to go to school, go to work, go to sleep, go home, change."

New York is actually Hassan's third stop since leaving his home in Yemen. He spent four months in San Antonio, Texas, studying English, then several months in Augusta, Georgia, studying computer information systems. A Yemeni friend in New York, Aman, convinced him to make the move to the city, and he is now enrolled at a local community college. He hopes to earn a bachelor's degree in political science before returning to Yemen. For now, his nightshift salary pays his tuition and the few expenses he incurs when he is not sleeping, studying, or working.

It was Aman who arranged Hassan's employment at the deli. They share a room in Brooklyn, but hardly see each other. "We both go to school and so we have to manage our time." Aman works the dayshift, the same twelve hours as Hassan in reverse. The schedule leaves little time for a social life. "Sometimes I want to go out, have dinner, share some moments with friends. I can't do it, because I got nightshift. I have to be here at this time. And if I didn't sleep I would be tired at night. Every night. Seven days."

The phone behind the counter chirps and Hassan is on it by the second ring. "What's up, man?" He smiles into the receiver. He takes a pen and a pad of paper. "Cajun turkey, lettuce, tomato, Muenster cheese. Whatever you want, roll, hero, whatever. Hot. Salt, pepper, right? Some sugar?" He laughs—ha-ha-ha. "Just give him like twenty minutes, all right? I'll call you back when it's ready." Hassan pauses, listening for a moment. "All right, then walk slowly."

Hassan hangs up and the door swings open. A man enters with a large paper bag full of Italian loaves. There is no room on the deli counter, so he stacks them on an empty shelf under the *Daily News*. The delivery man turns to Santiago and goes into detail on the night's bread delivery in Spanish.

The door opens again, and an imposing figure pushes inside. He is tall, wide, and moving slowly. There is the pungent smell of someone with no place to go. "Good evening," he announces. He pauses, then says, "Or good morning," and moves to the refrigerator case.

Hassan pays the delivery man in cash from the register as the door opens once again. This time, it's a young, well-heeled hipster from the rapidly gentrifying Lower East Side. He shakes a few strands of hair from his face and marches straight up to Hassan.

"You got a package for me or what?" he asks.

Hassan smiles, "I told you, you got to wait."

The hipster glances at Santiago who is putting together his Cajun turkey sandwich. "No," he responds. "I'm saying, a package. Aman didn't tell you anything about that?"

Hassan stares back blankly.

"Really? Bullshit."

"I don't know anything." Hassan looks under the counter. "Is that yours?" He points to a cardboard box. It's not the hipster's package.

"Motherfucker." And he storms off to look for a soda.

The imposing man trudges back to the counter and puts a forty-ounce can of Colt malt liquor in front of Hassan. He pays in change.

Hassan looks under the counter again. "Hey! Verizon?" He comes up with a package. The hipster shuffles over.

"You lying to me, or what?"

"No. I didn't know. I just saw it right now." Hassan pauses, "Can I see your ID?" He laughs—ha-ha-ha. "He didn't tell me about it, I just found it."

The hipster eyes the package. He is disappointed. "Aw, it's a fucking modem. Fuck."

"Modem?" Hassan asks. "You have a router upstairs? A wireless modem?"

Later, Hassan confirms that several nearby residents have packages delivered to the deli. Their mailboxes are too small for large packages or they are rarely home during daylight hours, so the store that never closes serves as a convenient way station. It is one way New York City remains a network of small communities where trust is still in circulation. And it has been that way for some time. In the early 1960s, the journalist and activist Jane Jacobs wrote in *The Death and Life of Great American Cities* about the common practice of leaving extra sets of keys with local shopkeepers, and the role these characters played in maintaining block-based social networks. Then as now, stores that stay open all night are particularly important in this ongoing attempt to forge a relative sense of community.

Today, that block-based social network, organized as it so often is around the all-night deli, is reciprocal in a way Jacobs could never have predicted. Hassan's question about the modem was not idle curiosity; he gets his homework done online by using the wireless networks of the tenants above the store—with their permission, of course.

The phone rings again. "Lucky Deli," Hassan says into the receiver. "What's the address?" There is a long pause. "Are you okay? What?" After a few false starts, Hassan gets a name and an order. "It will be ready in about twenty minutes." He hangs up the phone and shakes his head. "Sometimes we deliver in the nighttime. She asked me for a six-pack of beer, a sandwich, and wheat crackers. She doesn't even know what she is saying. I'm not even going to tell Santiago."

As a practicing Muslim, Hassan does not drink alcohol, but he has learned the fine art of dealing with drunk customers. "I see a lot of drunk people do a lot of bad things that they do not even mean," he says. He tells a story about two men who stumbled into his store a couple of months earlier. "They were drunk. They didn't know what they were doing," he explains. Hassan noticed they were slipping candy into their pocket, but decided not to confront them, hoping they would simply leave. Unfortunately, they did not. "They tried to attack me, but I defended myself."

Hassan looks around behind the counter, "I've got some stuff here." He finds what he is looking for—an aluminum baseball bat. He holds it up with a wicked grin. "There is another one there." He points over to Santiago who reveals a wooden bat with a noticeable crack on the handle. "I broke it on his face," he says, referring to the drunk assailant. "I had to defend myself because he started attacking me. I was so patient. I knew they took something, but I didn't mind. I thought, 'Just go away.' But when he attacked me, I had to defend myself."

Hassan called the police that night, something he hesitates to do very often. "Once the police came, I got into the car and we searched for them on the next block. Like three blocks down, we found them." The police arrested the two men, and Hassan found himself in the middle of judicial bureaucracy. "I don't have time for these problems," he explains. "When you go to school you don't have time to sleep, and you call the cops, they will call you again and again, interviews, witness, go to court, a lot of procedure. I try to avoid that."

Three young men push through the door. They are underage and seem to be the only sober customers of the night. They loiter around the candy until one of them speaks to Hassan with some familiarity. Hassan looks confused. The young man pauses. "Yo, I saw you today or the other guy?"

"No, the other guy."

"I saw the other guy?" He is embarrassed, but Hassan laughs it off—ha-ha-ha—putting him at ease.

Hassan and Aman do not look alike. Aman is taller and thinner than Hassan, but to most of their customers, they are interchangeable. Just as the deli itself is interchangeable with the dozens of Yemeni-owned convenience stores that line the streets and avenues of New York City. But Hassan and Aman are friends, and wouldn't mind seeing each other more than the half hour during their shift change. Hassan says, "A couple of weeks ago we had a man who worked here during the nightshift, and me and Aman worked during the day, six hours and six hours." He smiles. "Very fun. We slept very good and went out. We did a lot of things." His smile fades. "But," he continues, "we fired that guy, because he is not good at this business. So maybe we're looking for somebody."

The door opens and another stranger pushes through on his way to the beer case. Hassan adds, "The boss said there is somebody coming soon."

———

"I love this food."

Hassan is seated at a large round table at Sanaa restaurant on Atlantic

Avenue in Brooklyn. It's a Saturday night in February and the temperature has dipped below freezing. Soon Hassan will make the trek into Manhattan to take his shift at the Lucky Stop Deli. He doesn't have a winter coat, but the cold doesn't seem to bother him. For now, he is surrounded by plates of hummus, falafel, tabbouleh, and malooga. The waiter arrives with two more plates of spicy beef and liver. Hassan smiles and tears off a piece of malooga, a Yemeni flatbread. "My mother made all this kind of food." He scoops up a mouthful of liver with the malooga and says of the food, "It's not the same."

Hassan's mother still lives in Yemen with his father and older sister, though it has been more than a year since he last saw them. He has two other siblings who have also left home, a brother in California and a sister in Belarus. According to Hassan, a good life in Yemen is possible with the right kind of experience, but that experience is rarely available in Yemen. "If you have the opportunity to leave," he says, "anybody would leave."

The diaspora of Hassan's siblings is not the same forced migration that characterizes so many others on the nightshift. Hassan's father was a military pilot who now works for a commercial airline. They are part of the middle class in Yemen, with a nice house and a car for Hassan when he turned sixteen. Theirs is a migration of opportunity, a chance to accrue social and economic capital before returning to Yemen, where a foreign education can be highly valued. As Hassan explains, "Three years, or four years ago, when I was in high school, I knew I was going to come here. Even my father and my family told me that you can get good opportunity here. Because my father studied aviation here, in California."

Following in his father's footsteps, Hassan joined the military in Yemen, serving during the relatively peaceful period since the last civil war in 1994. It was his military contacts that facilitated a diplomatic visa to the United States. He recognizes that it is not always so easy for his countrymen to travel. "It's harder to come here because of visa regulations, expenses. They will not let you get in unless they know who you are and who has got your back. Like a government, like trustworthy people."

Hassan avoided many of the indignities and delays other Yemenis face when applying for a visa, but he could not avoid the more intimate frustrations of prejudice once in New York City. Working the nightshift in a Manhattan deli brings him face to face with a broad spectrum of human ignorance, and it is not always easy to take, especially when confronting the post-9/11 racial epithet *terrorist*. "Sometimes people say, 'You're a terrorist.' And I think, 'What am I doing here?'" His response is usually to remain silent, but his frustration is difficult to contain. "I think to myself, 'Listen, Hassan, if he says that, he's stupid. I have a good job, a good school. I'm fulfilling my dreams. Whatever he says, I don't care. He's doing the wrong thing.' And that makes me feel better."

Fortunately, not all of those who stop in for a forty-ounce malt liquor or a can of soda are so abusive. Not even most. "I met a customer," Hassan recounts, "he had a small sign on his shirt that said, 'Get together for all immigrants.' He gave it to me, actually, in the store. When I asked him why he did this, he said, 'We are a nation of immigrants. All of these regulations are wrong.'"

The restaurant is getting busier, filling up with an eclectic mix of Arabic-speaking men, a few families, and a sprinkle of English-speaking white couples from the adjacent upscale neighborhoods. Hassan likes to guess the origin of each customer as they enter, laughing at the telltale Yemeni or Egyptian accent. This particular strip of Atlantic Avenue boasts a relatively high concentration of Yemeni immigrants, though Hassan lives several miles away. His cousin lives upstairs, so Hassan puts in a to-go order to bring up to him before he leaves.

Dinner out is unusual for Hassan, who spends most of his time studying, working, or sleeping. His impression of New York is little more than just that, an impression. "First I came here for a visit in March," he says. "It was really nice. Lots of things to do. Now . . ." He trails off, searching for the words to express his disappointment. "Work is tough, studying. I'm not having fun."

Hassan describes his routine, a relentless cycle since he works seven nights a week. Work from 11 PM to 11 AM and sleep from noon to 4 or 5 PM. On days he has class, it's back to Manhattan by 7 PM. Otherwise he spends his time studying. "I'm very tired. The hardest part is when I get up. For me, it's okay. I can work. But somehow, I'm so weak getting up, I can't do it very fast. The alarm clock can ring for hours, and I don't care.

I don't even hear it. Sometimes, I turn it off and I'll say I'll sleep for ten minutes, and then three hours pass."

At work, Hassan fights the sleep with coffee. "Yeah," he says. "That's for damned sure. Three cups." And he keeps himself entertained by engaging the customers, laughing with Santiago, dancing, and listening to music. But his only friends are his roommate Aman, whom he never sees, and the few regular customers whom he sees only while on the job. "The nightshift is an easier job," he says. "But when it comes to life, the opposite. If I work in the daytime, I would enjoy the nighttime, going out or something. With the nighttime, you sleep in the daytime and if you have any appointments you are going to miss them just to work on the nightshift." Even on weekends, when classes are not in the way of socializing, he finds little time to see friends. "Usually on the weekends, what I do is the laundry and homework. But the most important thing that I do is sleep a lot. Twelve hours." He shrugs and adds, "I'm lazy I guess."

The waiter brings Hassan two large plastic bags filled with take-out, some for his cousin upstairs and some to share with Aman as they change shifts. In those few shared moments, he and Aman will compare notes from their classes earlier in the day. Aman will complain about the classes he was forced to take, and Hassan will play the pros and cons of different areas of study. "I'm not sure what to do," he admits. "I like politics. International relationships with other countries. I started with Liberal Arts because it has a lot of majors inside. So I take math classes, history, physics, science. Besides that you can take music, English, everything."

For Hassan, the credential is his ticket home. "I'm planning to stay here a maximum of five years," he explains, "until I finish my education. Then I will go back, get married." It is a refrain heard from most recent immigrants. The well-laid plans for a speedy return home. For many, though, "home" becomes a fuzzy concept as roots sink into new soil and the links to distant family become thin and hard to maintain. But something rings true with the way Hassan presents his case, keeping his eye on Yemen, with little thought of staying in the United States long-term. "For me," he says, "I'm not thinking about a green card. And I don't have to keep my money in a bank account so I can go home. I don't need that, because I already have a house there in Yemen. In Yemen, everything is good. My purpose is to have an education. It's not about a good job or not. Here it's hard for me, but my parents keep telling me, 'You're still young, you have to work hard. Then one day you will taste that what you did is very nice.'" He thinks for a moment, then says, "What is that thing people say when you do it the hard way? It's like 'easy come, easy go.'"

Hassan pushes back from the table. Outside the temperature is dropping and he steels himself for the wind. Gathering up the food for his cousin, he heads for the door. "I'm still young," he says, exiting into the red glow of the restaurant's neon sign. "I have to do it. I have an opportunity and I have to use it very carefully." He steps onto the pavement. "I don't want to mess it up."

# EIGHT: I DON'T KNOW WHERE IS THE KEYS

tell you the truth, I've been here fifteen years and I don't know where is the keys!"

Sunny, 42, cackles at his joke and pushes his paper hat off his forehead. He looks a dozen years older than he is, easily weighs two hundred pounds, and has a distinct bulbous nose and ruddy complexion. Tonight he wears a black Rick James t-shirt, black pants, and tennis shoes. Turning back to the grill, he expertly manages several orders at once, flicking his free hand to the beat of his metal spatula and the Arabic music overhead. It's after 2 AM on a Saturday night in late May, and the late-night rush at Sunny's Brooklyn deli has just begun.

Sunny's deli sits on a busy avenue, snugly sandwiched between a subway entrance and an underground pool hall that's hardly noticeable save the small crowd at its door day and night. Like most neighborhood stores in New York City, Sunny's makes most of its money off the cigarettes and lottery tickets it sells to on-the-go pedestrians. But deep inside, past the racks of magazines, the cases of soda and beer, and the shelves of dusty canned goods, there are a few tables and a well-worn counter where Sunny offers up everything from beef burgers to homemade falafel every night.

Tonight there is a steady stream of customers, with more on the way as the night tips toward dawn. Sunny dances in dizzying motion between the counter and grill, filling orders and lifting spirits. Overhead, a small television hardwired to the New York Lottery channel displays winning numbers and a patina of grease and smoke covers handmade signs. Most announce menu items, but one reads "All the hot food will be taxed." The space fills and patrons come in less and less sober, barking orders at Sunny. He takes it in stride, placating impatience with a gap-toothed grin, a practiced banter, and an infectious hiccupping chuckle that sounds disarmingly similar to that of Popeye the Sailorman.

"At 4 o'clock, forget it," Sunny says, his English tumbling out in a thick Ramallah accent. "You can't even talk to me, it's like a tuna fish in here." His malapropism of the more familiar "sardines" still captures nicely the tightly packed crowds that fill the narrow space after the bars and clubs begin to close on a Friday or Saturday night. He motions toward the front of the store where his partner and two or three Yemeni employees man the register for the goods on the shelves. "Monday to Friday, their business at nighttime is like $500 or $700," he explains. "It's not bad." Sunny smirks and leans in close, "But on the weekend, I kill! From 10 o'clock at night to 5 in the morning, almost two grand." With a sly shrug of his eyebrows, he adds, "It's like big business."

Whether called bodegas, delis, or corner stores, these small businesses do indeed mean big business. According to the Bodega Association of the United States, there are 25,000 such stores in New York City, generating annual sales of more than $7 billion and providing more than 65,000 jobs. And they are almost always independently owned by immigrant entrepreneurs.

According to a 2007 report from the Center for an Urban Future, foreign-born New Yorkers have always been more likely to start their own businesses than native-born. In some neighborhoods, the rate is two to one. As of 2000, the foreign-born population was still only 36 percent of the city's total population, yet half of all self-employed workers in New York were born outside the United States. Immigrants from Syria, Afghanistan, Iran, Israel, and Lebanon all start businesses at more than twice the rate of native-born New Yorkers, in some cases four times the rate.

And yet, recent immigrants face many more obstacles to opening businesses than native-born entrepreneurs. Aside from the universal problem of credit and capital, which is exacerbated by their recent arrival, newcomers face language barriers and a labyrinthine bureaucracy that requires a hard-won cultural literacy. For immigrants from the Middle East, these barriers have become treacherous in the wake of September 11, 2001. Detainments and deportations immediately after 9/11 effectively shut down dozens of small businesses run by and employing newcomers from predominantly Muslim nations.

The orders have started to pour in, but Sunny remains unflappable. In an uncharacteristic moment of carelessness, he knocks several dishes to the floor. The crash of thick porcelain almost drowns out the loud Jordanian music and the impatience of waiting customers, but only for a moment.

"I'm sorry, not my fault," Sunny says to no one in particular. "I'm the one gotta pay for it, it come out of my pocket anyway."

---

"It's my granddaughter. She's on the phone."

Approaching 1 AM on another Saturday night, Sunny's four-year-old granddaughter cannot sleep. He laughs into the phone and offers a few soothing words. Sunny's graying hair is freshly cut but he sports a day's graying stubble on his chin. His paper chef's hat has a blue stripe tonight, his black t-shirt advertises vintagedj.com, and his pants are crisp Tommy Hilfiger khakis. He hangs up and says with a broad smile, "She wants me to bring her a cheeseburger for breakfast."

Sunny has not been at work long tonight. He usually arrives after 10 PM and eases into the late-night rush. It's quiet for now. He leans both arms on the counter and gazes up to the front of the store. A few patrons dash in and out, grabbing cigarettes or soda, but the back is empty.

"I'm Palestinian, from Ramallah," he says. It's as much a statement of fact as it is a subtle political provocation. He was born in 1964 and lived through the Six-Day War in 1967 that annexed the West Bank to Israel. But Sunny, who chats easily with a few Israeli regulars in Hebrew, does not allow politics to interfere with commerce. He spent part of his youth in Jerusalem, but left, with his family, in 1978. For the next several years, Sunny crisscrossed the Western Hemisphere. "I lived in Brazil three years. I lived in Venezuela two years. Then I lived in Costa Rica for a year. Then I moved to Puerto Rico for a year. Then I came to the United States." Somewhere between those ports of call, Sunny spent a year in Italy working in a Sicilian flea market. That's where he met his Sicilian wife of twenty-six years.

They settled in Queens, had kids, and Sunny put his globe-trotting business and language skills to good use. With bedding purchased from a Jewish wholesaler, he became a door-to-door salesman to mostly Latino clients. "I bought the stuff for $15 to $18, then sell them for $89," Sunny explains. For most of his clients, he arranged payment plans as low as $10 per week. Soon he had $280,000 in debts to collect, which he sold for half price to another Palestinian. "I don't know how the guy got $140,000," he says. "I didn't ask him."

With a fresh supply of capital, Sunny searched for a more stable investment. He found it in this tiny store, run then by a Yemeni immigrant. "When I came here," he says, "they already had the business running. But Yemenis, they don't know nothing about food. They know how to sell candy, magazines, lottery, beer, soda, that's all." At first, he made only $120 a night. He offered to reinvigorate the prepared food side of the small business. "I said, 'This restaurant in here, we can fix this.' I look at the worker; he didn't even know how to make an egg. I thought, 'I know these people. I know how to figure them out.' I said, 'Listen, I am a man with five languages, you know? I can make this business up to the sky.' " The Yemeni owner offered Sunny a partnership for $150,000. He countered with $80,000 and a promise to turn at least $70,000 in profits. "The guy talked to his partner, and he said, 'Okay, we'll do it on paper. If the business doesn't go, you owe us $70,000.' " He accepted.

Sunny plastered the neighborhood with fliers to lure customers. "I tell them I make shawarma, falafel, hummus, this, that, burgers, cheeseburgers, cheese steak, turkey burger." After a year, Sunny was turning a large profit and his partners forgave the $70,000 debt. "Because we are Muslim," he explains. "We trust each other. Now, this place is worth no less than $1 million and a half. You don't touch this place for less. Not even $100,000 less, you won't touch it. Because this is an $80,000-to-$90,000-a-week business. Twenty-four hours."

According to Sunny, much of the revenue from that twenty-four-hour schedule comes from the nightshift. It's one reason he's almost always behind the counter from 10 PM to dawn. "In winter," he explains. "I never see the daylight. This has happened two or three years straight. I never see the daylight."

After several years, Sunny's social relationships, not to mention his sleeping and eating habits, have conformed to this commitment to the busiest hours of the night. "Well, my family gets used to me, you see," he says. That usually means arriving home from work around 8 in the morning, spending some time with the various members of his extended family who live in his three-story house in Queens, then sleeping, usually from 2 to 9 PM. "My wife, she wakes me up with a cup of coffee, that's my cigarette," he says. "I drive to work at 10, 11 o'clock. From 11 to 5, six hours, not bad."

When he is not working, Sunny prefers to spend time with his family at home. "The Arabic people are different," he explains. "The Arabic, the Palestinian, we like to have the family together. We don't like to separate." For Sunny this distinguishes Arabic families from the average American family. "Here, they see their mother when Mother's Day comes. Sometimes they say, 'Yo Sunny, I don't see my mother for the whole year. Mother's Day is today, I gotta send her flowers.'" Sunny chuckles and offers his standard verbal cue that he thinks something just isn't right, "Hello!"

Though Sunny feels somewhat disconnected from the U.S. emphasis on highly mobile, nuclear kin groups, he feels more closely allied to the extended kin networks maintained by his Latino neighbors and his wife's Italian family. More sedentary, agrarian economies, such as those in rural Latin America or the Middle East, support and even depend on large family networks. Sunny sent two of his children to Ramallah for five years to live with his mother, learn Arabic, and study the Koran. But as the postindustrial economy of the United States becomes the new global incessant economy, such traditional kin arrangements lose much of their salience. Mobility becomes an economic necessity, a quality at odds with the obligations and responsibilities of traditionally large families.

As kin ties become stretched across oceans and borders, migrants like

Sunny employ an array of techniques to maintain the connections. Most often this takes the form of capital that seems to flow more freely across borders than people do. Thus, Sunny supports family in Ramallah, as well as his wife's family back in Sicily. Though her parents passed away a few years ago, her brothers still run a small business that Sunny helped finance.

But as kin ties stretch, cultural ties can often snap in the process of dislocation. Sunny's wife, raised Catholic, not only learned how to prepare Palestinian dishes for her new extended household, but also eventually converted to Islam. Sunny says it had little to do with him. "I don't push her. She talked with my mother. She talked with Arabic friends. She went to the mosque. She looked. She read books. I never did ask her about it. I never told her, 'You have to be a Muslim.' " After ten years of marriage, she awoke one morning and proceeded to dress in the traditional head covering. "I said, 'What are you doing?' She said, 'You don't know? I took the Shahada yesterday.' I didn't force her, she did it herself. I give her more respect, but I didn't force her. We used to love her the way she was."

A young man enters, a girl on each arm. He gives a nod to Sunny and orders, "Grilled shrimp and cheese fries, Hakim." Sunny smiles and turns to the grill. After a few minutes he slides a plate of french fries topped with a dozen shrimp and smothered in American cheese over to the young man. "There you go, boss," he says.

Later, Sunny says a lot of young men order the shrimp to impress their dates, but the biggest sellers are cheeseburgers. "Friday, Saturday night, you're talking twenty-four in a case, maybe 150 burgers: 90 on Friday, 60 Saturday. Turkey burger, maybe 90 or 100. My order comes on Monday, seven cases of burger, four turkey burger, twenty-four each in it. Thursday, ten cases burger, ten cases turkey burger. Every week." That, along with the occasional platter of shrimp or shawarma, adds up to a healthy profit. "Like the falafel, I make it myself, it is almost all profit. I buy a big thing of chickpeas for $23 and it makes 500 sandwiches, $5.95 a platter."

One item Sunny does not offer is pork. "We don't sell no pork," he says. "Pork is not halal." He hesitates, and adds, "I mean, the burger is not halal, we get it from the company, but it's beef. Turkey bacon, beef bacon, turkey sausage, beef sausage. I mean, you know, we don't have to touch pork because pork is very nasty, man."

Sunny's aversion to pork is something he shares with his Yemeni partners, along with the religion that inspired the taboo, the Arabic language, and a social network that links the Arabic-speaking world to the United States. His own migration story might be unique, but the links between the United States and the Middle East, especially in New York City, are familiar, if not strained by recent geopolitical events. In the two decades prior to September 11, 2001, the Arab population in the United States nearly doubled. There is no firm data yet on how 9/11 has affected this trend, but tighter immigration restrictions have no doubt hampered new migration from the Middle East.

And yet despite the racial profiling of newcomers from the Middle East, immigrants from Arab nations are not monolithic and their migration experiences can be quite distinct. Sunny explains some of the differences between the Yemeni experience and that of a Palestinian. "The Yemenis come over here, and they worked very hard. But when you come to get a visa from Yemen to come to here, the American consulate over there, in Yemen, they want to know where is this person going to go, how is he going to eat, how is he going to drink, who is suppose to be in charge of him? And someone gives them a piece of paper from the bank, 'I have $1 million and I am in charge of him to come over.' For Yemeni it's very difficult." According to Sunny, the politics of emigration are very different in the West Bank. "The Palestinian people, it's different," he says. "The Jews want you out of the country fast. 'You, you want to go to America? You want a visa?'" Sunny pounds a fist on the counter as if stamping a passport. "Just leave please."

A young man stumbles into the back of Sunny's deli. "How fast can you make a cheeseburger?" he asks, the alcohol in his system causing a slight slur in his words.

Sunny sizes him up, then says, "Two minutes, my friend."

He turns to the grill and the young man sits down hard on one of the stools. He pulls out a wallet and a mobile phone, then barks at Sunny, "Two minutes, nigger."

Sunny turns back to the counter, "Why do you want to disrespect me?"

"Two minutes," the young man replies. He pulls out a bill from his wallet. "See this dead president? I want it in two minutes."

The young man is obviously drunk. He begins a muddled tirade about the war in Iraq then gets a call on his phone. Sunny turns his back on him.

Later, Sunny says, "In the daytime everybody is nice and lovely. Everyone is nice, give me that, give me this, thank you, I appreciate you." He shakes his head, and continues, "In the nighttime you don't see 'thank you,' 'appreciate you' after 1 o'clock. You say, 'Fuck you, give me fucking shit.' White and black, the same thing. You know? 'Yo, yo, shit, give me my fucking onion, man.' You know what I am talking about?" After a beat, he adds, "Hello!"

Sunny's mistrust of the night and those who frequent its hours began from the moment he opened his grill in 1993. "In 1993," he says, "you can't even walk here after 10 at night. No fucking way. No way." At the time, this section of Brooklyn was only beginning the slow climb out of the economic depression that had plagued most of the city since the 1970s. According to Sunny, the decision to remain open throughout the night had little to do with increased revenue, at least in the beginning. "We tried to close," he explains. "We go home like normal to our wife, to our children. We bought an alarm and everything. But they came in from the roof. They studied three days. The first they worked on the hole. The second they got to the ceiling. The third day they went in."

After more incidents of breaking and entering, Sunny and his partners decided to stay open and guard their merchandise in person. Though he's invested in expensive security cameras that he can watch from his computer at home, he says they don't help. "The camera will help when everything is over and the FBI come and say, 'Oh, is this the person?' Tomorrow he'll come here with a different face, different teeth, different hair. I know them all. I see them today with afro, and the second day I see them bald-headed, you know."

Staying open all night meant a radical reorientation to the community and customers, characterized most clearly by a paradoxical combination of dependence and mistrust. Unfortunately, the simplest way to manage the perceived threat was to racialize their fears and inscribe them onto their late-night customers. As Sunny says, "Our customers in here are almost like 70 percent black and 30 percent white, and any time they have a chance, they bust the place and go in."

Those first few years, Sunny describes nonstop violence that he indirectly attributes to the racial profile of the neighborhood in the early 1990s. "There was a fight every night," he says, "Not one white person on the streets back then." But Sunny's assumptions about race and its relationship to violence come back to haunt him in the aftermath of September 11, 2001. As an Arabic-speaking Muslim, Sunny was suddenly thrust into a social and political world that assumed he was linked to terrorism—at least more likely linked than say, an African American from the neighborhood. In a special 2001 issue of *ColorLines*, a newsmagazine covering race and politics, a report revealed that although 80 percent of Americans opposed racial profiling before 9/11, almost as many supported racial profiling when applied to those assumed to be Arab or Muslim after 9/11. The political climate change was palpable enough to prompt Sunny's joking response to a question about his personal life: "I've got nothing to hide. I'm not a terrorist."

If September 11, 2001, turned the tables of racialized violence on immigrant entrepreneurs from the Middle East such as Sunny, it also transformed the way Sunny viewed the community around his deli. As he says, "9/11 brought a lot more white people." And yet, he is quick to point out that during the night, especially on the weekends, white customers are just as likely to cause trouble as any other racialized ethnic group. He recounts one recent episode, "A couple of white guys came in and said, 'Yo, we can drink beer with our food?' I say, 'One or two, no problem.' They tried to bring a six pack. 'No, don't bring a six pack.' 'What the fuck is wrong with you, I'm spending money here!' I mean, what do you want me to do? I said, 'Sir, you make everybody do the same as you, I can't do that.' 'Well, I ain't finished eating and I'm drinking my fucking six pack, so shut the fuck up.'" Sunny raises his eyebrows and adds his signature, "Hello!"

For Sunny, part of the problem lies in the persistence of drugs and other criminal activity that continues to plague the area despite the recent demographic changes. "It doesn't show, but it is full of drugs in this area," he explains. "Big heavy dealer drugs in this area. I can walk you around and show a couple of houses. The people are in and out, out and in, even though the police station is there, they don't do anything about it. It's only one block from here. Sometimes you see them waiting on line, like they were in a restaurant, to get the crack and heroin."

Another factor in Sunny's ad hoc theory of violence is his own culturally constructed notion of "respect." Much of this idea of respect is organized around gender, particularly in regard to women and the ways men objectify them. "The women," Sunny says, "they come here and the ladies have no respect for themselves. The ladies, they come showing a lot of things, in the miniskirt, and them guys are like, 'Baby, you looking good.' The guy will come out, 'Hey, man, who do you think you are, that's my lady.' And there they go." Sunny's idea of respect also includes his own social position in regard to his customers, especially as they inhabit/invade his space. "At 4 o'clock there will be like forty people in here. 'Yo, I came here first.' 'No, I was here first.' And there they go. So many times I sweep blood in here. No respect."

After more than a decade behind the counter, Sunny has had time to develop his ideas about violence, race, and the community. But he has also developed a peculiar orientation to his customers; one that suggests another paradox: respect born out of a persistent mistrust. As he explains, "They give me a lot of shit, they cuss, they fight, but they never put their hands on me. They never do. Because, this happened a couple of times, they tried to come behind the counter, but I have my knife and I have a stick, a police officer gave it to me. And I said, 'If you step one more time I will hit you, I will cut you up.' You know?" The result is a confidence, however unlikely, that he has somehow earned a place in the surrounding social order without actually returning the same respect. "I know how to handle them," Sunny claims. "Because, I have to be a nigger like him— excuse my language. I have to know how to talk to them. I have to be one of them. 'Yo, chill out, hello. Lean back. Why you doing that bullshit like that, Hakim? You know what I'm saying? Stop that bullshit. Hello.' I gotta do like street language. Everybody has a level."

The nightshift abuse from customers, and his confidence in "being one of them," is one reason Sunny still works the nightshift himself. "You think I don't want to go home to be with my wife and kids?" he asks. "I'd love to do that, but sometimes we got no choice." He is convinced new employees would not last one night on the weekends on their own. "People come to work for one week, and when they come to the weekend, they go home at 2 or 3 o'clock. They just leave. 'Hello, finish your job.' 'No, fuck that.'" According to Sunny, new hires are especially easy targets for his typical nightshift customer. "When they see you are new, they like to make you nervous, to fuck with your mind."

Of course, when Sunny speaks of new hires, he speaks specifically of Yemenis or perhaps, in a pinch, Latinos. "Yemen or Spanish," he explains. "You see, Spanish people, Mexican, Guatemalan, Puerto Rican, Dominican, they are waiting for their check. You give them food for free, he feels good. He works hard. You give him $450, a couple of months later you give him $50 more, $500, he says, 'Oh, thank you, you are a good boss.' You know what I am saying? You make them feel like, you know, comfortable." Though he offers no health insurance or traditional benefits ("We don't have any of that bullshit," he says), he does occasionally take employees to a Manhattan club with bellydancing. "Just appetizers and ouzo cost $300," he says proudly.

According to Sunny, African Americans and ethnic whites are not so easily pleased as employees, though for quite different reasons. The implication is that although African Americans are more likely to sort out for themselves how little they are paid in comparison to the volume of business (and, according to Sunny, more likely to steal the difference), ethnic whites would never need a job that paid so little in the first place. "Listen to me," he says, "the Arabic people, especially the people from Yemen, can't put a black guy behind the counter. To put a white guy is impossible; he isn't going to stay one day."

And yet, despite his fragile peace with night customers, Sunny himself is not immune to the violence that he says erupts regularly. "I had to break up between a couple of people. He was beating a kid, 21 years old, beating him up, jumping him. And I come to break it up, and the guy he have brass knuckles. He start to hit him and the kid put his head down. He hit me. Thirty days, man, I was sucking on a straw. I used to weigh like 230 pounds. I lost to about 190, 195." He pauses, smiles, then adds, "I was looking good, looking handsome."

Perhaps the deepest contradiction of Sunny's racialized view of violence, particularly as it relates to the surrounding community, is found in how and why he chose to enter into business in this section of Brooklyn in the first place. As he explains, a Palestinian friend, who owned a Key Food grocery store nearby, told Sunny, "This is where the business is." In the late 1980s and early 1990s, social welfare programs, including food stamp programs, meant a consistent and dependable source of revenue for small businesses in economically marginalized communities. "He told me a lot of black people on welfare," explains Sunny. And indeed, he and his partners benefited greatly from the community's persistent poverty.

Today, much of the government assistance to the poor has been reduced or eliminated, leaving many thousands of working poor and unemployed families with no safety net and nothing to offer the small businesses that once depended on their monthly checks. Fortunately for Sunny, the end of public assistance dovetailed with the rise of gentrification, which increased with the influx of middle-class whites leaving Manhattan in the wake of 9/11. His business has survived, even thrived, as the neighborhood has changed. According to Sunny, however, there are reverberations from the deli's beginnings. Referring to the children of welfare-dependent parents who frequented his store in the early 1990s, he says, "Now those kids are big. I know them all by name." The government support may be gone, but Sunny can still capitalize on the social connections forged in his early days on the avenue. "Now one of them gives trouble up front, they call me on the intercom, I come up and say, 'What are you doin'? You disrespect me?' And they say, 'Sorry, okay, sorry Sunny.'"

---

"The weekend is very tough for me, man." It's dawn, Sunday, in mid-September, and Sunny sits at one of his own tables, an open Heineken in front of him. He looks as though he's on a tropical vacation: short-sleeve blue shirt, unbuttoned to the chest, navy pants, black shoes. Though sitting, he remains in perpetual motion, shifting in his seat, shaking his leg. "You see, on the weekends, there is too much stress." Like others who work nights, Sunny often finds himself with a drink in his hand first thing in the morning. Technically, it's at the end of his shift, which is when many people relax with a drink. But for those who work nights, it means they're often the only ones drinking while everyone else around them has coffee. "Saturday morning," says Sunny, "I have six Heineken. And when I go home I mix a nice, beautiful Chivas Regal with Sprite, two mixed drinks. Then I sleep like a baby."

Despite the weekend stress, and his fear of leaving the deli in the care of employees, Sunny still thrives on the work. "I tell you something, for me, if I take two weeks off, I can't wait to come back to the job and start working. Oh, man, I'll be like, 'I want a taste of it.' I don't know why. I'll be so bored. I take two weeks off, and I sit. If I don't find something to do, I will go crazy. Me and my wife, we argue every day. Just talking, like, bullshit. You know? But if I come to work, I feel better."

Sunny can afford to stop working. He estimates that he takes home between $8,000 and $10,000 a week, after paying employees and overhead. "I like to work, but in ten more years, I would like to retire." He stops, revises his plan. "Maybe five years more. I'm only 42 years old. I worked hard in my life." If his vacations are any indication, he will not take well to retirement. His version of "not working" might involve returning to door-to-door sales. "I want to do something walking, where I have to walk, door to door." He adds a qualifier, "but all on the first floor, because it's good to walk when you're older."

While he thinks about leaving the business sometime in the next decade, any hope that one of his children would take over has slowly withered. "I tell them, 'Here, take the keys. Own your own store. Run the business. Put $2,000 clean in your pocket every week.'" But as Sunny tells it, their answer is always, " 'No, dad, I'm not going to work like that, no.' They want to go to be a pharmacist, or like a doctor, you know? Lawyers. They don't want to work. They want to go to school, college. You know?"

For Sunny, it's all about the work and enjoying the fruits of his labor. "I make a retirement plan for myself. I don't want to think about the government giving me the tax—$1,000 or $1,400 a month. You think I'm gonna wait until I'm 63 years old to get a $1,500 check? I don't think so. All the Arabic are like this. Fifty years old, already millionaire." Sunny fully intends to follow that path, especially after years of toiling on the nightshift for customers he still finds difficult to understand and even harder to respect. "I'm 42, if I'm not a millionaire when I get to 50 years old, I'm gonna go burn myself," he says. "What do you think?" he asks, motioning to the empty tables and his well-worn counter. "Working hard like this?"

# NINE: ALL NIGHT ON THE STREET

**M**oments past 2 AM, on a cold December night, several young women in short dresses stand by a taxi's doors ready to step in before the passengers inside have paid their fare. They are on 14th Street in the meatpacking district, where the soundtrack of the street is a loud, low bass from passing cars and the clubs that line the street. Hundreds of people crowd the sidewalks, and the streets themselves feel like an extension of nightclubs. There is one soundless pedicab, but it is lost in a rush of passing cars, their thunderous engines and honking horns, the occasional shrill siren, and the mass of raucous pedestrians. It's a shocking contrast from the serene feel these streets will have in a matter of hours.

This is the New York night as playground for the young urban professionals who live most of their time in the day. Some wait in lines behind velvet ropes, some slip in through back doors. Everything is sleek, nothing is too high concept. The guys wear suits, some in tuxes, the shirttails out. The girls all wear dresses that resemble one hanging in the window of Stella McCartney's 14th Street shop. They all laugh and talk and click click click in their high heels across the sidewalks.

The chattering crowds gathered in and out of greenish pools of mercury-vapor and fluorescent lighting are descendants of New Yorkers who braved the night on city streets in the mid-nineteenth century. Then it was oil and gas that lit the sidewalks and made possible a collective, public nightlife after centuries of curfews and armed watchmen on patrol. According to the geographer John Jakle in his book *City Lights*, the new lighting technology enabled, and even encouraged, leisure activity at night, especially for men. The most famous, and genteel, destinations for nighttime entertainment, the nightclubs of the nineteenth century, were "pleasure gardens" such as Castle, Vauxhall, and Niblo's. They combined landscaped grounds with live music, theater, and the wonder of gas lighting.

Considerably less genteel were the saloons, dance halls, and theaters on the Bowery of that same era. The Bowery was an infamous stretch of lower-class nightlife that attracted working-class men, many of whom were involved in the meatpacking trade that was, in the early nineteenth century, concentrated on the Lower East Side. Caldwell in *New York Night* describes the "unhinged urban hoedown" of the Bowery in terms that could easily apply to the modern meatpacking district: thumping music, the steamy scent of street vendor food, peddlers, performers, and motley crowds sweeping into and out of saloons. There was even a familiar class distinction among the men themselves: the Sporting Men, foppish young dilettantes with their "affectations of culture," and the Bowery B'hoys, working class brawlers known for brawn and "proletarian swagger." Though today the distinction might more aptly apply to the Sporting Men of Wall Street and the Bridge and Tunnel B'hoys of Long Island and Jersey who crowd the busy sidewalks around West 14th Street.

Then as now, artificial light has a way of compartmentalizing nightlife. But the history of public lighting has proceeded in fits and starts, expanding and constricting the activities of urban citizens at night. Jakle argues that the earliest forms of public lighting were less a form of helpful illumination than an anticrime measure. Whether the lanterns of the eighteenth century, with their publicly employed lamplighters, or the considerably more automated gas lamps of the nineteenth century, street lighting was meant to ward off criminals who depended on the cover of darkness. As Ralph Waldo Emerson wrote, "Gaslight is the best nocturnal police." In fact, in Europe, public lighting was so intimately associated with state authority over the streets that street lamps were some of the first victims of violence during the French Revolution. As Wolfgang Schivelbusch points out in *Disenchanted Night*, loyalists were often hanged from lanterns as a symbol of the revolutionaries' defiance of the state.

Inevitably, public lighting also provided an extension of the day into the night, both for work and pleasure. From oil lamps to gas lights to electric lighting, technology increased nighttime activity throughout the nineteenth and twentieth centuries. By the time the old gas companies merged with Thomas Edison's Illumination Company to form Consolidated Edison (ConEd) in 1936, New York City was ablaze with electric public lighting, enabling the birth of a truly twenty-four-hour incessant economy. As Melbin contends, the technology may have been too effective for our own good. With the birth of artificial illumination and night work, we are exposed to lower levels of light for longer periods of time. As such, we produce less melatonin than did our agricultural forbears and can postpone sleep more easily. We are also more vulnerable to the health risks of reduced melatonin.

But in addition to labor and leisure, public lighting is still connected to the early concern for public safety, particularly in regard to surveillance and crime deterrence. Jakle points out that as street lighting became standardized, street lamps stood in for more cops on the beat. And as the technology became more refined, new applications were found for policing the night through light. Vapor technologies, such as mercury vapor and sodium vapor, were found to emit particular wavelengths, creating a greenish glow or harsh yellow. Indeed, sodium vapor's nearly monochromatic yellow was so unpleasant as public lighting when introduced that cities took them offline. In the 1970s, when crime was on the rise, authorities hoped that yellow, a symbol of caution, would deter violence on the streets—they quickly became one of the most common street lamps in the United States.

Of course one other vapor lighting technology dominates the city at night: neon. And in the meatpacking district on a Saturday night, flashing neon, a symbol of revelry and lowered inhibitions, wins out over the sodium vapor lamps overhead. Walking these streets, or just about any on a Manhattan Saturday night, one can almost always spot the clubs from several blocks away. Either there's a neon sign or, if it's one of those clubs without a sign, there's the smoke of a street vendor's cart parked nearby.

---

"I spend all night on the street."

Jahi, an Egyptian in his early twenties, stands behind his kebab cart on Gansevoort Plaza—the intersection of Gansevoort and Greenwich, Little West 12th and 14th streets. It's a little before 2:30 AM and this section of the meatpacking district is still bustling. There's a giant new Theory store where Woolco used to be, a fitting symbol of how fashion has replaced food in the district. The cobblestone streets remain but instead of meat trucks rolling across them, they're jammed with taxis full of customers. People are everywhere. The quiet of the side streets gives way to the throbbing bass of the clubs, the horns of taxis and limousines, and the fragments of conversation the revelers scream to one another and into their phones. Above it all there's a giant Budweiser billboard of beautiful people partying that reads: "Expect Everything."

"I work just only on weekends," Jahi says with a chopped yet melodic Egyptian accent. He works 10 PM to 5:30 or 6 AM, always on this same corner, four days a week. By "weekends" he means Wednesday through Saturday. "They don't come to the club Sundays," says Jahi, "so I have Sunday, Monday, Tuesday off."

On the nights he's not working, Jahi says, he parks his cart in a garage, but he's always in the same spot. "Nobody can come here," he says proudly, "just only me." He has permission from the city and the nearby restaurants to operate his cart, and he pays $500 a month for the privilege to be here. "The city talks with the restaurants here," he says, "you know, because I make a big smoke." He points to all the smoke coming from his grill. He points to his permit and says he pays $6,000 for it every year. "Just to get the permit," he stresses, "$6,000." The cart itself costs about $10,000, and the cart works twenty-four hours. Jahi elaborates, "Now it works here. Just here, in the night. Then in the morning I leave it in the garage and clean it, and another guy go and take it to midtown."

It's cold now, though, so in another month they'll take the cart off the street and leave it inside until spring.

The food, says Jahi, is all chicken, all comes prepared from the garage, and all has to adhere to the city health codes. His bestsellers are shish kebab and hotdogs, equally popular. "All of the guys like this. And all of them, if you go to the club and drink, you become so hungry, you don't care what you eat." He says that the food is good, however; he eats it. "Don't worry," he adds, "it's healthy. I lose my life if I make it not healthy for you, if you get any problem and you call. I will be in trouble. They come every, like, every month or couple of weeks, to check the cart, to see that I have this." He demonstrates a wet rag and a dry rag. "This is wet, and this is dry. After I finish any order, I just clean this and this dry. To keep everything clean."

As he talks, he scrapes clean his grill. A girl interrupts him, her voice laced with alcohol, "Hey, do you have a restroom?" A few girls buy some chicken kebabs and flirt with him. Some customers return asking for hot sauce and salt. The only salt he has is from the pretzel warmer, which is very hot. He gives some to the girl and it burns her hand, but she laughs. "I told you it's hot," Jahi says. She thanks him. He responds, "You're welcome, sweetie." Another girl approaches with a distinct swaying gait, saying, "I lost my wallet. Did you find a wallet?" He tells her, "Sweetie, no, I don't have it." She says, "I never did this in my life. I lost my wallet."

Girls stumble across the cobblestones and on the sidewalks in their stilettos. Some guys help carry their dates across the minefield of cobblestones. Other girls take off their shoes. When one guy leaves his date stranded on the sidewalk to fend for herself in her heels, she stays there and shrieks out after him, "You deserted me." He strides easily across the cobblestones. "You deserted me," she screams again but he never looks back.

All around the intersection, guys try to hail taxis but cannot. They are all occupied. One guy is fortunate enough to have his own car, but lacks one of the beautiful girls as his date. As he drives by in his sedate sedan, he yells out to a blonde woman who is walking alone and talking on her mobile phone. "Hey!" he yells. "You! I know you." She does not turn to look at him. He makes another pass through the intersection, yelling, "You!

Hey! I know you. You with the blonde hair and the phone, I know you!"
She never acknowledges him. She continues to talk into her mobile phone,
walking past another guy who is also on his phone. "I HAVE LIKE FIVE
PEOPLE," he bellows into his phone. "CAN WE GET IN?" Almost in
response, a young guy who looks as though he's in his teens says to his
friends, "See, I'm fucked up so bad, you wanna hear a funny story?"

Jahi talks about what it's like to deal with drunk people every night.
"A lot of them," he says, "they give me fucking hard time about nothing.
Sometimes about the price." He tells a story about a guy who asked the
price of a shish kebab, and when Jahi told him it was five dollars he ac-
cused him of ripping him off. "I said to him, 'This is the deal. I don't put
my hand in your pocket to take the money. You like it, it's five dollars,
take it. You don't like it, that's it.' So to me he says, 'It's okay,' and he give
me ten dollar and go. A lot of funny situations like this. He'll start fight-
ing with you and then he pay more than you tell him and go." Jahi laughs.
"And some of them, they just take it, and go, without paying nothing.
He's just fucking drunk." Some pay when he reminds them, others pay
twice and walk away before he can say anything.

And then there are the pretty girls. "A lot of them," Jahi confesses,
"they say, 'You are so handsome. I like you.' And if she comes the next
day, does she even remember me? And some of them asking about," he
pauses, "very bad things to do with them. Some of them, 'I wanna hot
dog.' 'Can I have a hot sausage?' I say to her, 'Yeah.' She says to me, 'Do
you not want to give me your own hot dog?' I say to her, 'Look . . .' And
she says to me, 'You can do it? I come with you.' I don't know, but some
of them talk serious about that. Because I know, before I come here, a lot
of guys who were working for this take a lot of girls. But it depends on
the guy. For me, I just care about my business. They're drunk. That's why
I don't like to play with any girl because maybe she get me in trouble or
something. Even if she don't make problem, I scared about her, because
if she like to do this with any guy, she have something bad, like disease
or something. If she don't care about herself, I should care about myself."

Just a block or two away from Jahi's cart, the ghostly remains of the
old meatpacking district sulks in the shadows. Once the largest center for
beef production in the country, New York City was host to dozens of

stockyards, slaughterhouses, and processing plants in the nineteenth and twentieth centuries. One of the largest slaughtering districts in the city was moved in the 1940s to make way for the United Nations building. Labor strikes, competition, and sanitation laws conspired against the industry in the second half of the twentieth century, until most of the trade was concentrated around West 14th Street. In recent years, even that small foothold has given way to real estate development. Now, a faint, hazy light from overhead lamps coats the squat brick warehouses and loading docks, and even the sounds of the city seem muffled. A sign at the London Meat Company announces, "Jobbers Welcome," but no one is around to welcome them at this hour. The most visible presence are the signs of gentrification, such as a van for a company called Robbins Wolfe Eventeurs with the motto "Events Perfected." As the *Villager* described the trendy area in summer 2006: the corporations are coming. A commercial development group known as the Meatpacking District Initiative recently announced its goal to support the district's functioning as a twenty-four-hour "ecosystem."

For the homeless people who still panhandle here at night, the district has always functioned as a twenty-four-hour ecosystem: meatpacking plant by day and dormitory at night, though that may not be what the Initiative has in mind. "Years ago," says one formerly homeless man, "prior to 9/11, there were lots of homeless here. 9/11 changed everything, in terms of how the police treat the homeless." Since then, he adds, a number of the old meatpacking warehouses have been demolished, but a number of others have been converted to restaurants and clubs.

"I have a good job," Jahi says, "but after this restaurant opens I will have a hard time." He points to a building directly in front of him and says, "They already have one upstairs, but this one is new." He plans to move a little farther down the block. He's been doing this, he says, "a long time." Then he adds, "I've just been here for one year but my brother, he been here for ten years, and he take this spot seven years ago." Now, says Jahi, his brother owns five carts; he's "like the owner." He gets 35 percent and his brother gets 65 percent of whatever he makes. So at the end of a busy Saturday night he gets $100–$150.

About his pay, Jahi says, "It's enough for me." He adds that he's not looking for more than this right now. He was trained in physical education, physical rehabilitation, and massage in Egypt, but is not qualified yet in the United States for those jobs. He laughs and admits, "I don't like this work. For me, it's the very first year, I don't have experience here in the city, and I should be beside my brother, because he cares about me. So after I get my experience and my ability to depend on myself I will go my way but first I have to do this work."

A homeless man approaches Jahi's cart to solicit one of his customers. "Listen," the man says, extending his arms widely, "this is my living room!" He says that he can earn "maybe $200 to $300" tonight. "It depends in the crowd and it depends on what day," he says like a businessman. His strategy is to always ask the men. "Not the girls," he says like he's outlining his business plan. "I talk strictly to men. And when it's couples, I rap, romantically." He's here all the time, he says. "I'm like a boomerang—every time you throw it, it always comes back."

"These guys," says Jahi, "some days they make more money than I make. Every day he make big stories, but he's the same guy. I hear him come here and say to them, 'Do you mind to buy some food for me?' They leave me money. After he leave, 'Don't give me any food. Give me the money.'" Jahi has seen homeless people wearing suits who tell people that they lost their wallet and just need to borrow $20 but will return it if they can have a phone number. In one day, says Jahi, they can "make $100, or $500, because this area, there's a lot of tourists here. They don't care about ten dollar or twenty dollar just in one night." He says he's seen the guy who just came to his cart do this. "This his work," says Jahi. On whether or not people should give them money, he says, "If you don't like it, don't do it." The same goes for those who "keep singing funny song for you," says Jahi. "If you like it, pay him, if you don't like it, don't pay him." He laughs again and says, "Yeah, in just one year, I see a lot of new stuff here in this city."

Two women approach and ask, "Have you got any E's or coke? Ecstasy or cocaine? Do you know where I can get some E's or cocaine from? We're from England and we're drug addicts!" Before long they're leaning suggestively into two guys wearing hooded sweatshirts. The four of them disappear around a corner.

On the street at night in New York City, anything goes and all are equal. A homeless man can make as much, if not more, than a street vendor working the same streets. Tourists and locals alike drop money for kebabs, taxis, clubs, restaurants, and drugs. Some will sleep outside. Others will return to warm hotels or homes. Still others won't sleep at all, until daybreak.

An exterminator on the nightshift says he loves his job precisely because of this spectacle. "I'm working at night," he said, "in one of the greatest cities in the world, where entertainment is nonstop. I observe people, that's what I get a kick out of. Movies, sitcoms, and reality television don't do it for me. But watching a six-foot-five black guy in a red dress with stilettos and a wig walking in Chelsea—and nobody gives him a second look because, hey, it's Chelsea—that to me is interesting. That's normal. That's everyday. You should hang out on Ninth and 14th, because there's all the transvestites right by the meatpacking district. Sit around there for a couple of hours and just enjoy the show."

Issues of class are seen starkly at night, when it becomes more obvious who has a bed to return to and who does not, but they are also inverted. The geography of Manhattan shape-shifts; a working industrial district becomes a playground. There is also, in the night on the street, another, unexpected inversion. Whereas other jobs increase the isolation of the workers, these jobs on the street allow for a strange intimacy. In his first year in New York, Jahi has so many offers for, um, relationships that he has to spend much of the night declining them.

On 14th Street just east of Eighth Avenue a dozen people wait in line for tacos at the El Idolo II street vendor. It's a few minutes past 3 AM. The hungry people jostle for position and consider their orders. The van, which is the size of a bread truck, sells everything from beef to chicken to pork to tongue. The girls teeter from foot to foot on their high heels. Across the street, on Eighth, there's a store called Shoegasm. A young guy passes by the taco van and says to his friends, "I'm too fucked to mess with it. It's too far to walk."

Down 14th Street, just west of Seventh Avenue, the Donut Pub is open twenty-four hours and has been since 1964. They're too far from the meatpacking district to get as much business at this hour as the street vendors, but once the bars close at 4 AM they will become the pub of choice on this street. For now, at 3:15 AM, the man behind the gleaming counter, an immigrant, claims that at the Donut Pub at this hour, "Everything fresh." At this hour, the donuts may be fresh but the customers are "too fucked to mess with it."

# TEN: CALL IT A NIGHT

At 3:30 AM on a brisk November night, dozens of bodies are strewn about the waiting area of the Long Island Railroad (LIRR) in Penn Station. Couples lie passed out in each other's arms, young women sulk in clusters of three and four, and young men vomit into trashcans. These are the casualties of Manhattan nightlife waiting for the nightly "drunk train" to carry them back to the Long Island suburbs.

A backlit board of train routes and their track numbers shines overhead, and the few alert passengers wait impatiently to learn the track number for the next train to Long Beach. Several strands of white twinkle lights hang overhead, premature holiday decorations. Metropolitan Transit Authority and state police officers stand nearby, bemused by the display of semipublic drunkenness, especially the young women who've long since ceased to care whether or not their tiny dresses are covering anything important. One young woman passes by, talking to her friends about her high heels, "I'm seeing stars but I'm not taking mine off."

Penn Station, on the west side of Manhattan just south of Times Square, is a city within the city. There is a main street with its row of shops, half of which stay open around the clock. There is a police station and a small army of officers on patrol. There is even a plaza, a place to gather if not actually interact. And there is, of course, plenty of transportation—it is the busiest train station in North America. There is all of this, and despite the baroque muzak piped into speakers throughout the warren of passageways, there are few places more deadening to the senses in the nighttime city.

It was not always so.

New Yorkers of a certain age knew Pennsylvania Station as a stone temple to transportation. Starting in 1902, it took nearly a decade for legions of laborers to complete, and when it was finished it had consumed a half million cubic feet of granite, hundreds of buildings, and eight acres of real estate. From 1911 to 1965, Penn Station welcomed travelers to New York City with soaring columns and the full force of the sun piercing a web of iron and glass 150 feet overhead.

Built to last for generations, it barely made it past the age of 50. The efficiency of air transportation undermined the dominance of railroads at midcentury, and office space was at a premium. It took less than a year to dismantle the old building and only three to sink the new one into the ground. The destruction of Penn Station outraged many New Yorkers, and inspired the founding of the Landmarks Preservation Commission that would eventually save Grand Central Station from a similar fate. Pete Hamill, in his book *Downtown*, writes of what it was like to pass by the demolition in 1965. "I was not alone," he writes, "gazing at this immense act of municipal vandalism and whispering, *You bastards. You stupid goddamned bastards.*"

Now Penn Station is a maze of underground platforms serving Amtrak, the LIRR, and the New York City subway system. Low-slung corridors serve the various levels, connected by a range of chain stores and eateries, a handful of which stay open all night. A diverse crew of nightshift workers keeps the trickle and flow of off-hour commuters fed and entertained until the last train whisks them away.

A number appears on the big board in the LIRR waiting area, the 3:49 to Long Beach, track #14. The lifeless partygoers miraculously rouse themselves and herd down the steps and onto the departing train.

The train itself is overcrowded and already starting to smell of sweat, liquor, and the pungent odor of alcohol-infused vomit. Young women sit on their dates' laps, and dozens stand in the aisles. Some are jostled into sleep again; others recount the misadventures of a night on the town.

"Where ya been? In the city? Whadya do?"

"Fuckin' clubbed it up. It fuckin' sucked."

A girl of no more than twenty coughs into her mobile phone a few minutes past 4 AM, "I think I'm gonna call it a night."

The train rolls out into the night air just past Atlantic Avenue in Brooklyn and continues out to the edge of Queens, stopping here and there along the way. Conductors make their way down the crowded aisles, doing their best to check for tickets and collect the fare from those who did not purchase a ticket in the station. Inevitably, someone refuses to pay. This time it's Vince, a thickset young man still pulling from his last beer in a brown paper bag. Two more conductors appear from either end of the car, large men who somehow look even larger in their boyish uniforms and pert conductor hats. Vince unwisely challenges their authority. The train makes an unscheduled stop and the three conductors manhandle Vince off the train, along with a couple of his friends. The conductor explains, "He didn't have a ticket and he didn't want to pay for it. That's what happens when you get a little beer in you." With the excitement over, the conductor is able to laugh about it. "It's all right," he says. "We don't like to throw them off but he wanted to get thrown off. Usually they're just blah blah blah, but if they get up," he pauses, then adds simply, "He got in my face."

The train rolls past the edge of the city, out onto Long Island. The crowd thins and quiets down with each stop.

Valley Stream, 4:23 AM.

Lynbrook, 4:26 AM.

Beer, pizza crusts, and other detritus litter the floor, along with a fair amount of bodily fluids. A few guys standing near the door recount some of their favorite drunk train stories, most involving sex on the train. Like the couple who stripped bare and had sex in the seats of a crowded train. The reaction of the crowd? "They threw money at them."

Two couples in their forties sit near the end of one of the cars, scandalized by the carnival on display. They are on their way back to Oceanside from a fortieth birthday party in Manhattan. One of the women tries to speak, but hiccups violently, the other describes the scene back at Penn Station: the couples passed out on the floor, the young kids getting sick, and one girl she remembers in particularly bad shape, "A Chinese girl, oh, excuse me, Oriental." The men accompanying them say nothing, amused grins on their faces.

Oceanside, 4:32 AM.

The train pulls into Long Beach at 4:45 AM with only a few passengers. The others disembarked all along the line, trudging home to sleep off the night. After a few minutes, a new train pulls out of the station heading back into Manhattan. Cups of coffee replace cans of beer, and the clubbing clothes have been changed for briefcases and hard hats.

Jill, a bright-eyed, red-haired conductor in her forties, makes her way down the aisle of the jarringly quiet train punching tickets and greeting passengers. "Good morning," she says with a smile. It's the end of her nightshift on the LIRR and she is looking forward to a day off. With a laugh she says, "I say 'Good Morning' all night long. It's morning twenty-four hours a day!"

Jill's been on the job for seven months and does not seem to mind the nightshift hours. "It took me awhile to get my train legs," she says, standing firm against the swaying of the fast-moving train, "but I have them now." Before this she worked days for a large company and never worked a weekend. "It was a normal job. I wore suits, stockings." But according to Jill, there was no future and, as a single mother, the job at the LIRR offered opportunities for advancement. "I wanted stability and look what I got," she says laughing.

Her shift varies day to day, but she works six and sometimes seven days a week. As winter approaches, conductors who've been on the job longer will return from vacation and her shifts will become even more unpredictable. Usually she works the overnight shift, or the occasional "half night," 5 AM to 1 PM. She admits this variability can wear on her. "I lose track of days, hours."

But she can always tell when it's approaching 4 AM, especially on the weekends. "I heard the kids were pukin' all night," she says, referring to the train that pulled in from Penn Station. She also heard about the incident with Vince. None of it seems surprising, she's seen it all herself.

"Halloween. That was the night you had to ride the train! That was the best night to ride the train. It was like a circus train." She laughs and recounts stories to rival those of fellow passengers. "I've seen girls helping out their boyfriends," she says. "She just holds up the ticket." She shakes her head and says, "I mean, we all like to do that in the privacy of our own homes, but . . ."

The train rolls through the same stations it passed on the way out before it plunges into darkness beneath the East River. Penn Station is moments away.

# ELEVEN: I JUST WORK HERE

Late one muggy, summer Saturday night, or, depending on your perspective, early Sunday morning, Ahmed stands with his hands in the ice of a beer display case trying to cool off. He has bronze skin and an easy if timid smile. Though in his thirties, his graying sideburns and mustache make him look a bit older. He is minding the counter of a nondescript newsstand on the LIRR concourse in Penn Station. Behind him, two or three men browse the hundreds of magazines on display. Before him, a handful of waiting passengers mill about the cramped corridor. The air is thick and close.

"Punjab is very hot," he says in a soft, barely audible Punjabi accent, "but in here they turn off the air conditioning at night."

A homeless man approaches and tries to buy a giant can of Budweiser. Ahmed raises his voice from a whisper to something just barely audible, "It's after 4. It's Sunday. It's closed." The man shuffles away without a scene.

Ahmed bent the truth. Anyone can buy alcohol from his store at any hour, despite city ordinances to the contrary, but according to Ahmed, some customers cause too much trouble. "Sometimes," Ahmed explains in his quiet whisper, "when they're drunk, the customers fall over the hotdog machine."

As he cleans the outside of a display case full of twenty-four-ounce beer cans, he explains the legal system that allows this loophole: several different police forces cover the station including the NYPD, New York State Police, Amtrak Police, and, since September 11, 2001, the National Guard. Significant overlap covers the street level concourse and the platforms, but the LIRR level falls between the cracks. People can drink alcohol if it's covered—and many stores on this level, including Ahmed's, supply brown paper bags for that purpose—so you can drink in the station. In fact, the LIRR operates its own beverage carts on the platforms. Sales of beer, wine, and liquor total more than $300,000 a year in profits.

A female officer in uniform stands nearby. She's young, perhaps in her twenties, not much older than the girls in their stilettos stumbling through the station. She has very pale skin, more so in the fluorescent subterranean light, and a softened native New York accent. She confirms Ahmed's description of the laws and adds that they can arrest people if they're too "drunk or rowdy" on the grounds of violating open container laws. There's no judgment in her tone, nor in Ahmed's. They state this as they would give directions to a tourist. She adds gently, "There are some nights when you feel like you're working on the psych ward."

A woman overhears this and, this being New York City, she comments. In a movie-star voice, breathy and nervous, she says, "I'm a medical student. I hope that New Yorkers will always have the freedom to buy alcohol, that we would not have our civil liberties curtailed in any way." She exhales her words like a 1930s Hollywood starlet, then disappears.

For the past six years, as long as he has been in the United States, Ahmed has worked the nightshift. At newsstands. Though trained as an engineer in Pakistan, he says a newsstand was the only job he could get in New York. He first worked at a small one here in Penn Station, then his boss, he says, promoted him to this larger location. It's not much of a promotion because it did not entail extra pay, only more customers.

He works six nights a week, from midnight to 10 AM on weeknights and midnight to noon on the boisterous weekends. That's fifty-four hours a week, without overtime pay, benefits, or health insurance. Ahmed earns $6.75 an hour before taxes. "I don't mind the nightshift," he says, "but I'm trying to get a job in MTA or other city job." Weeks later he's shifted his focus and says he wants to drive a taxi like some of his friends.

"New York is okay," Ahmed says, smiling, "lots of opportunities." He came to New York, leaving behind his wife and extended family, for the promise of those opportunities. Back in Pakistan, a good job earned about $150 a month. Here, despite the difficult hours, he can make ten times that amount.

But it has meant sacrifice. Ahmed and his wife have been apart since he moved away. A plane ticket to Pakistan would cost him 222 hours of labor. "It's very expensive to visit," says Ahmed, "$1,500 for return flight." By living in Queens and enduring a long commute, he and his roommates can pay just $1,100 per month for rent, which is inexpensive for New York City these days. But it is not enough to afford easy travel between continents, especially when he is obligated to support his family from afar. By living and working in the United States, he's able to send back $300 a month. His father is deceased, but that $300 helps support not only his wife, but also his mother, brothers, and sisters. If he cannot visit, at least his money can.

These international social linkages, shored up by wire transfers, keep Ahmed neither here nor there. His social life is stretched across oceans and time zones, requiring constant maintenance of connections that can go years without physical contact. This phenomenon is certainly not new—it is as old as migration—but the nature of its lived experience, the velocity of its maintenance in the global incessant economy, is qualitatively different. It is, in a word, transnational, and it makes notions of identity, nationality, and, in particular, patriotism complicated, abstract, and often useless.

It is one paradox of transnationalism that Ahmed only started thinking about returning to Pakistan for Ramadan precisely because he became a U.S. citizen in early 2006. With citizenship comes freedom—the freedom to move physically across borders he has long since traversed in every other way.

Each night, Ahmed engages customers in his own quiet way. Once, he has to call the police when a drunk woman cannot remember that she ordered three hotdogs from him and refuses to pay. Another night, a drunk man tries to buy beer with change ("pennies," Ahmed whispers), but when Ahmed counts the money it's only sixty cents, so Ahmed won't sell him the beer. "The guy called the police," Ahmed explains softly with a slight smile, "but the police just said he had to pay for the beer."

Ahmed, with his navy knit PepsiCo shirt, khaki pants, and gentle de-
meanor, seems out of place in this late-night bacchanal. All the more so
because he's a practicing Muslim who doesn't drink or smoke. (Well, he
confesses, he drank once after giving in to pressure from friends.) He
takes his breaks in the pizza place a few doors down, where the back room
is crowded with men playing drinking games and watching action movies
on the wall-mounted television. But Ahmed keeps to himself, standing
alone to eat an apple as a late-night meal. "I like to have something
healthy to eat," he says. His store boasts a sizable pornography section
popular with employees and customers alike, but Ahmed doesn't join
them. Instead he talks about his plans to return to Pakistan for Ramadan.
"It's the best time to go."

He does have his indulgences, however. He splurges for cable television. "I like to watch twenty to thirty minutes after work," he says, "especially the Pakistani channel."

On another night, edging toward 4 AM, two cops flip through gun
magazines, and Lamine, the West African manager from a bakery down
the corridor stops in for the *New York Post*. He knows it doesn't arrive
until 4, but his bakery will receive the daily bagel delivery soon and he's
hoping to read the paper during the calm before the chaos.

"Not yet, my friend," says Ahmed with a shy smile.

--------

"I just work here," says Lamine. "This is not my career."

It's just after 1 AM on a summer Monday night, and the West African
employees at the bakery are busy baking, glazing, and cooling rolls and
other pastries. Lamine, 31, is perched on a stool at one of the four tables
in the back of the bakery. He has a shaved head, a thin mustache, a tuft
of a beard, and an elegantly pointed nose. He wears the latest style jeans
and a perfectly pressed checked shirt.

Lamine came to the United States from Senegal in 1994. "In America they do a lottery, every year. That's how I applied and came here," he
says. "I won the lottery." He worked at the bakery for six years, from
1998 to 2004, but quit after disagreements with the management. He returned to Africa briefly, and when he arrived in the United States was

asked to come back to the bakery. "They said everything was going to change," Lamine says, "but they didn't do anything." He gave his two weeks notice and went to work days at Home Depot. He had health insurance, but made less money than at the bakery. In December 2005, the management at the bakery changed and they called him again to return. Lamine explains, "He called me and said, 'The management was the reason you left. I need your help, because the guy who worked here at night, he couldn't handle it. You know how to do everything.'"

Lamine took the job managing the bakery from 10 PM to 6 AM, but kept working forty hours a week at Home Depot. When he first came to the United States, like many of the West Africans who work with him in the bakery, he worked nights and went to school during the day, so he was used to surviving on little sleep. After a few months, however, his boss at the bakery said, "You could leave that other job and I will pay you more money." So he did, giving up the health insurance there in favor of the additional money at the bakery. "I am on Medicaid," explains Lamine, "and I get more money here. I had to look at the difference, one had insurance and the other had more money. I had to choose one."

On the nightshift, social networks can be more concentrated and visible than on the dayshift. At Lamine's bakery, all of the employees are West African. One young man in his early twenties cleans the glass cases that will hold the bagels to entice morning commuters in a few hours. In response to how it's going, he says, "A-okay," then smiles. He's in the United States on a student visa and has been taking English classes for seven months. "That's what my teacher taught me today, to say, when you ask how it's going, 'A-okay.'"

Lamine explains how he recruits other West Africans to work in the bakery. Often "a friend of a friend" is the only recommendation one needs. Referring to a recent Senegalese hire, he says, "I knew a guy who knew him. He told me his friend wanted a job at night, and I told him, 'Okay, bring him.'" Another West African, from Burkina Faso, wanted to work full-time and Lamine arranged it. Friends of friends, or nonkin social networks, have always proven effective in finding employment at every level of the labor market, something the sociologist Mark Granovetter describes as the "strength of weak ties." Another West African bakery employee, from Côte d'Ivoire, explains it this way: "We see each other here and we help each other. I see it with my teachers too. They are from England, and they all know each other. When someone says they want to hire someone, we know people."

The bakery usually has fewer customers and more employees than the other stores in Penn Station at night. Also, much work takes place off-site, with the bagels arriving at 4 AM already baked, and the raw dough for the other pastries arriving ready for the ovens. While much baking, glazing, rotating the breads between the ovens and the cooling racks, cleaning, and other work remains to be done, Lamine manages the place calmly and competently. Everyone has a job to do, and everyone does it. No one seems to need much direction.

When everything runs smoothly, Lamine has time to take a break. One night he strolls over to another bakery, also owned by the same company and staffed at night entirely by West Africans. The coffee in his bakery, he says, is "too strong." Another night some of his employees peruse a large bag of jeans and shoes that one of them brought to sell from his store in the Bronx. Those not in school have side businesses. As Lamine explains, "Everybody does something else." Other than Lamine, they each earn about $8.00 an hour.

They are almost all in school. Throughout New York City, immigrants working nights are often a highly educated group. Lamine first worked the nightshift to go to school. When he initially came to the United States, he worked days in a Bronx children's store but that left little time for school. Though the pay at the bakery was not much initially, it freed up his days to study and take classes in telecommunications at the City University of New York's Lehman College. "When I graduated from school," he says, "I kept the job."

The bakery job was a way to provide money while he went to school, nothing more. Lamine says he does not send money to family in Senegal since two sisters live in Europe, one married to a diplomat, and both send money home. "Now only my mother and older sister are in Senegal." Still, Lamine recognizes that even a nightshift job at a bakery in Penn Station pays more than most unskilled jobs back in West Africa. "Some people," he admits, "they call you and say, 'I need this,' and you know what you left back home. Over here the money is like this," he says, loudly snapping his long fingers, "and over there you have to work months to get a salary which compared to here is like a week. In Africa you might live in a family where only one guy works to take care of more than ten or fifteen people. And only one guy works. It is very difficult."

Though he is now a manager, he does not intend to stay in this job much longer. He wants to go back to school, he says, "and have more experience." Lamine makes a distinction between "work" and a "career." "I am not too interested in being a manager here," he says. "I graduated with a degree in telecommunications. That is a long way from being a manager in a bakery."

---

"Drunk people like to steal the tip jar."

Alam cleans out the popcorn machine for the night at a small café a few doors down from Lamine's bakery. He wears jeans and a short-sleeved, striped, button-down shirt. He has olive skin, dark hair, and expressive brown eyes. He is soft-spoken and slight, but like all nightshift employees on the LIRR concourse, he spends much of his shift dealing with customers under the influence of alcohol.

Alam is the manager of the café, though he still works a long shift, 8 PM to 6 AM. He has a flexible schedule, some weeks working as few as four days. And for Alam, the nightshift has its entertainments.

"I'm 35," Alam admits, "But if anyone asks me, I say 31, especially if it's a pretty girl." Alam says that his favorite thing about working nights is watching the girls on the weekend. "You can't do that in the daytime," he says, "not like in the nighttime. Friday and Saturday night, the girls come. They are crazy. They are drunk."

But Alam rarely actually speaks to any of those who brush past his café. "I don't speak English the proper way," he says. He feels that in English he fumbles in the briefest of exchanges. This is one reason he prefers the nightshift, when New York City is free from the frenzy, the hard edge, and the overachiever tendencies of the day. Alam, in fact, says he could earn more than his $8.50 per hour on the dayshift, but it's too busy. "It is so much headache to have so many customers. It is easier at night."

In the wake of the fiscal crisis of the 1970s, New York City underwent significant economic changes, most noticeably in the form of globalization and its by-product, deindustrialization. According to Saskia Sassen in *The Global City*, deindustrialization created a new economy for New York City organized around producer services such as global finance and insurance. That left thousands of semiskilled laborers scrambling to fill positions that required new skills and higher education.

This change in the economy did not slow the influx of new immigrants, but it did radically reorient the way those newcomers were absorbed into the economic life of the city. A century ago, immigrants were the brawn behind industry, working in factories but also contributing to the physical fabric of the city such as the original Penn Station of which this newer, uglier version is but a painful reminder. Now, however, with deindustrialization, immigrant labor creates less than it cleans, cooks, and toils as the quiet cashier. Recent immigrants are at a distinct disadvantage in the new economy. The alternative is the nightshift. The nightshift is to immigrant labor what industry was a century ago.

Alam works the nightshift in Penn Station because, as he says, "What else can I do? There's a language problem."

On another hot summer night, Alam sits in the back of his café. The large seating area is closed off for the night, crowded with bright red tables and chairs that will be full by the morning rush. With Sheryl Crow singing "If It Makes You Happy" overhead, Alam takes a deep breath, eyes closed. In a low, rhythmic voice, he begins to speak. The words are Bangla, and there is a music in them that fills the empty space. It's a love poem that Alam learned in Dhaka, the capital of Bangladesh, when he studied the revered art of reciting poetry. The cheap plastic furnishings and garish lighting seem grossly out of place.

The words fade, and Alam opens his eyes. "It means," he says, "I love you so much. I think so. I don't know the proper English. It's like a sad story. It's better in Bangla."

Alam left Bangladesh for New York City in 2000. Like many others, he left behind a wife and extended family, though he has been able to visit once or twice. "Bangladesh is a poor country," Alam explains, "a lot of people there. One person has a job so a lot of people can eat. It's very hard. Most people think about this place like heaven, not only Bangladeshi, a lot of people think this place is heaven. It's true. If I work in my country like this, I can make, monthly, $200. I can make over here, $2000. So it's a lot of money." He sends money back to his wife, daughter, and mother.

Alam received his green card when a previous employer at an Indian restaurant sponsored his application. "I am a good chef," he says, "but I left that job because you are in front of an oven . . . for like eight hours. It's not only hard, it's like hell." His green card, officially titled Form I-551 and a form of Lawful Permanent Resident (LPR) status, entitles him to work and travel in and out of the United States, but the cards expire after one, two, or a maximum of ten years. At that point, green card holders can reapply for a new card, but many consider the reapplication process an undue burden.

For Alam, it is difficult to live away from his wife and daughter, but, he says, "That is the life." Later, less guarded, he becomes more vulnerable and speaks, in the second person, about what it is like to live and work in New York City while his wife and daughter are in Bangladesh. "If she is like a Bangladeshi girl," he begins, then jumps ahead a little in the narrative, "you come over here, like in 2000." He continues, shifting the geography of the narrative to Bangladesh: "You love her, and you marry her." He shifts the narrative's geography again, placing himself in New York and his new wife in Bangladesh: "She is waiting for you." He explains, "You marry her, and after a couple of months you came back again to New York to work. You have a green card. You cannot bring her when you want. There is paperwork, it takes maybe five years, six years." His wife "loves it over here," says Alam, but "she cannot come now. The visa is so tough." Since they have a young daughter, he tries to return every year or two for several months.

Like many immigrant nightshift workers, Alam is part of a global flow of human resources, where geography is painfully real in its ability to physically separate, but otherwise an abstraction that has little bearing on individual identity. Alam, sitting in the back room of his café reciting Bangla poetry, is where New York and Dhaka meet, overlap, and belie the very idea of bounded territories. The new global incessant economy has provoked a shifting geography that affects goods as well as people; it is a world system where capital flows in one direction and people flow in the other.

In this socially and politically fluid economy, immigrants as labor are interchangeable, dispensable in the eyes of employers because there are a thousand more waiting to render the same service. But the night offers a unique problem to those same employers, the problem of trust. Incessance requires continuity to run smoothly, and nightshift workers are less likely to be viewed as interchangeable. This is one reason Alam is able to travel back to his family for months at a time and still return to his job in Penn Station. As he says, "They know me very well."

———————

Half past 4 AM on a summer Friday night, the bars barely closed, a pack of girls struts past a man cleaning the floors on the Amtrak level of Penn Station. He is in his middle fifties, balding, and what hair he has left is snowy white. The girls stop him, slurring. All seven share the same bottle-blonde hair color. One trails her fingers seductively along the side of his cart of cleaning supplies. She speaks to him, out of earshot of her friends, who've begun their wobbling walk toward their train. He smiles at her, like a father, says a word or two, and returns to his work. She jogs a little, bouncing in all the right places and some of the wrong ones, to catch up with her friends. In an Eastern European accent she says, laughing, "I wanted to see if I could borrow his broom." Later, laughing himself, he says in a Turkish accent, "They were Russian."

Raif has gentle brown eyes and a wrestler's build. He's cleaned the floors on the Amtrak level for more than twenty years, always at night, so he's seen his fair share of young women on their way home after a night on the town. Since arriving from Turkey in 1981, he has successfully provided for his family, with both children now in college, bought a home, which he rents out, and maintained a day job as a building superintendent for two decades. But living the American Dream has come at a price. "I ask myself," he says, "Why did I come to the United States?"

Thirty-five years ago, when he was twenty-one, he was in Turkey dreaming about living in Switzerland or Germany. He was working as an electrician, making a good living and on track to retire early like many of his friends. "Usually," he says, "people come to the United States because there is no job in their country, or a bad life, or something. In my country, my life was excellent. I never thought of the United States, never. Never thought of coming to the United States to work."

His wife, also from Turkey, had other plans. Her family had first come to the United States in the 1960s. After several years of moving back and forth between the United States and Turkey, she met and married Raif, but she never intended to stay in Turkey. Shortly after their marriage, she returned to the United States and applied for a green card on Raif's behalf.

"Then I came here," says Raif, "and oh my God, it was no good."

He did not speak the language, did not yet have a green card, did not yet know anyone beyond his wife's family. "Their life was here. My father-in-law, mother-in-law, they all lived here. I had nobody here. No brother, no sister, no friend." The only answer he has for why he came, and stayed, is, "My wife likes it here, a lot."

One of his first jobs was in his brother-in-law's butcher shop. Again demonstrating the "strength of weak ties" in finding employment, Raif heard about the custodial job at Penn Station from a customer at the butcher shop. "I will bring you an application. It's good money," Raif remembers him saying. He filled out the application and took it in on a hot day in August. "With no English," Raif adds. The interviewer hired him on the spot. He started that same morning, not much more than a year after he arrived in New York.

Three weeks later Raif switched to the afternoon shift, and soon after that he was working the nightshift. "At first," says Raif of the nightshift, "it was very hard. No sleep. In the daytime, you can't sleep because there is too much noise outside. Cars, horns, even the little birds. Upstairs tenant makes noise. I even bought ear plugs."

Soon after starting the nightshift job at Penn Station, Raif found a position as a superintendent in an apartment building in Crown Heights, Brooklyn. The day job meant a free place to live and no bills: "no rent, no gas, no electric, no telephone." Sleep remained elusive, but he decided to keep the nightshift job. "Working the nightshift was good for me," he explains, "because in the daytime I stayed home."

The arrangement freed up his income from cleaning the floors at

Penn Station. Combined with his wife's salary, which was double his since she was a U.S. citizen who spoke English, he was able to purchase a home in Brooklyn as an investment. "Then," says Raif, "my wife became pregnant." When the baby arrived, his wife stayed home for a year. "Then with the second pregnancy," he says, "my wife quit her job permanently." Without her income, Raif felt he had to continue to work both jobs, day and night.

Working two jobs for twenty-four years has provided for his family but it has cost Raif a great deal. "Maybe my hair turned white too early. Maybe I can change my hair to look younger. But my wife," he adds playfully, "no, no, no, she is jealous." His tone turns more serious. "The nightshift," he says, "is no good for the body. I'm not sick, but maybe the average life is 70 years old, 80 years old, and I will only get to 65 years old, I don't know. There is some tiredness in my life, because when you don't get sleep, your eyes go like this," he closes his eyes halfway in an exaggerated expression of fatigue, and "your face goes white."

There is also the added burden of working underground. "There is no fresh air," Raif says. "Penn Station, you know, is underground, you don't get any fresh air. Eight hours at work, plus the subway, that's ten hours everyday underground. Just the walk to my house, two blocks, I get some. I wake up 7 or 8 o'clock and it's dark outside. Just Saturday and Sunday I see the sun, get some fresh air, go some place, have a picnic."

Raif is not shy about his bitterness. In some respects, Raif is the so-called model minority, the immigrant laborer who scraped and saved, bought a house, and raised a family. But for Raif, there are few days he would not trade it gladly for the life he could have had in Turkey. America has provided comfort and security for his family, but little else to persuade him life would not have been better back home. And for Raif, Turkey is still clearly home. Unlike the shifting geographies of so many immigrants caught up in the transnational flows of goods and people, some like Raif never lose their sense of place, and displacement, in the migration experience. America may be a land of economic opportunity, but it makes no promises.

For many native born, this is the crux of the immigration "problem": newcomers as economic freeloaders with little use for citizenship in the classical sense. But such a critique depends on an equally classical notion of nationalism as territorially bounded. For hundreds of millions of people around the world, that notion has lost all currency. And its devaluation is largely a product of a global incessant economy driven by U.S. prosperity. Where once the United States was an international symbol of political liberty, it has become a transnational symbol of economic opportunity. And, then as now, it makes no promises.

"I work two jobs for twenty-four years, two times twenty-four, that's forty-eight years I've been working." One gets the sense that Raif's said this before, many times. "In my country, the retirement age is 47. You start early at like 18 years old, you can retire at 37 years old, 40 years old, 43 years old." Raif is 56. "I told my wife, 'If I worked in my country, I would be retired right now. Ten years ago.'" He adds, sadly, "I'm still working, but my friends my age, they are all retired, they are enjoying life. But I am working hard," he says, adding, "two jobs!"

Raif takes a breath, his eyes unfocused, his voice soft. "You come to United States for a good life. You make money and have a good life. My life is okay, there is no problem, no money problems. But in my country, one job is the same as two here. If I work one job here, I can't make money."

Though he has been in the United States for twenty-five years, though his son, he says, lamentably is "American," he still refers to Turkey as "my country." He dreams about a retirement that would allow him to live in both countries. In Turkey, he says, "the American dollar is a lot of money. It's like the President's life when I go to my country. When I retire, I will go to my country and have a President's life."

––––––––––

On a weeknight just after midnight in Penn Station, a police officer handcuffs a young white man in a button-down shirt and navy pants. He mumbles incoherently and the cop replies, "I told you not to sit in that particular chair." It's quiet enough to hear the classical music that runs on a twenty-four-hour loop, serving as a sort of soundtrack to the tableau that plays out here each night. Such as the gaggle of drunk guys speaking Spanish, talking about their night out, one of them urinating on the floor that Raif will have to mop soon. Or the white guy that sees them and says into his mobile phone, "Seems like it'd be a great place to just come with a video camera and stay all night." Or the three national guardsmen and two Amtrak policemen who converge on a drunk, 20-something male as he flops out of a Red Cap Service booth. The five uniformed men tell him and his friends to leave.

Law enforcement is omnipresent in Penn Station. There are officers everywhere, but they are outnumbered exponentially by gigantic cans of beer and the partygoers who consume them. They are also outnumbered by the homeless population, especially in winter, which finds in Penn Station what the sociologist Mitch Duneier in *Sidewalk* refers to as a "sustaining habitat," where all they need is provided in one single place.

Raif explains their sustaining habitat this way: "A long time ago, there were not too many homeless people. But a city judge gave an order—cold weather, rain, snow, Penn Station accepts homeless people. Not to lay down on the floor, just stand up. Somebody would sleep on a garbage can or somebody would sleep on the handrail. Sometime I talk to the homeless. I ask them why they come to Penn Station, leaving the nice weather. Outside there is nice fresh air, why stay here? They say, 'No, no, I am very safe here. I am scared outside. I am scared of the shelter. It is a very safe place, Penn Station, a safe place.' And sometimes the businesses give food to the homeless, the homeless eat good in Penn Station. It is home, their home."

Recently, the MTA created a program, MTA Connections, that offers referral services to homeless people taking shelter in the subway system, including Penn Station. If they couldn't kick them out, they could at least gently persuade them to enter the shelter system instead. Blue-jacketed Homeless Outreach workers cruise the station in pairs, tackling the delicate task of picking out the homeless from the disheveled revelers on their way home. One outreach worker, Will, a compact African American man in his early forties, patrols the LIRR level greeting everyone with a cheery, "Good morning!" He says it's their policy to always say "good morning" no matter what time of night.

Under Giuliani, at the time Duneier wrote *Sidewalk*, the city tried to legislate an end to this sustaining habitat. But in 1999 a judge ruled that Penn Station was a public space and that homeless people are as free to hang out there as anywhere. "You haven't lived," one Penn Station officer says, "until you've seen somebody bathing in a toilet." They aren't around as much in the summer. "They're out there with their forty ounces," he says by way of explanation. But they're all over the place in the winter.

Penn Station is overseen by neither city nor state law enforcement, but both and, therefore, really neither. The homeless are maligned by just about everybody, but they are allowed to stay in this sustaining habitat. The same officer who snidely assumes the homeless are "out there with their forty ounces" says nothing about the suburban 20-somethings sprawled on the floor of the LIRR waiting area vomiting into paper bags. The feeling is reminiscent of anthropologist Victor Turner's concept of "liminality," that in-between status, something neither wholly this nor wholly that. With the different levels, Penn Station is neither wholly above ground nor below. And it is, most important of all to the nightshift, neither really night nor really day. Even in daytime, there is no sunlight. At night, there is the sense in other places—in a diner, a taxi, a deli, anywhere outside—that when the sun starts to rise the day has dawned. But in Penn Station the sun never comes; it is always night.

Raif knows this in-between place better than most. After twenty-four years of not getting enough sleep, he daydreams about what it would be like to work only the dayshift. "The dayshift starts at 6:30. Maybe I wake up at 5 o'clock. Come to work here. At 2:30, I'm finished, and after 2:30, I'm free—sleeping, shopping, anything. And nighttime sleep is good, like four or five hours of sleep, that's very good, five hours is enough. Daytime sleep, five hours is not enough. Good sleep, I come to work strong, but no good sleep I come here weak." Whether it is school for the kids, doctor's appointments for his wife, or the constant complaints of tenants during the day, Raif never seems to get a good day's rest. "Then I come to work, oh, very hard. I want to sleep."

He smiles, a rueful smile, then confesses, "Sometimes, I see the homeless people sleeping and I think, 'My God, I want to be this guy sleeping.' Sometimes I think like that, like I want to be the homeless sleeping here."

1:48 PASSENGERS ARRIVING FROM STATEN ISLAND

1:51 77TH STREET STOP ON MIDNIGHT RUN

2:05 CHEYENNE DINER

2:13 AMTRAK DEPARTURES AT PENN STATION

# TWELVE: EVERYONE IS THE SAME DOWN THERE

**A** few meters beneath the junction of Flatbush and Nostrand avenues in Brooklyn, the No. 2 train trundles to a stop at the end of its long trek from the farthest northern edge of the Bronx. Air brakes explode like a gunshot, and everything settles into a momentary silence. Then, the doors clatter open and a few dozen weary passengers disembark. A jolly, prerecorded announcement reminds everyone, "This is the last stop on this train. Everyone, please leave the train. Thank you for riding with MTA New York City Transit." Within the half hour it will roll out again, heading up through Brooklyn and the west side of Manhattan and into the Bronx. In the meantime, George, the train's conductor, steps up to the street level to catch a bit of fresh air.

George, 50, has a genial, freckled face and short, almost auburn hair. A fatherly-looking African American man with one daughter, a spunky twenty-year-old in college, his is a calming presence. He joined the Metropolitan Transit Authority (MTA) in 2004 after a dozen or so years of managing a Brooklyn department store. After two months of dayshift training and "posting" with another conductor, he put in for a dayshift assignment close to home. But new hires rarely get their first choice. After rotating through a couple of different rail lines, George was assigned the No. 2 train on the midnight shift.

"You have to be able to adapt to different schedules," he says, describing the rotating shift work of MTA personnel, "but there is no difference in terms of pay or rank." He pauses, then adds with a wave of his hand, "Everyone is the same down there."

The MTA is the latest iteration of various private and public institutions that have managed all or part of the New York City subway system since it began operation in 1904. It opened under the auspices of the Interborough Rapid Transit Company (IRT) and quickly expanded to more than 123 miles of routes shared with the Brooklyn Rapid Transit System (BRT). By the time the Independent Subway System (IND) opened its routes in 1925, three competing subway systems served the city. In 1953, the entire system was consolidated under the New York City Transit Authority, which in turn came under the authority of the MTA in 1968. Today, the New York City subway system maintains 26 train lines, 468 stations, 660 miles of track, and more than 4 million passengers on an average weekday. It is not the largest or the oldest system in the world, but it is the only one that operates on a twenty-four-hour schedule—and it has done so since opening day.

Though the subway system officially opened in 1904, there is, as with many things in New York, a quirky marginalia to that history. In 1870, before electricity and one year after the completion of the first transcontinental railroad in the United States, a secret pneumatic-pressure-powered subway car ran several hundred feet under Broadway. As Brian J. Cudahy explains in *Under the Sidewalks of New York*, Alfred Ely Beach, unable to obtain city permission in the era of Boss Tweed, had crews dig the tunnel under cover of darkness on the nightshift.

On a Tuesday afternoon in December, George slides into a booth at Carville diner in Brooklyn. It's a staid design, nothing like the old railroad car diners, which might have been more appropriate given his second career with the MTA. George was born and raised in New York City, Harlem to be exact, though his parents were from the South.

Today is one of his two days off a week, and George looks tired. He has not been with the MTA long, and he is still adjusting to the odd hours of the nightshift. "The midnight shift is especially hard because I get home so late in the morning," he explains. George has Tuesday and

Wednesday off, but if he gets home too late on Tuesday, he cannot salvage much of the day. "So you really lose a whole day," he adds. "You only get a day and a half off."

There are three shifts for MTA conductors: AM, PM, and midnight. But the train schedules dictate a certain amount of flexibility in start and end times on the shifts. The PM shift straddles the evening commute, with conductors working into the night, and the midnight shift typically runs from 10 PM to 5 AM. But late at night, track work slows most of the trains and almost all of them run local, stopping at every platform, after 11:30 PM. The runs become a lot slower, which is one reason the midnight shift is actually popular: conductors know they will make fewer complete trips.

Fewer complete trips mean fewer things can go wrong. Trains are designed to carry only two employees, the operator and the conductor. The operator controls the speed and braking of the train from the lead car. The conductor, tucked away in a special compartment midway down the train, controls the operation of the doors and stays on the alert for any potential hazards. On the No. 2 line, most of the trains are newer automated models with computer-controlled announcements and safety mechanisms. In fact, the trains are so self-sufficient there is a move to change all titles to "conductor/operator" given the reduced need for human labor on the trains.

"I don't think that will happen," says George. "There are too many safety issues." He tells a story to illustrate his point. It was midnight in the Bronx, and the No. 2 train was stuck between stations. Like most trains in the New York City subway system, the No. 2 moves above ground in the outer boroughs. This meant that, at that moment, a few hundred passengers were stuck a couple of stories above street level. After two hours, they were becoming impatient.

"I had to keep making announcements, trying to calm the passengers down," says George. "I would make an announcement and then communicate with the operator, asking him to speak to them also. I think they were getting tired of hearing my voice."

Eventually, the train jolted forward and eased into the next station. "But there was a track problem," explains George, "and the operator needed to check it before anyone exited the train for safety reasons."

George announced to the passengers in his soothing voice that the doors would open, but no one was to exit the train until he gave permission. "The doors opened, and I looked down the length of the train." The platform was empty. Everyone stayed on the train. George smiles with a bit of wonder, "It was like a miracle. No one moved. They actually listened to me."

George is convinced the passengers would have ignored an automated announcement. "You need the human voice of the conductor."

Most nights, however, are uneventful. Late at night, well after the commuters have spilled out of the system, the long ride from the Bronx to Brooklyn can be strangely quiet. "Around 2 or 3 in the morning, there is hardly anybody out there," says George. "Sometimes you can count the number of people you pick up at a stop."

For those few passengers after 11:30 PM, there is a curious algorithm to navigating the system. Even native New Yorkers can find it difficult. Local trains may skip some stations, and express trains may stop at every platform. Some trains may not run at all, and some may take you into Brooklyn in order to get across Manhattan. The A train may run on the F track, or the No. 5 on the No. 2., or the Q (labeled a J) on a mysterious route that resembles something akin to an M train. Or an R train may sit in the station with no announcement as to why. More startling than all of this is that no one complains. Some people have to get to work, but no one is in a hurry.

The slower pace allows MTA workers greater attention to detail than possible during the pandemonium of daytime commuting. Thus there is the off-hour maintenance that wreaks havoc on the regular routes. Maintenance trains roar past the platforms, battered and heavy-laden. Garbage trains creep through the system and take on cargo at every station. Cleaning crews attack the platforms with power hoses and mini-Zambonis, scrubbing the dingy tiles until they smell of bleach and herding the few waiting passengers like scared cattle.

Of course, there is also the heightened sense of vulnerability that comes with being anywhere in the city after dark. Underground, fear is democratic. Everyone is the same down here, and anyone can end up alone on a station platform. A scavenger can haul a coil of copper wire from a construction zone, across the tracks, and up onto the platform in plain view of a dozen tired passengers. LED messages, hardly noticeable during the quickened pace of day, warn in flashing red letters, "It's always chain-snatching season so don't flash your jewelry," and "Awake is alert." Even the rats are emboldened to come up from the tracks and hunt for food left behind in the day. A red sign on an uptown E platform depicts two huge, hideous black rats. "Rats," it reads, "Let's stop them . . . in the building, on the block, in the subway, in the park." On a Manhattan-bound Q platform in Brooklyn at 4:15 AM, a grizzled MTA worker motions toward a rat lugging a brown paper bag up a flight of stairs. "Chain a' life," he says. Asked if the rats bother him, he replies, "Depends on the size. If they're big, you let them go first."

For George, there is a rhythm to the twenty-four-hour cycle on the subway. He describes how the morning rush dies down to a trickle midday, and how the afternoon rush dies down to a trickle after midnight. Sealed off from the changes in light from day to night, this rhythm blurs the clear boundaries between day and night found in most above-ground jobs. For George, who has worked all three shifts, the PM shift is the hardest. "Sometimes," he explains, "you start out in the Bronx and it's sunny. Then it is dark by the time you get to Flatbush."

George can still sense a change in the ride after dark. Traveling underground, it's easy to forget that this city never sleeps. "You get the sense the city is asleep," he explains. "And as you move into the morning, you can feel the city waking up." That intuitive sense of the slumbering city is difficult for George to put into words, but his conviction about the nightshift is firm. "The night is just different," he says. "The people are different."

———

It's 12:30 AM on a Monday night in late January, and the station platform at Flatbush in Brooklyn is still rather lively. Two MTA workers stand near a Metrocard vending machine emptying out the day's receipts. One of them is on guard, gun drawn, while the other removes the cash. A lanky, dapper man saunters past and into the waiting train. He wears a crushed velvet suit and a black feather boa. In one hand he carries a small bag with a white feather boa stuffed haphazardly inside, perhaps his spare.

On the platform, Will, the MTA Connections outreach worker from Penn Station, bounces down the length of the train, clipboard in hand. He is as cheery as ever, always ready with a "Good morning!" no matter how late the night. Two white women, a decade or so his junior, trail behind him looking earnest if slightly shy. They are volunteers for the annual street count of homeless individuals sponsored by the Department of Homeless Services. Thousands of volunteers have fanned out into designated areas of the city in hopes of estimating the number of those homeless who are not counted in the shelter system. Will is a team leader in the night's count.

Two months later, Will sits in a Starbucks near Bowling Green station at 8:30 AM. In the train station, morning commuters and fresh stacks of free *AM New York* newspapers have replaced the feather boas and drunkenness of night train riders. In the Starbucks, almost no one sits at the few tables to drink their *grande* coffees, giving in to the morning ethos of commotion instead of calm. Daylight in New York brings with it a different sort of citizen rule: stand still, even for a moment, and someone will yell at you for not ordering your coffee or breezing through the train turnstile or walking fast enough. Having just finished his eight-hour shift, Will feels energized by the caffeine-craving people in line for a latte on the way to work. "I didn't really want to work midnight to 8," he explains. "This was the shift that had Saturdays and Sundays off. Saturdays and Sundays are very appealing to a father. You make adjustments accordingly."

Will is in his third year with MTA Connections, his third year on the nightshift seeking out those who might need help with a meal, a safe place to sleep, or medical care. The Starbucks is next door to his organization's offices, and he likes the predictability of the atmosphere. It's something he's picked up working nights, an appreciation for the all-night franchises that offer up the same thing the same way every time. Spotting two coworkers in the hurried line ordering coffee, he laughs and waves at them. "They can handle the coffee," he says, "I can't."

They're younger, but Will, in his midforties, is equally energetic after a long night's work.

Like George, Will works the midnight shift, but Will's shift runs 12 AM to 8 AM. There are day and evening shifts, but the midnight shift has the largest team. "The night teams," explains Will, "do the bulk of the placements and finding of the homeless." His team has nine members, including the two women waiting in line for their coffees.

According to Will, finding the homeless can be easy at night, especially in winter. "You'll find them on trains that don't go outside," he says. "You want to stay warm, it's cold during the wintertime. During the summer, you'll find them on every line possible. But during the winter, the E train, the A train, that's the two main lines that they like." Will, however, does not spend much time riding the trains. Most of his outreach work takes place in the larger stations, such as Grand Central or Penn Station, or the so-called terminal stations, which means the end of a line, such as Flatbush Avenue.

The work is relational, generating trust with individuals who want or need help, but it can be limited by the nightshift hours. Will and his team spend much of their time shuttling people to drop-in centers, shelters, and hospitals with twenty-four-hour psychiatric evaluation centers. Unfortunately, not all social services are available at night. Will tells a story from last night. "We had a guy who wanted to do a detox. Well, it's 1:30 in the morning, there aren't any detoxes available. We can take you someplace, but likely as not, you're not going to stay." This can be frustrating, since night is the busiest time for the outreach teams. It also echoes Melbin's point about the decentralization of power on the nightshift. Top decision makers are at home asleep while lower-level employees bear all of the responsibility with none of the authority. "So much happens overnight," says Will, "but you can't communicate with other agencies overnight. You need management. Not just supervisors, but real administrative decision making."

Identifying who is homeless after midnight in the subway system can also be challenging. Will recounts an incident from early in his time with MTA Connections. Still adjusting to the nightshift schedule, he found himself dozing off on a station platform. "A sweeper came through and said, 'If you need something . . . ' " Will laughs, and recalls, "And when I looked at him we kind of recognized each other, and I said, 'You wanna know what? You just really demonstrated something to me. You cannot look at a person and assume anything.' " Will has learned to approach individuals with a light touch, crafting his words so as to avoid any assumptions. "I'd like to say it's not going to happen to me, and it probably wouldn't, but you never know. I'm sure some of these guys are sitting there wondering as we approach them, 'How did I wind up here? What am I doing here?' So you want to keep that in mind when you approach people."

Will is preparing to enter graduate school in the fall, a master's in social work, and then, perhaps, a PhD. It has given him a certain critical distance when it comes to homeless services, and he is not naive about the MTA's motivations in guiding the homeless out of the subways and into the shelter system. "I don't make any big decisions," he says, "but I don't think it's genius-level thought to say they just want cleaner trains for tourists." He stops, then offers provocatively, "But what's wrong with that?"

For Will, the value in the program is in the result, not the motivation. "The bottom line is that good things are happening for these folk. You might want the city as opposed to the transportation authority to take a hand in it, but you take it where you can. You make change as often as you can and where you can. If you wait for that particular moment in time where you say it's perfect, how many people have you neglected?"

It is a philosophy that keeps him coming back for more each night, though he often sees the same men and women over and over again. "Certainly, they're going to be back on the street," he admits. "But you want to do the best you can do at any particular moment. The best you can may not be the best that's available. The best that you can may not be the best possible. But you want to do the best you can do for that individual at that moment."

This is not Will's first nightshift job. As a young college student, he worked for the MTA as a nightshift bus driver. "I had the pleasure of driving out of the West 14th Street depot, driving the 14th Street crosstown, the 23rd Street crosstown, the 34th Street crosstown." He smiles broadly, as he does often, and continues, "The stress level, the amount of passengers, anything that you can imagine that's on a scale from 1 to 10 in the morning, is down to a 1 or minus 1 at night. There's no comparison. There's no traffic on the streets."

Not that he cared much for the job. In his words, "I haven't always been a people person." But he would never take the job today. According to Will, "The city is more dangerous now. It's not the same way."

It's a curious assessment. Will was driving his bus in the early 1980s, one of the worst periods of crime and economic hardship in the city's recent history. The mass transit system was notorious for random acts of violence and vandalism. In the years since, especially since the late 1990s, crime has dropped precipitously, as much as 60 percent in most areas of the city. The transit system has all but eliminated vandalism, and most riders feel perfectly safe. Areas of blight in and around the city, such as Times Square, have been transformed, safe havens for tourists.

And yet, for Will, times could not be worse.

"Because I get to be around it a lot," he says. He warms to his topic, but there is little passion in his voice, simply disappointment. "The façade of our city is that we've become highly civilized, that we've really gotten things under control, that we've quieted down. But I'll tell you right now, if you go to certain neighborhoods the heroin scourge has not lessened, methamphetamines are making their inroads as we speak."

Will takes up Times Square as an example. "It seems that as a city, we worry about appearances. 42nd Street? Look at it, ah . . . ," he kisses his fingers, "it's wonderful, Disney. But 42nd Street, to me, today is alien. The community of sex workers, the community of substance abusers, and the people who facilitate that—that hasn't disappeared. The drug war hasn't been won. But 42nd Street is Disneyland! That's not real. That's not how our city really is. That's how it is on the outside. I prefer my truth to be in front of me, as opposed to behind a smiling face and a plastic hat. It's different now and it's not as safe."

Will leans forward; here is his point: "These are things you see at night. You may not see them during the day, but you see them clearly at night. At night, things are relaxed. At night, there's less of a façade. Even

Disneyland has to put out their garbage from time to time. So that's the time of day the garbage gets put out. It's less sparkly. But there is an element that does come out at night. I'm sure just by sheer numbers there's twice as many criminals out on the street during the day than when I work, but you don't see them as clearly."

# THIRTEEN: THE REAL HARD CORE

**T**hese are the real hard core."

Barry, 59, nods in the direction of several homeless people asleep in blankets on the steps of a church. "These people are here sleeping every night," he continues. "These are the people who sleep here year round. This church really supports the homeless."

Barry is standing on a quiet corner of West End Avenue on the Upper West Side. It's only the first weekend in December and winter hasn't hit yet, but it's in the low thirties. Barry is an ox of a man, broad, athletic, and fair-skinned like an Irish boxer of long ago. Despite his age, he still has all his hair, a silvery blonde, and most of his strength. And after living on the streets of New York City for two and a half years, he still has a soft side, especially for those who are still homeless. He blames a gambling addiction for putting him on the streets.

He labors around the next corner like a fullback and spots more homeless people sleeping. This group sleeps in cardboard boxes covered in plastic. "These people are really tripped out," says Barry. "They're here every day."

Murray and a friend arrive just shy of 10 PM. They shake hands with Barry and stamp their feet against the cold. Murray is as big as Barry, completely bald, and black. He blames a drug addiction for keeping him caught in the cycle of homelessness for the better part of fifteen years. His friend is white, slight, and has neither the charisma nor the street smarts of Barry or Murray. "He's not homeless," Murray explains, "but I told him he might as well come with me." They are waiting for Midnight Run.

Barry and Murray both work for Midnight Run, an organization that helps the homeless in New York City by bringing vans full of clothes, blankets, shoes, and food. Most everything they bring is donated, and often brand name. "They're doin' it not as charity," says Barry. "They're coming out here and treating these people as their peers." Last week, Barry was complimented on his Kenneth Cole shoes, Perry Ellis shirt, and Calvin Klein suit, all from Midnight Run. All homeless people, says Barry, know when and where to wait for the vans. Barry is no longer homeless, and these days Murray is not what sociologist Peter Rossi calls "technically homeless" since he is staying with his friend. But they both depend on Midnight Run to sustain them. Murray's friend has an apartment but lost his job almost a year ago ("I'm agoraphobic," he says) and needs some warm things for the winter. While they wait for the vans, Murray and Barry discuss whether they know anyone asleep here tonight.

Barry explains that it is not difficult to sleep on concrete steps, when it is the only safe, warm place you can find to sleep. Statistically, homeless men tend to avoid shelters. In New York City this is especially true, with thousands of them sleeping on trains, in parks, on church steps, at the Staten Island Ferry terminal, wherever they are left alone. "One thing about having a homeless past," says Barry, who also has a corporate past, "I can now fall asleep within minutes, anywhere, anytime, any condition. Virtually any homeless man you see, in a library or any type place, they're gonna nod off, because you never get enough sleep."

About 10:30 PM, the Midnight Run trucks arrive. Their diesel-engine *chug-chug-chug* is the only sound in the still night. Barry and Murray discuss how often this group of volunteers does a run. "Back when we were really out here and all that," Murray says, "they would come four times a year." It's their favorite group, mainly because they bring such high-quality goods but also because the volunteers always take the time to talk to the homeless.

The lead volunteer, Ellen, steps down out of the truck. Next to the three big trucks, she looks especially small. She's all pastels: light hair, lavender parka, pale skin. But she's a powerhouse. She's been doing this for eleven years. She admits she's slowing the frequency some. "But I'll never give it up," she says chirpily. The inside of each truck's back door has a list of what that truck holds—jeans, shoes, thermals, sweaters, even soup and Clementines—and, within the trucks, the items are in boxes labeled by size. "You gotta be organized," Ellen says. "I tell them before we leave, 'You take out something from a box, they don't want it, you put it back in that box.'"

As Ellen explains her system, another volunteer recruits Barry to wake up the people on the church steps so they have a chance to get what they need. "I never knew that people slept at this church," says Barry. Midnight Run's executive director told Barry to be sure and wake them up. This policy is in sharp contrast to that of the New York City Department of Homeless Services (DHS) annual count of "street homeless." Volunteers for the DHS count are firmly instructed not to wake up anyone.

Current numbers are hotly contested, but DHS estimates there are about 35,000 homeless men, women, and children in New York City. In 1979, Robert Hayes, New York City's first legal advocate for the homeless, estimated the number of homeless men in the city at 10,000. Hayes argued the case of *Callahan v. Carey*, which awarded the right to shelter to anyone who requests it, and later founded the Coalition for the Homeless.

Midnight Run started in 1984 with a handful of volunteers making trips from the northern suburbs down into Manhattan at midnight. Decades later, most of the volunteers are still from outside the city. "When the Midnight Run started," explains Barry, "there would be one run. They'd get here at midnight, and go home at 5 in the morning." Now they begin much earlier in order to cover more territory. They only make runs in Manhattan, but do them year round, six nights a week, with Sunday breakfast visits to three locations. Six groups are out tonight. With its three vans, this group's caravan looks more like professional movers than an outreach to the homeless.

Barry and Murray explain how they learned about Midnight Run.

"Being homeless . . . ," begins Murray. Barry finishes his thought, "The Midnight Run finds you." Murray continues, "Being homeless, if you need clothes, you need to eat, you need toiletries . . . the Midnight Run."

It's a tough city to survive in, economically. Barry and Murray talk about how easy it is to lose your Medicaid coverage if you start earning over a certain amount. "That's why society is so messed up," says Murray. "You're either poor enough to get . . ." Barry interjects, "Well, you could take anyone, forty to a hundred thousand dollars, and depending on what their," he pauses, "out-go is, to me that's middle class, in New York certainly. Forty thousand, if it's a family, you're in trouble. But there's a lot of people like that."

Murray agrees. "Here in New York," says Murray, "it's very expensive." He thinks a minute, then adds, "I mean Manhattan."

Murray has been struggling for the better part of a year to find a studio apartment that he can rent with his soon-to-expire Section 8 voucher. Introduced by the 1974 Housing and Community Development Act, Section 8 divided government subsidies between incentives for developers of new housing and vouchers for eligible tenants. As the social policy scholar Joel Blau argues in *The Visible Poor*, however, there were never enough vouchers to solve the affordable housing crisis. Blau also suggests that by subsidizing market rates, the vouchers actually pave the way for inflated rents, allowing real estate developers to decline the subsidies in favor of market rents once gentrification takes root in a neighborhood.

"Why would the landlord take my voucher for $1,000 a month when they can rent it to some yuppies for $4,000 a month?" asks Murray. He says real estate brokers only show him "slum apartments," or apartments in neighborhoods that will not help him stay sober. "Let me tell you how the voucher thing goes," Murray says. Accepting the voucher will allow him to earn no more than $200 per month. "You get your voucher, but you have to stay poor for the rest of your life. You say to yourself, 'Do I want to take this voucher and live in one of these slum apartments and stay on welfare for the rest of my life?' Because your voucher is for the rest of your life. But that's not me."

Barry leaves Murray at West End Avenue and walks east. At 11 PM, he arrives at another Upper West Side church and finds the diesel trucks haven't made it here yet. Two people, tightly wrapped in blankets, lie sleeping on the church steps near the front doors.

An African American man, James, sits reading, waiting. He won't admit that he's homeless, though he's anxious for the Midnight Run trucks to get here before midnight so he can make curfew at the shelter where he's staying. "I'm an alcoholic," he says, "but I'm gonna get my life together." For no real reason, other than that he's sitting on the steps of a church, he adds, "I don't believe in religion. I believe in God." He explains that he's here to get some new coats for him and his wife, who lives with him at the shelter but is sick tonight. "You know what," he says, "street smarts is better than any smarts. Because, you know why, I can adapt in any environment." He references *Trading Places*, a film starring Eddie Murphy as a homeless man who, through a social experiment of two wealthy bond traders, winds up with the house, butler, car, and job of a successful trader played by Dan Aykroyd. Aykroyd's character turns to despair and crime. "Some people would kill themselves," says James. "Some people can't handle pressure."

Barry leaves James with a promise that the trucks will get to him before his curfew and continues his walk east. He arrives at the corner of 77th and Central Park West at a quarter till midnight. Midnight Run stops here every weekend. Barry says that everyone on the streets knows about this specific stop. "They always know," he says. "On Friday and Saturday nights, they know, year round, that people will stop here. There will be anywhere from thirty to seventy people." Tonight, however, there's hardly anyone around. Perhaps that is because it is freezing out now, getting colder by the hour. Barry tries to talk to some of the guys waiting for the run but it's hard for them to hear one another over the wind.

The three trucks pull up with a diesel roar. Ellen and her husband, Tom, climb down onto the street. Ellen tells Barry two stories about mistakenly assuming someone was homeless. One man wore flip flops and was shabbily dressed, but he turned out to be a doctor. Tom calls out, "I got coats in here." A dozen or so more men emerge from the shadowed park benches to claim things from the trucks. One guy says, "You got coats? That's what I'm lookin' for." Someone complains about the cold. A guy hears him and says, "They're calling for snow on Monday."

Yellow light glows from the lampposts along Central Park West. Tonight they are festooned with signs that say "New York Divided." They are for an exhibit at the New York Historical Society across the street, but seen from this vantage point—homeless men coming out of the shadows for coats and soup, doorman apartments overlooking the avenue—they speak to the city's ever-widening divide between rich and poor.

Standing near one of the trucks, Tom talks about his experiences as a volunteer with Midnight Run. He has been coming out for only a couple years, and on one of his first runs he helped hand out his own suits. Newly retired, he did not need them, so they filled almost an entire truck with them and brought them out one night. "This changed my mentality about homelessness," he says. "I used to think, 'Why don't they just get a job?' but that's for me. I can get a job, but I've been given the whole toolbox. They haven't."

Ellen says they have just one more stop after this. "It's a small one," she says. "We're gonna end up going to Penn Station because we have so many lunches."

Barry nods knowingly and says, "You can always go to Penn Station." It's one of the three sites for the Sunday breakfast trips from Midnight Run. "Or," Barry continues, "when it's warmer, Madison Square Park."

Barry remembers an icy winter night he spent in Penn Station and launches into the story. "Now when I was homeless," Barry says, "I used to be down there, and I used to say to myself, 'If I had a daughter, and she was wearing what these girls are wearing,' I'm tellin' you. There's no modesty. Dresses that are barely there, and high heels. Drunk and sprawled on the floor." That February night, he had recently had knee surgery. The shelters would not take him, says Barry, because he had a cast to his hip and they did not have elevators. So a friend suggested he come stay with him, requiring him to take the Long Island Railroad to get there. He spent the night in Penn Station before taking an early train.

"So I'm down there on the LIRR level the night before I'm gonna go up there," Barry recalls. "It's a Friday night. I'm on my crutches and there's all these drunk kids. I see this guy walking . . . and a twenty-dollar bill drops on the ground. I'm on my crutches and I'm like, 'I've got to get to that.' You know who sees it, one of those cleaning guys, but I'm gonna tell you what, I set the world's record on crutches. I put that crutch on that $20. He goes, 'You got it, huh?' And I said, 'Yes, I got it.'"

Around 12:30 AM, Barry says goodbye to Ellen and Tom and walks toward Central Park. Behind him stand the high-rise apartments along Central Park West. Beside him men clamor for coats on the sidewalk. Once upon a time, says Barry, Midnight Run would stop at the park and find a giant group of men there. "There'd be a hundred guys. Hundred guys. Sleeping inside a big, old bakery truck." He says there would be another forty or fifty in Riverside Park. The numbers are low tonight, he says, not because there are fewer homeless people, but because the police have cracked down on where they can congregate. "Everybody's spread out," he explains. "There are more homeless than ever."

Central Park is silent and empty except for the *clop clop, clop clop, clop clop* of a hansom cab. The glow of city lights hangs overhead, casting shadows through the thick canopy of trees. Though a light layer of snow covers the ground, the temperature is milder here. The trees block the biting winds that whip through the long blocks on the Upper West Side. Trespassing this most forbidden of spaces in New York at night, Barry feels no fear.

Though he never slept in Central Park during his years of homelessness, Barry has friends who have. He says it is not as dangerous as people think but that you do have to sleep in groups. There is always the threat of violence, but not always from other homeless people. "Groups of teens," he says, "are the worst." A group of teenagers mugged him once late at night. The most dangerous place he slept was in Battery Park. "I slept in the fort, in the parapet, because you were sheltered from the wind and rain."

Barry says he also slept on "Park Avenue." By Park Avenue, Barry means Christ Church on Park and 60th. "I stayed there for a year on the front steps. It's probably the best situation for a homeless man in New York."

At the southern perimeter of the park, the silence evaporates with the noisy city. The clopping of hansom cab horses' hooves gives way to the honking of yellow taxis. Motorcycles, cars, taxis, and trucks whoosh by, free to fly faster in the night. Walking south on Park Avenue to visit the church where he once slept, Barry explains how he found his spot on the steps there. A man who still sleeps at the church invited Barry to sleep there when a spot opened up. There was a hierarchy dictating who could sleep there, and his friend called the shots. "He ran the show with the homeless people," Barry explains. "The guys there had all been there seven or eight years. There was someone that slept on the side steps and six guys that slept in the courtyard. They all know each other. They all watch each other's backs."

Barry gives a crash course in how to survive the elements when you sleep on the street. In the summer, he says, some guys sleep in the bushes near the subway grates. In the winter, wrap up in black plastic trash bags and use only certain types of cardboard boxes. At Christ Church, says Barry, there was another key factor: "I was under cover. I was on the front steps." His friend showed him how to master the art of sleeping rough. "We'd put the cardboard down, sleeping bags, quilts, and then a tarp over us."

Exactly at 1 AM, he reaches the oddly shaped church. Situated on a corner between larger buildings, the church is easily passed in a daylight trek through midtown. Cardboard dormitories, a half dozen or so clean, well-kept, and sturdy boxes, line the sides of the buildings that form a small courtyard. They too are easy to miss if you walk by too quickly. The color of the cardboard blends in with the sand-colored walls of the church. Nestled inside the courtyard, the sleeping men are protected from the bite of rushing wind and the sound of flying cars.

"These are professionals," says Barry. "They are completely encased." He explains how they hide the boxes by day. He also talks about who they are. "Six of those eight guys are Vietnam vets getting disability checks every month." One reason homeless men and women forge relationships with churches is that they can have disability and other checks sent to them via the church address. Another reason is that the churches will defend their right to sleep on their steps.

Barry explains how many Manhattan churches have used legal pressure to protect this right. As Murray explained back on the Upper West

Side, "Giuliani said it's against the law to be homeless. And the Supreme Court said it's not. The churches told Giuliani, 'Leave the people at our church alone; we allow them to sleep there.'" Barry elaborates on this with the example of Christ Church. "The church has a list of names," he explains, "that they give to the precinct, saying, 'Do not bother these men, or we will go to court.' Apparently, during Giuliani time, they tried to screw with them." Barry then describes how one of the church members is a lawyer in a prominent firm. "He just got on the phone and called One Police Plaza and talked to one of the Super Chiefs. 'Don't even think about it or we'll go all the way.'" Also, Barry adds, the precinct in this neighborhood does not bother homeless people much. "They have always been the type that they have better things to do than hassle homeless people."

This church in particular has a number of other benefits for the men who sleep here. "You're in one of the safest areas," says Barry. "But in other places, like Battery Park, one eye open, one eye closed." Another, not unrelated, perk to this place is that it's in one of the wealthiest areas of the city. When Barry began sleeping here, he says that other men told him, "When you wake up in the morning, look under the cardboard." Though sometimes there were as many as seventy men sleeping alongside him, he says, "Invariably, five out of seven mornings, there'd be a five, ten, or a twenty in your pocket." He mentions how the man who invited him to sleep on the steps, who has been out here at least fifteen years, could tell by the bags or containers that people carried what restaurant they had eaten at that night. "He'd go, 'Hey lady, you know you're not gonna eat that steak.' And she's like, 'You're right.' We'd be eatin' fillet."

Another advantage to sleeping on these steps is the way the men are treated the next day. In the morning, the church maintenance man wakes them at 6:15. "You can go in the church and wash up," says Barry. "They'll hold your bags, as long as you come and pick them up by 7 o'clock at night."

During the year that he slept here, says Barry, he would either wash up in the mornings at the church or at a nearby twenty-four-hour deli. "They knew my situation. I used to come in and buy coffee and they always let me, because they knew I didn't make a mess, and I always asked." He walks there now.

Just a half block away, the DelMonico gourmet food market is still open. "It's under where the DelMonico Hotel used to be," explains Barry, "but Trump bought and condoized it." Outside, fluorescent light illuminates the deserted sidewalk. Black rubber floor mats lie drying on top of white buckets, testifying to the hard work of the small nightshift crew.

Inside, the fluorescent lights hurt Barry's outside, night eyes. Heat lamps warm prepared foods in the silver trays of the buffet island. Steam hovers between the lamps and the various rice, meat, and vegetable trays. Nudging toward 1:30 AM, it's closer to breakfast than dinner time. Throughout New York City, however, it's easier to buy eggrolls on the nightshift than oatmeal. "Oatmeal," says the immigrant nightshift worker behind the counter, "only for breakfast. At this hour, no." They're blasting jazzy versions of Christmas tunes, first "Rudolph the Red-nosed Reindeer," then "Santa Claus Is Coming to Town." The TV in back blares a news segment covering a rally protesting the recent shooting and death of Sean Bell, yet another African American controversially gunned down by the NYPD.

Barry has not been inside, or had access to a bathroom, in more than three hours. The money in his pockets is cold. His fingers feel numb, his face wind-burned. The only warmth he has felt for hours is the occasional heat lamp he passed under at several midtown hotels. As cold as it has been tonight, it is that much colder when you are sleeping outside all night. When Barry arrived in the city a few years ago, it was still winter. Other homeless people told him where to get the right cardboard boxes, and blankets from Midnight Run.

Near the deli counter, Barry exchanges a few words with a man in his twenties. "He's homeless," says Barry, "or formerly homeless. He makes good money. He's a male hustler. He services both women and men. There are some times when he's been running around with a couple thousand in his pocket. He has got a drug problem."

These days, male hustlers and other sex workers do not walk the streets of New York City as much as they once did. Quality of life campaigns, which former mayor Rudolph Giuliani began and current mayor

Michael Bloomberg has continued, pushed them off the streets. Strolling districts, where prostitutes once lingered in order to find customers, have all been shut down. Tourists can now go to the theater in Times Square, walk around late at night, and never see a prostitute. But as Will, the homeless outreach worker for MTA Connections pointed out, that does not mean prostitution has disappeared. Sex workers have been forced to work inside, such as strip clubs, where they are not paid as much to dance as to take customers to private booths for sex. They are routinely arrested. They are frequently raped.

The sociologist Elizabeth Bernstein spent a decade writing *Temporarily Yours: Intimacy, Authenticity, and the Commerce of Sex*. She hung out with adult sex workers in San Francisco, Stockholm, and Amsterdam, and argues that structural factors in the global economy have shaped the way individuals make a living, including those who sell sex. Sex workers are as likely to be middle-class individuals pursuing PhDs and writing careers as homeless people in need of a fix. Their work, as Bernstein deftly demonstrates, is sometimes the first experience of empowerment in their lives. They offer, without shame, what Bernstein calls "bounded authenticity," sex as recreational instead of procreational, marital, or part of a lasting relationship. It has the illusion of authenticity for the customer, but is understood on both sides that it is bounded, that it is, ultimately, a financial transaction.

Barry says goodnight to the male hustler, steps back outside, and heads west. He admits that he still feels connected to the guys who have no place to go. It was not always so. "I had no compassion," admits Barry. "Now you gotta remember, I was working on Wall Street in 1981. Homelessness was a big thing even then. I had no compassion. My retort to them would be, 'Get a job.'"

Barry stops on the corner of Fifth Avenue and 59th Street. The Plaza Hotel looms overhead, undergoing renovation into upscale condominiums. To his left, Apple's new glass cube welcomes computer shoppers twenty-four hours a day in front of the sleeping F. A. O. Schwartz toy store. Across the street, Central Park swallows up any remaining light.

"That was before I was out here," he continues, "and learned what it's all about."

# FOURTEEN: I'M HERE ALL NIGHT

I'm here all night," Ricardo says, chuckling from his shoulders, his eyes dancing. That sly grin suggests he has much more to say.

Ricardo, 49, a round man in a full-length overcoat, is pacing under the awning of a stately stone building. He is a doorman. His brimmed hat caps a cherubic face, and his thin salt-and-pepper mustache accentuates his slightly impish smile. The heat lamps overhead are warm enough, but he moves anxiously to and fro as if waiting for someone. Waiting for hours.

After midnight, the Upper West Side of Manhattan falls into a quiet slumber, deeper and more complete than most neighborhoods on the island. Just two decades ago, the long, uninterrupted blocks between Central Park and the Hudson River were crowded with drug dealers and sex workers. Today, they are crowded with doublewide baby strollers and delivery boys peddling their cargo from boutique grocery stores. Night has taken on the character of its residents, leaving the streets to the empty taxis that troll the avenues and the doormen who mark off some blocks in hundred-foot increments.

With the clock creeping toward 1 AM on this last night in November, Ricardo explains how he took up his post as doorman at this Upper West Side building more than twenty years ago. He had only recently arrived from the Dominican Republic, and though he spoke some English, it was a distant second to his native Spanish. "I started out in maintenance," he explains. "I work a lot with my hands. Construction, all kinds of repairs." But it was not long after he was hired that the superintendent was fatally shot in his on-site apartment. "I was working for the super, and this guy he had a girlfriend, a married woman. She left her husband and was living with him. Then the husband he came here one day and shot them both." The building hired a new superintendent and promoted Ricardo to nightshift doorman.

The new job meant union representation and a new uniform. It also meant more contact with tenants and the public, but the nightshift kept such interaction to a minimum. Ricardo was still a recent immigrant, and still more comfortable in Spanish.

"The union, they paid for my English, so I took English classes for free," Ricardo explains. "I spoke English when I lived in the Dominican Republic, but here I went to school. I went in the morning, every day, from 9 o'clock to 12 o'clock, every day. I was there four years." His instructor took a special interest in his education, offering private lessons and extra tutoring. "She gave me more help because I am Jewish and she is Jewish, so she helped me a lot."

Ricardo is a Dominican Jew. That is to say, he is Jewish and from the Dominican Republic. Like the Jewish diaspora in Argentina and Cuba, Jews in the Dominican Republic are part of a long history of religious persecution in Spain. Ricardo's grandparents emigrated from there in the early twentieth century, before Franco's reign. In 1979, Ricardo continued the sojourn north, crossing the Mexican border into the United States as an undocumented immigrant.

"I came here illegally to this country. I came through Mexico, Nicaragua," he says in Spanish. The words tumble from his mouth in the familiar rhythm of native speakers from the islands. After almost thirty years in the United States, he is now a citizen and speaks English fluently. When he speaks the adopted tongue, it is with the music of his native Spanish.

A young couple hurries into the building. Ricardo offers a friendly tip of his hat, but says nothing. He claps his hands together against the increasing cold and looks out across the street. There, under the awning of another high-rise building, stands another doorman in full dress uniform. Ricardo offers an energetic wave, and his counterpart waves back.

"That's James," explains Ricardo. "A very good man. He is my friend."

James, an African American man in his midforties, stands at attention near the glass revolving door of his building, still waving over to Ricardo. The glass and steel building towering above him is three times the size of Ricardo's and requires a staff three times as large. His clear, piercing eyes, close-cropped hair, and pencil thin mustache decorate an angular, serious face. James is not tall, but somehow he makes an imposing figure. The rest of him is lost in his charcoal gray uniform. His voice is resonant and sure. "Ricky's a good man," he says, referring to Ricardo. "We look out for each other."

James took the job as nightshift doorman after losing a position at a company that went bankrupt on Long Island. The hours appealed to his desire to spend more time with his children. "I wanted to be involved in my kids' life," he says. "Like when they were younger and they were ill, I was home. I didn't want a babysitter watching them. I would do so many different things. We would go to the museums. My oldest son, he said, 'Daddy, I appreciate what you're doing, 'cause I know it's hard.'"

Family is a topic James does not grow tired of, nor is his faith, his church, and what he considers his calling as a Christian in his job as a nightshift doorman. "I had one lady who walked up to me and said, 'Are you a religious guy?' I looked at her and said, 'Why do you say that?' And she said, 'The way you carry yourself.' I said, 'Yes.' And she said, 'I was telling somebody I knew you had that tendency. You're a serious person.'" James manages a smile, and says, "There's a time for everything. I like to laugh, you know. But I'm serious in a lot of things. My mind is always going. I mean, especially when you have God in your life."

James has put that faith to good use over the past fifteen years on the job, especially as the neighborhood has changed so dramatically. "Ten years ago there were homeless people all over the place," he says. "There was Bunny. She was a young woman, but she looked old. I would buy her cups of coffee from the deli and let her come inside to get warm. One day she knocked on the door and said, 'James, I can't take it anymore. I'm getting into a program.' Months later she knocked on the door again, and I said, 'Who is this?' I didn't even recognize her. She had become a counselor in the program and turned her life around." He recounts more stories of other men and women, some of whom found their way off the street, and some who did not. "I've been able to have a lot of relationships with the homeless at 2 AM."

As James warms to his topic, he slips into the cadence of a preacher, hitting certain syllables for exactly the right emphasis. But he also knows he's on the job and is careful not to offend those who do not share his worldview. "This job gives me the opportunity to minister to a lot of people," he explains. "When I walk down I meet some of the other doormen and they say, 'Hey man, there's something different about you.' But I've learned to be wise. I have to feel you out before I say anything. You know, through the years you grow wiser. I know certain people I'll just pray for silently."

A middle-aged woman trundles out from the elevators with a small terrier. "Hi, how're you?" James asks, then turns his attention to her dog. "Hey, Whiskey," he says, reaching down to pet Whiskey. The dog ignores him. "You forgot about me?" James asks, affecting a hurt tone. The woman chides the dog, "This is Dennis. You know Dennis. You see him all the time." James smiles, ignoring the fact that the woman got his name wrong. She lingers and he asks again, "How you doing today?" She responds with a few words about the weather and wanders off with Whiskey.

---

"The nightshift is something you have to get used to," says James. "It's an adjustment."

It's 8 in the morning, and the two doormen have slipped into civilian clothes and met for breakfast at a cramped diner one block from their posts. There are few tables in the space, most of them filled with their tenants. Few of the tenants seem to recognize the two men out of uniform. Ricardo looks smaller out of uniform, James leaner. Ricardo wears a black parka vest over his gray sweatshirt and faded jeans. He slumps in his seat, his shoulders hunched over, but the glint in his eye suggests he's as likely to pounce as fall asleep. James sits erect, at attention, dressed in a buttery leather jacket, black cords, a black leather cap, and rectangular Phat Farm eyeglasses.

James continues, "My wife and my kids, they look at me and they say, 'I don't know how you do it. From being up all night, from going to sleep around 5 in the evening, and sleeping for several hours, then coming back.' Because sometimes I get three hours sleep. You get used to it after a while."

Like many on the nightshift, James and Ricardo use their off-hour schedules to their family's advantage, providing childcare during the day when their spouses are at work. When Ricardo arrives home after his shift, his first duty is to shuttle his three children off to school. It's a complicated routine, as each of them—two sons and a daughter, ages 9 to 13—attends a different school.

James smiles and says, "Oh boy, I remember those days." His three sons are much older now, in high school and college, but as he explains, "I used to do the same thing he's doing."

When James signed on for the job as a nightshift doorman, his greatest concern was not the hours, but the uniform. The gaudy suit bedecked with epaulets, tassels, and brass was not something he felt comfortable wearing. "For me, it took an adjustment. I felt like I'm in the military," he recalls. "I put the uniform on and it's double-breasted and then I put the cap on and I'm like, 'Oh boy.'" He's gotten used to the idea, but it took some time. "I was a little embarrassed. But I realized in my mind that this is the job that I had to do. So I just adapted. Now, it's no problem."

The sociologist Peter Bearman, in his book *Doormen*, discusses the role of uniforms in the occupational prestige of the doorman trade. He argues that aspects of the uniform represent the purity of the profession as a "clean job" relative to other blue-collar trades. Still, Bearman points out that any uniform in the American labor market, especially the service sector, conveys low status. Not surprisingly, many doormen, and even some tenants, admit their discomfort with the idea of uniforms.

But uniforms serve a critical function and it has little to do with the perceptions of passersby. Bearman suggests that the central problem for doormen like James and Ricardo is the contradiction inherent in such personal contact with tenants who are socially quite distant in the American class system. Discretion is highly valued in doormen because they are privy to the most intimate details of their tenants' lives. And yet, there is a yawning class divide that contradicts this intimacy. A clear boundary marker is needed in what could be murky social territory; enter the uniform, and the gaudier the better.

Both Ricardo and James admit to feeling invisible to their tenants when they are out of uniform. Ricardo explains, "When they see you working and they say, 'Hello, hello,' and then you put on the change of clothes and they look the other way." James nods in agreement, "Yes, yes, yes. They don't recognize me with civilian clothes on. But I am the same way with the uniform on and without."

This problem of social distance is true for all doormen, but it seems magnified on the nightshift when the job involves much less contact with the tenants in their building. There are five hundred apartments in James's building, and at least as many names and faces to remember as they pass in and out. "Not working the day, I don't really get a chance to see all of them," he explains. "I've stopped many where they've been like, 'I've been here twenty years,' and I'm like, 'Sorry, I don't know you. You still gotta show me your ID.'"

This disconnect between nightshift doormen and most of their tenants has a series of consequences, from altercations with tenants they do not recognize to a tightening of the purse strings when it comes to customary tipping. As James says, "The guys during the day, they receive a lot more in tips than I do." That said, sitting in the cramped diner filled with tenants from his building, he adds, "I'm not really into it. I appreciate what's given."

Ricardo laughs. "Some of them are very hard," he says. "Sometimes $3, sometimes $5. Very economical."

James interjects, "Sometimes I tell them, 'Look, I get a paycheck every week and if I don't see you that often I feel funny taking from you.' I say, 'I'm here to help you, I'm here to assist. And at the end of the week, if I put in my time, I'm getting a paycheck.'" James smiles to himself, then says, "I remember, there was an old lady and she used to always give change. She would give like five dimes. But I even appreciate the little things. I appreciate the gesture."

The gesture of a tip is one way tenants acknowledge the paradox of interpersonal closeness and social distance. But they are also acknowledging the peace of mind that doormen offer, not only in terms of personal service (something dayshift doormen offer more consistently), but more critically in terms of personal safety (something nightshift doormen presumably offer in lieu of more tangible services).

Jane Jacobs once described the importance of eyes on the street for city safety, especially after dark. Neighbors and public characters can create a network of vigilance to keep the perception of danger, if not danger itself, at bay. All-night delis like the Lucky Stop on the Lower East Side receive packages for neighbors, offer a familiar face at any hour, and help foster an organic, mutually constituting urban community.

But for many quiet stretches on the Upper West Side, there are no all-night delis. Not unlike the American suburb, where two-car garages have replaced front porches and houses have turned inward, the high-rise apartment buildings of upper Manhattan offer little in the way of public characters or a network of vigilance on the long blocks between Central Park and the Hudson River. After dark, doormen are the last live eyes on the street, paid substitutes for public characters.

It is a responsibility that James and Ricardo take seriously, if for no other reason than their own safety.

"If I don't see him at the desk," James says in reference to Ricardo, "and I see somebody at the door, I'll give him a call. We look out for one another."

"You have to be very, very careful," says James. "One guy I had to drag out of the lobby because he was following these young girls in here. I'm looking at him, and the guy's like, 'I'm not leaving.' I said, 'I'm calling the police,' and he falls out on the floor. He said, 'I'm not moving.' I had people coming in and looking at me. I grabbed him by the collar, opened the door, and dragged him outside."

James also describes a fight in front of a popular restaurant a few doors down. "I heard a guy say, 'Gun!' And you don't know what they're gonna do 'cause we're right there. But thank God, nothing happened. You have to be alert. And I usually lock the doors after a certain hour."

"We're playing with our life!" says Ricardo. Slipping into Spanish, he says again, "We're playing with our life! And the residents don't recognize that. The president of the building doesn't recognize that. And neither does the union recognize that. You are risking your life." Warming to his topic, he switches back to English, "You know, on this street, in the nighttime, there are a lot of delinquents walking. Going for the bus, going for the train, crossing the park. It's not easy."

Ricardo makes $21 an hour for his nightshift at the door but, for him, it is not enough given the risks of working through the night. "Sometimes they pay overtime, but they should pay double because the nighttime is very hard. The doorman doesn't have good security, only the telephone. You have a problem, you call the police. If someone comes with a gun or something like that, it's dangerous."

James nods in agreement, adding, "During the day, it's busy. But at night, it's a different atmosphere."

But James and Ricardo are not the only ones doing the watching. The surveillance cameras that dot the city are there in the lobbies of their buildings too, a fact that gives Ricardo pause during his shift. Of the many techniques he uses to keep awake, one includes prayer. "I like to pray in the morning, at 3 o'clock in the morning, or 2:30," he says. "But up in the corner, you know, the camera is watching me." He grins, then laughs with his whole body. "I worry about the camera, I do."

According to a 2006 survey by the New York Civil Liberties Union, there are more than 4,000 surveillance cameras in Manhattan. That's up from 769 only seven years earlier. Whether the increase correlates with September 11, 2001, or the technology has simply reached some critical mass, cameras now record even the most mundane activities of millions of New Yorkers every day. They are in every diner, deli, airport, hospital, and train station; they are on street corners and inside building lobbies and stairwells; they are even on the dashboards of most taxis. And though the cameras silently record twenty-four hours a day, they are somehow more noticeable at night. With fewer people distracting attention, and less pressure to conduct your business and hurry on, the unblinking eye of a surveillance camera, or two, or ten, mounted on a cramped deli ceiling makes buying even a soda somehow feel suspect.

This mute judgment of activity, angled overhead and recording every move and sometimes every word, is precisely the point, and the more obvious the technology the better. Indeed, for the New York City Police Department, surveillance cameras are the new street lamps, augmenting if not replacing the cop on the street. Claiming that cameras installed in public housing reduced crime by 35 percent, the NYPD plans to set up more than five hundred surveillance cameras throughout the city. In some cases, the police have set up mobile surveillance stations, small booths on pneumatic lifts that raise flood lights and cameras two stories above the street, pointed in every direction throughout the night in so-called high crime areas. Like public lighting at the turn of the last century, cameras are assumed to deter crime by exposing, and now recording, activity. But where lighting had a dual purpose, both to light the way for law-abiding citizens and to serve as eyes for state authorities, surveillance cameras serve only the latter purpose, recording the activities of everyone equally, from would-be criminals to doormen saying their nightly prayers.

With increased risk and social isolation, not to mention lower tips and the surveillance of their surveillance, neither James nor Ricardo claims to enjoy the nightshift. James has worked his post long enough to earn a dayshift schedule, but there is a logic to the nightshift that makes sense for now. "I could have been on 4 to 12," he explains, "but I would never see my family. I like to sit down and eat dinner with my family, find out what's going on in the house. With my wife working 8 to 4, we'd be just passing by, and I don't want to do that."

Ricardo, however, is less philosophical. "I never had the chance," he says. "I don't have a friendship with the president or the superintendent, so I don't have the chance."

For now, they both work the night, making the schedule work for themselves and their families. Most of the night is passed a hundred feet apart, each in the doorway of his building, maintaining his watch until daybreak. There is too much distance and too little time for even minimal conversation, so their contact is reduced to gesture.

"We see each other," James says, "and we go like this . . ." He clasps his hands together and bows. "Sometimes people will be walking by and wonder, 'Who is he doing that to?'" But James clarifies, "It means, that's my brother across the street."

Ricardo cries out, "You know what it means? It means, God bless you."

2:41 NEON SIGN AT SKYLIGHT DINER

2:49 MIXED EMOTIONS

3:03  OPEN 24 HOURS

3:37 TACO VENDORS IN WEST VILLAGE

# FIFTEEN: NIGHT BOAT WEEKENDS

W e call this the money boat."

Billy, 42, a nightshift deckhand for the Port Authority, makes his rounds through the cabin of the *Alice Austen* between dockings. The *Alice Austen* is one of two smaller ferries that run the nightshift between Manhattan and Staten Island. It's after 2 AM on a hot Saturday in late August and the ferry is still full of summer tourists. While they chatter away in various languages and snap photos with pocket cameras, the ferry steams out of the Staten Island terminal and heads toward the open harbor. There is no moon out tonight, so the ship will plow through the water at nearly seventeen knots, making the trip between the two islands in a little less than a half hour.

"For a job as a deckhand on a ferry," Billy continues, "this night boat weekends is the worst job in the place, but the money is better. You get two-and-a-half days built-in overtime every check."

Billy was born and raised in Brooklyn but lives on the water. Sporting a graying goatee these days, Billy has spiky black hair and a set of rugged good looks. He's fished tuna and bluefish in the open sea past the narrows, worked on tugs in the New York harbor and the Governor's Island ferry to Manhattan when the island was still an active military base. The few jobs he's held on land—including driving a hansom cab in Central

Park—were always between gigs on the water. But the small-scale fishing industry is dwindling, most of the work in the harbor has shifted to New Jersey, and the military base closed years ago. After four years on the nightshift for the Staten Island Ferry, Billy is enjoying the steady paycheck, if not the tedium of the job.

"Used to be you couldn't get on this night job unless you had seniority," Billy explains. As the ferry nears Manhattan, he will walk the short ramp and prepare the gangplank for passengers to disembark. A few minutes later, the *Alice Austen* will be loaded down with new passengers and heading back out into the harbor. Billy leans against a rail near his post, arms folded, more than a little bored.

"It's turned into a shitty type of job, basically."

Both the waterfront and harbor have long played important roles in the life of the city, and yet it is easy to forget that New York is surrounded by water. As Phillip Lopate points out in *Waterfront*, more than a few New York writers have helped forge a literary connection to the water: Walt Whitman, Alfred Kazin, the sociologist William Kornblum, the inimitable Joseph Mitchell. But by and large the city has turned its back on the ocean, architecturally and culturally; it has little of the urban synergy that West Coast cities still enjoy with the Pacific.

There was a time, of course, when the harbor and its port were integral to the development of industry and the growth of the city. The port became the largest and busiest in the world, providing employment for countless thousands of New Yorkers. Those employed by the port, many of whom were recent immigrants, spent their lives hauling cargo off the boats that came and went day and night. The harbor too was critical, both to transportation and to the insatiable appetite of a growing city. In *The Big Oyster*, Mark Kurlansky details that New York was world famous for its oysters well into the twentieth century, raking them up from the bottom of the harbor and exporting them far and wide.

The water also made New York at night possible. In *City Lights*, Jakle reveals how as early as 1792, New York City street lamps were lit using spermaceti, a substance obtained from the heads of sperm whales. In early 1880, the first commercial installation of Thomas Edison's electrical lighting system occurred in the New York harbor on a steamship called the S.S. *Columbia*. Electric lights would not illuminate land-based industry for another year.

Today, however, the New York harbor and its port have declined in significance, both for shipping and in terms of the city's connection to the water. The current fascination is with bridges and tunnels, not ships and boats. Yet, industries change. This is not new. The city is loyal to no one. The *New Yorker* writer Joseph Mitchell described the old-time oyster bedders and lobster baymen whose work became unprofitable in the changing city. According to Kurlansky, with increasing pollution, the last of the New York oyster beds closed in 1927. Despite recent attempts to clean up the New York waterways, few are willing to risk the toxins found in the handful of oysters that still cling to the garbage dumps beneath the surface of the harbor. Even the original Fulton Fish Market, after the fish started arriving primarily in trucks instead of on boats, was shut down and relocated to the Hunts Point Market in the South Bronx.

"We're supposed to make continuous rounds," Billy explains. "Suspicious packages, suspicious people. This is more people normally than we have at 2 AM going to Manhattan." He walks from aft to stern, scanning the rows of seats and occasionally peeking through one of the porthole windows into the blackness beyond. He casually points out one of several security cameras mounted on the ceiling of the cabin. "They have cameras all over the place," he says.

Billy started working on the ferry in 2002, a year after the terrorist attack of 9/11 radically transformed the lower Manhattan skyline and the city's attitude toward security, especially on the water. Though the life of the city has slowly turned its back on the harbor, the open water that surrounds the archipelago of New York City represents a vulnerability no less exploitable than the air itself. From the National Guard troops that patrol the terminals to deckhands like Billy, all must maintain constant vigilance against an unknown threat. And staring out into the night from the portholes of the *Alice Austen*, one senses that vulnerability in the vastness of what cannot be seen.

But the view from the ferry reveals more than the city's defenselessness. To starboard is the busy Port of New Jersey. Cranes rise like skyscrapers against the faint glow of Newark, Jersey City, and Perth Amboy, and several lumbering freighters wait patiently through the night to load and unload cargo. To port, Brooklyn is dark and has been for years.

The difference between the two ports has not always been so apparent. The well-known 1954 film *On the Waterfront* focused on the port when it still spanned both the New York and New Jersey sides of the Hudson. Lopate describes how the Port of New York, once the largest in the world, lost out to Elizabeth, New Jersey, when the Port Authority sought to root out organized crime. James Sanders in *Celluloid Skyline: New York and the Movies*, attributes the shift to "containerization"—a new mechanized method of offloading cargo that required fewer workers and a larger facility. However the shift occurred, the New York longshoremen endured injury and illness, a lack of steady work, strict codes against working other piers, and what Lopate describes as "a debilitating pattern of idleness and drinking," until their jobs disappeared completely.

As shipping has declined, the men and women who make their living on the water have turned to what employment is available. Like Billy, many have turned to the Staten Island Ferry, even if it means walking the deck a hundred times a night.

"To get this job you need two years of deck experience on a boat—fishing boat, tug boat," says Billy. Some come from the pleasure boats that circle Manhattan, and others from the U.S. Navy. "Some guys have AB tickets, which is an 'able-bodied seaman' ticket," explains Billy. "Some are for in-shore and some are for open water. I don't have any of that anymore." Billy came to the job with more than enough experience, though he had let his Z card expire. "It's just a merchant mariner's document," he says. "It wasn't a qualification for the job, not when I got it." After a few years as a provisional hire, he was upgraded to a permanent civil service employee.

Billy's job on the ferry consists of three nights on the boat, one night in the terminal, and three nights off. His shift is consistent: Thursday through Saturday are spent on the ferry itself, and Sunday nights are spent on land operating the bridge that connects passengers to the upper level of the terminal. Billy explains the awkward calculus of nightshift labor, "The other night crew on this boat works Sunday night for Monday and they get off on a Thursday morning. We come in Thursday night for Friday. They do four nights on the boat, but there are only seven days a week. So we do three plus one." He smiles at the complexity of his explanation and says, "See, I tell people I live eight days a week, and they look at me like I'm crazy. I work four nights, I get off Monday at 6:45 in the morning. I don't go back to work until Thursday night at 10:30. I have four full days off and I work four days. It's like living eight days a week."

The twisted logic of nightshift schedules can spell disaster for performance. According to Billy, "You're not allowed to do more than twelve hours on the boat in one shot. They say if you agree to it then you can, but I won't agree to it. If there is an accident, they'll ask you why you were on the boat for more than twelve hours. I don't do it."

On the afternoon of October 15, 2003, there was in fact a tragic accident involving the Staten Island Ferry. The assistant captain, Richard J. Smith, was alone at the helm when he passed out, causing the ferry to slam into the pier on the Staten Island side. The crash killed eleven people and injured dozens more. Though the accident occurred in the afternoon, fatigue was a factor.

On the nightshift, fatigue is just one of many factors that can lead to accidents, and in some cases, catastrophic disasters. Bhopal, Three Mile Island, Chernobyl, all of these are associated with industrial accidents that cost thousands of lives, and all occurred on the nightshift.

Melbin suggests that information about potential problems falls through the cracks during the changeover from dayshift to nightshift employees. This gap in information, he asserts, led to the 1984 catastrophe in Bhopal, India. A worker on one shift checked a gauge and decided it was normal. A worker on the next shift checked the same gauge and also decided it was normal. Both readings were normal, but the increase was not. Since there was no one to compare the two readings, no one knew that the pressure had increased fivefold within a half hour. The resulting 12:40 AM rupture and chemical leak killed 2,000 people and injured 200,000.

The 1979 reactor meltdown at Three Mile Island in Pennsylvania was not due to information lost between shifts, Melbin explains, but to the fact that management was not on site. The time lost rousing management at

4 AM meant a "routine" emergency became what the economist Kenneth Fortson has described as "the worst accident in the short history of U.S. commercial nuclear power."

Seven years later, at 1:23 AM on April 26, 1986, another reactor meltdown caused massive loss of life: Chernobyl. This accident was again due at least in part to a communication failure. The information lost occurred not during a shift changeover but, according to a 2002 Nuclear Energy Agency report, between those conducting a test at the nonnuclear part of the facility and those in charge of the nuclear reactor.

Fortson attributes such accidents not to the faulty transfer of information or lack of management, but rather to the "inherent physiological implications of late-night work that make off-hours jobs more hazardous than daytime jobs." Performance impairment is at its highest as the circadian cycle is at its lowest point in the early morning. In short, circadian rhythms affect job performance.

Billy knows this well. "I usually get sleepy around 3 or 4 in the morning," he says. "Your body has a clock. It says at 3 o'clock in the morning you're not supposed to be up walking around."

Billy laughs and adds, "Unless you're sitting in a bar getting drunk— you never feel that clock then." Here as everywhere there is a close kinship between alcohol and the night. Not unlike Penn Station, Billy says that one benefit of working the nightshift is the spectacle of humanity commuting to "the city" for its nightlife. As he explains, "The one perk about working on the weekends is you get to look at the women all night. Especially the weekend, you see them going to the city and you see them coming home." For Billy, the entertainment is in the contrast between the beginning and the end of an evening. "Some of them look gorgeous getting on, and they look like wet noodles getting off."

The ubiquity of alcohol in the incessant economy also means that commuters do not even have to leave the boat to get their fix. Billy points to the snack bar at midship on the *Alice Austen*. "They serve beer here," he says. "I wouldn't allow it, but they do. At 4 o'clock we shut it down. Used to be, you could have it all night."

Between the occasional drunk passenger and the boredom of walking the cabin all night, the nightshift job on the ferry lacks much of the romance of life on the water. Like most of the other crewmembers, Billy works the ferry for its consistency but remains a seaman at heart. For him, that means working on his nights off as a nightshift deckhand on the *Brooklyn VI*, a sport fishing boat that runs out of Brooklyn.

"It's extra money," he explains. As a deckhand on the *Brooklyn VI*, Billy receives tips from customers for help with their rigging and cleaning their catch. "I haven't taken money out of the bank since early June. It's cash, cash, cash." But the work is largely seasonal; hence the importance of holding onto year-round employment on the ferry. "It depends on the people, on the number of people," he says. With the cold winds of autumn there are fewer customers willing to brave the elements on the open water, so fishing trips begin to dwindle after Labor Day. According to Billy, "You might get a couple of nitwits, but I don't even want to go out in crappy weather. Nobody wants to sit in the rain all night, that sucks."

The *Alice Austen* is cutting back its engines and easing toward the ferry terminal near Battery Park in Lower Manhattan. In the distance, off starboard, the Statue of Liberty glows green in the darkness, and overhead the city skyline casts its brilliant light over the water.

Billy is getting ready to guide the bridge onto the gangplank for the passengers to disembark, but he is thinking about fishing. "They're going tuna fishing tomorrow night," he says. "Twenty-four hours. They'll leave at 6 tomorrow evening and should be back 5 or 6 the following day."

The passengers begin to crowd the exits, waiting for the ferry to dock.

"We used to go two or three times a week on twenty-four-hour trips," Billy continues. "You could make $2,000 or $2,500. You don't go out and do that anymore. You go out and you're happy if with thirty-five people you caught sixty fish. That's a banner trip. We used to go out and catch two hundred fish."

Billy slips on his gloves as the ferry enters the terminal. He mentions that the *Brooklyn VI* is set for a night run on Tuesday and the weather looks promising.

"If we sail," he says, turning to the gangplank to let the passengers off, "I'll be there."

# SIXTEEN: NIGHT FISHING

**W**e're just off of Seabright, New Jersey."

It's a Tuesday night in June and Billy, the deckhand from the ferry, is moonlighting on the *Brooklyn VI*, a bluefish boat that operates out of Brooklyn's Sheepshead Bay. Tonight he wears a navy hooded sweatshirt emblazoned with the *Brooklyn VI* logo and the traditional fisherman's oilskin overalls known as skins. The 110-foot boat pulled out of the bay at 7:30 PM, passed under the flight path of JFK airport, and ran due east for two hours through six-foot swells. By the time it anchored in the shallows of the Atlantic Ocean, the sun had set and the horizon had disappeared in the darkness.

Billy and another deckhand work the deck. Some nights, they'll help customers bait hooks, fillet (dress) any fish they catch, and help untangle the occasional backlash, where the line gets caught up in the reel. Other nights, when the fish are biting, they'll mostly gaff, using a long metal hook to help haul the fish up out of the water and onto the deck. On a good night, they'll get tipped well for all their work.

"It's not a lotta money," Billy continues. "You pay a bill with it, but this sucks." He's referring both to the steep swells rocking the boat from side to side, and the fact that no one is catching any fish. Deckhands earn most of their income from tips, but no one tips if they don't catch fish. Customers pay $45 each for the trip plus a $5 contribution to the pool for the biggest fish of the night. On a rainy night like this, with only fifteen customers, even the boat's owner could lose money on the trip, which costs him about $750.

"Last night was good," says Billy. "It went fast. We only had fifteen people on, but we had the fish too. I went home this morning and I stunk. I always say if you don't stink, you made no money." Still, even a good night is a grim reminder of how the sport fishing industry has declined. "Used to be, years ago, business was better. But now, no one is fishing."

For decades, charter and party boats full of people eager to catch bluefish, striped bass, and tuna have departed from Sheepshead Bay to fish in the harbor and off the Jersey coast. Already in the 1920s sport fishing charter and party boats were part of life in New York. In his essay "The Bottom of the Harbor," from the collection *Up in the Old Hotel and Other Stories,* Joseph Mitchell describes Sheepshead Bay as "the principal party-boat port." He depicts Emmons Avenue, where the piers jut out to hold the boats, as a place "many people consider the most attractive waterfront street in the city," an avenue that "smells of the sea, and of beer and broiled fish."

Though today Emmons Avenue feels less like the waterfront Mitchell described—retired men watching the boats go out, fishing for crabs, quarreling with one another—there's no denying that it still smells of the sea. Down the avenue from the twenty-four-hour El Greco diner that serves more BLTs than beer and broiled fish, there are still several piers that jut out into the narrow channel that leads to the bay. Top-heavy party boats and sleeker sport fishing boats bob and sway in the water, some with misleading signs such as "Blues 7 PM to 7 AM." *Blues* here refers not to music but to bluefish, and each night the boardwalk is sprinkled with captain and crew half-heartedly hawking the night trips to passersby. Across the way, the Loehman's department store and new high-rise condominiums remind them that their days are numbered on this stretch of the avenue.

The 110-foot *Brooklyn VI* can accommodate more than 150 customers lined shoulder to shoulder around the narrow deck. On a busy night, after collecting money and distributing bait and tackle, deckhands spend most of their time cutting lines and helping with tangles. Tonight, though, there are only fifteen lines in the water and the rough sea has the boat spinning in a wide arc around the anchor, making it easy to snag a line under the hull.

Halogen lamps above the deck light up the surface of the water around the boat, but beyond that it is inky black. In the distance there is the faint speck of another bluefish boat, and even farther, the dim lights of the coast, but the steep swells keep such reference points on the move. A few minutes after they anchor, someone vomits in one of the two bathrooms. Chuck, a thick-set, convivial deckhand, tours the deck calling out, "Mirror, mirror on the wall, who's the palest of them all?"

One passenger flops face down on a bench in the galley, a likely suspect for the mess in the bathroom. The rest wait in groups of two and three for some action on their lines. There is little chatter on the boat, and for a while the only sound is the crackle of a radio and the play-by-play of a Mets game at Shea Stadium. When someone does finally bring in a fish, it is Alanna, a five-foot-tall young woman in green skins.

"Atta boy, girl," says Chuck as Alanna heaves another bluefish onto the deck. Before he can move in to help, she clamps down on the flapping fish with the heel of her rubber boot and wrenches the hook from its throat. With a practiced move she scoops up the catch by the gills and drops it into a barrel by her side. The male customers on either side of her scowl at her good fortune. She smiles sweetly. "Must be beginner's luck," she says as she baits another hook with a chunk of herring.

Alanna is no beginner. She's been out on the bluefish boats since she was 8 years old, and worked as a deckhand since she was a teenager. In her early twenties now, she's a schoolteacher at a Brooklyn Yeshiva and married to a boat captain. But she has made an art of playing into the stereotypes of women on boats. As a deckhand, presenting herself in this feeble way often meant bigger tips for less work from the mostly male clientele. As a fellow passenger trying to catch some fish, it often means deflecting overtly sexist banter. It also means refraining from commenting when male customers use ill-advised techniques, such as trying to catch bluefish by using shots, or weights, on their lines.

There is another tug on Alanna's line, but she does not look happy.

"Dogfish," she scowls. She can tell by the way it feels on the line, and sure enough, a few moments later she pulls a small, brown, speckled shark out of the water. Chuck comes over to help, and she lets him. The horns of the dogfish, its prickly spine, can sting, causing headaches and nausea. Chuck throws the dazed shark back into the water. Up in the air-conditioned wheelhouse, the captain, Tom, is on the radio to the other bluefish boat anchored nearby. He learns they are pulling in nothing but dogfish. "They're a pain in the ass," Billy says of dogfish. "They take over your slick and if they don't thin out, you've got to pick up and move. You can't catch those all night." Dogfish, despite their name, are actually small sharks that give birth to a small litter of five or six offspring every other year. With the number pulled over the railing of the *Brooklyn VI*, it is no surprise that they are endangered and must be thrown back.

One by one, the other customers put their rods into metal slots along the rail and return to the galley. They're letting their lines drift to see if they might catch something while they watch *According to Jim* on the television. Some brave the offerings of the small kitchen manned by a teenager who fries up frozen burgers and sausage and pepper meatballs.

With fewer passengers on deck, the night takes on an almost peaceful quiet. It calls to mind the origin of the maritime term *graveyard shift*, which referred to the graveyard quiet on a ship after midnight. (Though nautical sounding, the terms *lobster shift* and *lobster trick* referred to the nightshift on newspapers.) The only sound is a macabre, rhythmic thud against the hull as it pitches against the swells of the ocean. In the water, lit up by the lights above deck, schools of squid pass under the boat, along with bits of garbage. At the edge of the light, dozens of tiny storm petrels, or what the deckhands call bonita birds, flit around the boat for the chum that Billy tosses onto the water's surface to attract the fish.

Eventually, only Alanna and the deckhands remain on deck but even they are waiting for Tom to blow the horn. When it blows three times, they know they are heading back to the bay. Alanna has the high hook for the night, meaning that she caught more than anyone else on the boat: eight bluefish. She'll give them to Billy and Chuck to sell for a little extra cash. None of them actually eats bluefish. As Billy says, "I call them turds that people eat."

Many of the night customers come hoping to pull in bluefish, which they then plan to sell in low-income communities throughout the city first thing in the morning. These tend to be neighborhoods with few fresh seafood outlets and fewer controls over the quality of goods sold illegally from the trunks of night fishermen. But after years of pollution in the New York harbor, the Clean Water Act of 1972 is finally having its effect and the fish bought in the informal economy of economically marginal communities is at least cleaner than it used to be. And fish pulled from further out to sea, such as those on the *Brooklyn VI*, are cleaner still. But as Kurlansky suggests in *The Big Oyster*, most of the fish from the harbor is consumed by the poor "who are probably eating poisoned food."

Aside from contamination, the culinary qualities of bluefish are lost on Billy, Chuck, and Alanna.

"The best way to cook a bluefish?" Billy asks. "Slap it on a board, spice it on up, throw it in the oven, cook it for about four hours, take it out, throw the fish out, and eat the board."

Alanna adds, "He could have done it better. You know, you gotta add lemon . . ."

Billy interjects, "I know, I know, I was doing the quick version."

"We've got time for the long version," Alanna says, rolling her eyes at the tedium on board.

"Oh, I forgot," Billy replies, "we're stuck here."

---

On a damp weeknight in September, Alanna and her husband, Ben, are in a deli in Sheepshead Bay. The pastrami piled high on rye bread, this is a delicatessen of which the newer New York delis, bodegas, and corner stores are only a dim reflection. Ben's dirty blonde hair is tucked under a cap turned backward. The growth of his stubble competes with his goatee and, combined with his bloodshot eyes, makes it clear that he's gone more than a few days without much sleep. Alanna, her long hair dyed brown since her last trip on the *Brooklyn VI*, is neatly dressed for a night on land, with lots of sparkle from the wedding rings she didn't wear on the boat. She was all set for another night on the water, and had even convinced Ben to come along after his day job as captain on another boat. But the night run for the *Brooklyn VI* has been canceled. High winds coming up from the south pushed the sea outside the harbor into fifteen-foot swells, too dangerous for the 110-foot boat.

Alanna started fishing as a child. Her father was a regular customer. "It was kind of like my own little haven," she says now. As she got older, Alanna began working the boats, particularly the *Pastime*, during the summers. "There's a lot of old people out there, they're not so nice to women. You know, 'Women don't belong on fishing boats.' I hated going out daytime."

The night boats were a different crowd. Ben, twelve years her senior, worked the decks when Alanna first started coming out to fish. Now, he is a captain with fifteen years of experience. In that time, he has formed some strong opinions about the differences between day and night customers.

"You wanna see the zoo, you gotta be there on a Friday or a Saturday night," explains Ben. "You have your Dominicans, and your Colombians, and your Russians, and," Ben pauses, which he does often, considering his words, "your Puerto Ricans, and some Mexicans thrown in, just for flavor."

"It's true," interjects Alanna.

"And all of them are in their own little separate sections of the boat," Ben adds, "All of them are drunk. And the tension is just building because they all hate each other."

One reason for this ethnic tension on the boats stems from the difference between subsistence fishing and recreation. A 1997 study of fishing in the Upper Mississippi Delta, by the sociologists John F. Toth Jr. and Ralph B. Brown, found that blacks fished within a "subsistence framework" whereas whites fished for leisure. Both blacks and whites fished for social reasons, but blacks tended to use the actual *fish* to extend social networks (for example, having a fish fry or selling the fish) whereas whites used *fishing* to extend social networks (for example, the camaraderie of being on the boat together). This has less to do with skin color than with distinct histories of economic advantage, but it helps explain why Ben, Alanna, Billy, and Chuck, all ethnically white native-born New Yorkers, fish to have fun, but the Colombians, Dominicans, Puerto Ricans, Mexicans, and even Russians they describe are there to catch fish.

"Like the *Brooklyn*," says Alanna. "It's always been a meat boat. It was always about, 'We gotta catch the most bluefish, gotta be on top, gotta be number one.' The *Pastime* was more like, everyone was going out to catch fish, but at the same time it was more family-oriented."

Ben smirks at Alanna. "What boat were you fishing on?" he asks.

"I was in the back, where were you?"

"You weren't paying attention," says Ben. "There were nights, in the years I was there, you had fifty to sixty people on the boat—on the *Pastime*—every one of them was catching fish to sell."

"I'm not talking about them," argues Alanna. "I'm talking about hungers."

*Hungers*, according to Ben and Alanna, is boat slang for customers who don't care much for the boating experience, but are there to pull in as many fish as possible.

"People who are there to . . . ," Alanna says, thoughtfully.

Ben interjects, ". . . Kill 'em all. Kill, kill, kill."

According to Ben, the night brings out the hungers, and none of them seem interested in cleaning fish for sale or eating and even less interested in tipping deckhands.

"Fifty-six people," he says. "This is the reason I went to days. Fifty-six people on the boat one night, all-out slaughter on fish. Nonstop gaffing from the time that we anchored the boat to the time we went home. Not one fish cleaning job. Zero. Made four dollars that night."

Between the tight-fisted hungers and those Ben refers to as "class B" deckhands, it is a wonder that boats still leave the dock at night. For the owners, however, the night runs remain profitable. As Ben explains, "Most of them make more money at night, because you'll have more people cramming on the boats at night. Even though the deckhands make less, the boat owners make more. In the daytime, it might be the other way around. The boat owners might not make anything. The nights might actually support the days, but in the daytime the people tip more."

Still, there are those such as Billy who only work the night. Some because their "other job" leaves few other options. But others do so, according to Ben, because the dayshift will not have them. "There are like categories," he explains. "The upper deckhands, like the better-class ones, will all be in the daytime. The class-B deckhands, the new guys and people you just can't have around day customers, you put them at night."

"They're distorted," adds Alanna.

"Or very harsh," continues Ben. "Or severe drug addicts. They really can't be shown in the daylight to people in a business setting."

"So you throw them at night," says Alanna.

"The nightshift is definitely a more interesting class of people."

"Maybe that's why I liked it more," says Alanna. "It's more fast-paced."

"No," argues Ben, "it's because it was less mainstream than anything else you could possibly do."

"Well, yeah, think about it," says Alanna. "I'm a typical Jewish girl going to Jewish school. I wear skirts. And I was so culturally shocked by everything. It was insane for me. It was my wild part. Because in the daytime you don't get that. It's boring."

Ben agrees. "Night fishing definitely satisfies a blood lust, if you have a penchant for that. Just, kill, kill, kill."

After Ben shifted to days, he took on extra work at nights running the party boats that leave from the same dock. Some of the boats used to be bluefish boats in the bay's heyday, but the runs are shorter. "It's a paddle-wheeler that they charter out for parties," explains Ben. "We go out for four hours and that's it. Leave at midnight and get back at 4, and we herd them off as fast as we can and then we go home. That's a nice, quiet job."

Alanna is not convinced. "There was a shooting last year," she says.

Ben confirms the incident: three men waited for the boat to unload and then fatally shot two people on the pier. "But that was just the one incident," he says. "Since then we haven't had any problems." Besides, he adds, the boats are chartered with five professional security guards and the police are always on the alert when the boat is coming in or out. According to Ben, this has as much to do with heightened security since 9/11 as with the shooting. Like the Staten Island Ferry, the dinner boats are subject to the Maritime Security levels. "Homeland Security has us on a high alert for hijacking," he continues. "We have to search everything going on the boat. Every cooler, every package, everybody gets patted down walking on the boat. Everyone's bag gets searched. No liquids can be brought on the boat." He admits the rule against liquids helps bar sales, but adds, "it's a security level issue."

In the summer, Ben works weekdays on one of the bluefish boats as either captain or deckhand. On the weekends, he adds a few nightshifts on the party boats, spreading himself over the twenty-four-hour cycle. "Friday night," he explains, "at 5, I go to sleep for about three hours. Then I go back over and get on the paddle-wheeler at 10. Load the people on the boat, leave at midnight, come back in at 4. Go home, relax for an hour, go back at 6. Do the fishing boat again until 4 or 5 in the afternoon. Go home, get another couple of hours sleep again, go back to the paddle-wheeler again at 10, stay until 4 in the morning. Go back home. Do the fishing boat again the following day. And then hopefully the afternoon trip on Sunday is a 6 to 10 o'clock trip. So I can get that out of the way early, get home by 11, and go to sleep to wake up at 6 the next morning and start the week all over again."

If all goes well, a summer schedule like that will earn Ben between $1,600 and $2,000 per week. But the hours cut into his sleep. As with the ferry, there are regulations about working a boat with a certain amount of rest. "It used to be you could only work twelve hours straight," Ben says. "So if a boat left the dock, the captain on duty could only be on duty for twelve hours and then you would have to have somebody to relieve him. But the way the regulations were worded, as soon as that boat hit the dock, the twelve hour clock was reset. So even if you went back out an hour later, you could do the first twelve hours again before you needed to be relieved. I think recently they have changed that. But I am not 100 percent sure."

"Nor do you want to find out," chides Alanna.

"Not really, no," Ben says, sheepishly. But then, he adds, "It gets exhausting. You try to find an hour here, an hour there, to sleep. You get a little run down. But for the most part, you get used to it. I actually do it better now than I used to. When I was younger I needed more sleep than I do now."

Still, there is the occasional triple. "A triple is like a day, night, day or a night, day, night. Three trips in a row. Like with the fishing trips, one trip rolls into the next one."

"And the days blur together," adds Alanna.

Ben and Alanna have heard the stories of the 1970s, when the Sheepshead Bay fleet was the largest on the Eastern seaboard. "There were fifty-four boats leaving Sheepshead Bay daily on the ten piers," says Ben. It was before his time, but it is part of the lore of the bay. Dozens of boats went out day and night. There were bigger boats, and more of them.

"Like the *Tampa*," offers Alanna, "the famous *Tampa*."

"Yeah, the *Tampa*," says Ben. "It's down in Central America." Like many of the larger boasts, the *Tampa* was sold off as the number of customers dwindled over the years. Others, like the *Amber Jack*, were converted to party boats that are still chartered from the same pier. "People are not coming out as much," Ben explains. "You used to have the need. A guy would start off with a 65-footer. Then he'd carry full capacity every night. Then he'd get a 90-footer and a 100-footer, and keep increasing. Around the late '80s, people stopped going out with full boats. And after that they started downsizing. Instead of going up and getting a bigger boat the following year, they'd go from a 100-foot to a 75-footer."

The downturn in the recreational fishing industry is no doubt connected to the city's declining interest in the harbor, but environmental concerns have also had their effect. "The regulations are a big thing," explains Ben. "Somewhere along the line, they got the idea that in order to keep the biomass at a certain level, people like Greenpeace and environmentalists started suing the federal government, saying, 'You're letting them do whatever they want. They're destroying the fishery, they're destroying the environment, they're hurting the poor little fish. We must save them.' So they started putting in regulations and making arbitrary numbers as what they think the biomass should be and guessing as to what it is. I mean, they're trying to estimate how many fish are in the ocean, and they actually come up with a number."

"They" are the Mid-Atlantic Fishery Management Council (MAFMC) and the National Marine and Fisheries Services, which govern the east coast waterways. Between 2003 and 2007 the MAFMC reduced the harvest limit of bluefish in New York State from 26.8 million pounds to

inherited the business and, two years ago, he got a job with the Staten Island Ferry. Even though he was making money, he wasn't making enough where he could afford his medical insurance or put away money for retirement. So, he got a city job and he pays somebody else to run the boat on the days he has to be at work on the other job."

Ben himself has considered working the ferry, but he fears the tedium of the job compared to piloting a boat in the open water.

"It's boring," he says simply.

Alanna agrees, adding that Tom, the captain of the *Brooklyn VI*, cleans the bathroom on the ferry.

"He's a bathroom guard," confirms Ben, with a mix of pity and disdain. "At the end of the trip, he goes in and checks to make sure the toilet paper is there. Makes sure the toilet flushes. If it doesn't flush, or it's stopped up, he'll call the engineer and put an out of order sign up. That's his job." Ben shakes his head and continues, "He's qualified to take a boat up to 100 gross tons up to 200 miles offshore. And that's the qualifications you need to sweep a bathroom on the Staten Island Ferry."

Neither Ben nor Alanna feels terribly excited by the prospect of Ben checking the bathrooms on the ferry, but neither do they aspire to his piloting the ferry. Ben explains that few are willing to take on that level of responsibility. "You go from guarding a bathroom to being responsible for a 1,600-ton boat, and the lives of everybody on it, in strong currents and adverse conditions in the New York Harbor, for an extra $12,000 a year, I think it amounts to. That's why nobody really wants to run the ferry. A few guys just for the prestige. But most of them are very happy sweeping cigarette butts and putting the garbage out. If you do one overtime day a week, you make more than the captain."

Recently, Ben has been thinking a lot about Florida. A few years ago, he was paid to pilot the *Pastime* down the Atlantic Seaboard to a fishing port near Orlando. He and Alanna were both sad to see the boat go—they met on the *Pastime* and spent most of their summers on its decks—but the economics of recreational fishing forced the owner to sell it down the coast. The trip was bittersweet but eye-opening. He sensed that a fishing boat captain can still make a good living down in Florida.

"I spent four or five days down there when I brought the boat down, and it is just such a different atmosphere," says Ben. "The people are friendlier. Just everything is more relaxed. There's no tension, no screaming, you don't hear cars honking. It is just so nice. You walk down to the water and you see dolphins splashing next to the boat, manatees swimming by."

Ben pauses, then adds, "Actually, a manatee went swimming up the Hudson River a few weeks ago. But he was just lost."

# SEVENTEEN: DIFFERENT FISH, DIFFERENT PLACES

I t's gonna get in your clothes," says the parking attendant. It's bitter cold on the last night of February, but you can still smell the fish as soon as you drive into the parking lot of the Fulton Fish Market in its new home in the South Bronx. The market has recently moved to Hunts Point, a desolate, industrial promontory that juts out into Flushing Bay across the water from Rikers Island jail. The parking attendant's tone is friendly, playful even, but he's not joking. One trip to the fish market and you'll want to burn your clothes.

Inside the 400,000-square-foot market, the smell is stronger, the lights are blindingly bright, men speed by on forklifts at a dizzying pace, and massive amounts of fish sit on ice in wax-coated cartons. Vendor stands and floor drains run the length of the cavernous space. At the stands, salesmen with fierce hooks hanging from their shoulders open cartons, weigh fish, set out wooden baskets full of crabs, and generally prepare for the day. Though officially forbidden, not a few of them go about their work with a cigarette dangling from their near-purple lips. Their clothes, which they keep in lockers at the market, haven't seen a washer in a few days—the smell would seep quickly into any change of clothes—and many a salesman has pieces of fish and blood on the shoulder where he hangs his hook.

As in the original market, everyone knows one another, and strangers stand out. The frenetic pace of the forklifts and the swinging hooks seem choreographed, practiced, but deadly to those unaccustomed to the dance. For all the latent danger, it's a jocular, friendly place where eye contact, smiles, and jokes are as routine as the smell. It's 12:20 AM. The market has been open for twenty minutes.

A forklift driver named José says in Spanish that things might calm down around 2 AM, but that only reveals that he's new here. Things won't calm down because it's a Wednesday night and, in fish market parlance, that means it's Thursday. Thursdays are one of their two busiest mornings. Asked if there will be a lull tonight, a salesman with twenty-eight years of experience says, "Not on a Thursday, no." The restaurant chefs from Manhattan and seafood market owners from all over the city come to the market on Thursday mornings to buy fresh fish for the weekend. On Monday mornings they return to stock up for the week.

Thursday mornings were the busy morning at the original Fulton Fish Market, too. But even the familiar commotion—the smell, the lights, the flying forklifts, the cartons of fish—cannot make the new space feel like the old one to those who knew it well. "Every now and then," wrote Joseph Mitchell in "Up in the Old Hotel" in 1952, "seeking to rid my mind of thoughts of death and doom, I get up early and go down to Fulton Fish Market." The original market was operating in 1822 but did not occupy the buildings most recognize as the market until 1869. Fish originally arrived at the market by schooners and sloops, but eventually came in by trucks. By the 1990s, even as mayor after mayor was trying to push it uptown, it was the largest fish market in the United States and one of the largest in the world.

The Hunts Point Market, though a new home to the Fulton Fish Market, has been around since the late 1960s. It filled the gap left by Manhattan's Washington Wholesale Market, which operated from 1812 until 1967. By the 1990s, the Hunts Point Market was already the largest of its kind anywhere worldwide.

———————

At the eastern end of the market, near the loading dock and the garage where forklifts park in neat rows to be recharged, a gigantic grouper draws the attention of everyone who passes by. It has a two-inch-thick rope through its lip.

"How much do you think it weighs?" asks a burly white salesman.

A smaller Asian customer replies, "300 pounds."

"That's what I thought," says the salesman. "185. 'Course he's missing his guts," he adds, laughing. He tosses his hook back onto his blood-stained left shoulder and nods again at the grouper. Laughing, he says, "Atkins diet. No carbs."

Down the main aisle from the enormous grouper, a set of swinging doors leads to the Fulton Café, the only option for hungry salesmen or forklift operators. The Fulton Fish Market website conjures the image of a posh sit-down restaurant, but the Fulton Café is more of a standing-room-only deli. Still, where else can you get fresh popcorn shrimp at 2 AM? The young cashier is proud of the café. "We deliver to all the other markets," he says, "because they all say we have the best food."

A salesman, Pan, 32, orders coffee for his crew. He's slight, even in a bulky coat. He has shoulder-length jet-black hair, caramel skin, and tired black eyes. He admits that he sleeps only four or five hours a night, or a day. He wears a hat, a greenish parka, baggy jeans, and the ubiquitous rubber boots that all the salesmen wear. The back left shoulder of his coat has pieces of fish guts and blood dangling off of it at the bottom of his stainless steel hook. A normal hook, he explains, costs $20, but weighs a hefty three pounds. His hook, by contrast, cost $125. "But this one is handmade," he says proudly. "Stainless steel. No weight on it." Half the weight of the $20 variety, the lighter hook makes a long shift of lifting heavy fish that much easier. But the lighter weight is not all that Pan appreciates. Nonchalantly, he adds, "I got scratched with a $20 hook and got an infection in the brain. What they call meningitis."

While the cashier rings up his order, Pan says that though Thursday and Monday mornings get quite busy, good money is "not really" part of his life here. For that reason, he also works days making deliveries for a Japanese restaurant in Manhattan. "And I live in Connecticut, exit 40. An hour from here." He takes his order back inside the enormous market to the stand where he works. Coffee consumed, he resumes his job filleting tuna. He concentrates on the work, nods occasionally in response to a question from a coworker, and holds a cigarette precariously between his lips.

A few weeks later, Pan takes a break from his tuna filleting to eat grilled shrimp and salad with his boss and crew. He came to New York with two brothers twelve years ago. They're from East Java, Indonesia. "It's shit over there," he sneers. "A lot of people came over here. I've never been back. My mother is over there and she came over here one time to see my daughter. But I got my own family."

Pan has a wife and two daughters ages 2 years and 4 months. They live in Connecticut, he says, "because it's cheaper, and it's good for my daughters." Pan's wife doesn't work. "Before," he says, "she was a technical designer in Manhattan. She used to drive to the station and take Metro North to Penn Station, but not anymore."

Though his brothers work in a restaurant in Manhattan, Pan worked at the Fulton Fish Market before it moved up to Hunts Point. He first worked as a buyer for another fish wholesaler for two years, then, he explains, "I talked to this guy and he hooked me up over here."

Nearby, an artist, Naima, stands on a metal staircase overlooking Pan and sketches him at work. Wrinkled and thin, Naima looks to be in her midseventies. She wears no makeup, her hair pulled back in a bun, a full-length charcoal gray parka, and a colorful knit scarf.

"The market has been the main subject matter for my entire painting career," she says. Naima started sketching the original fish market as an art student in the mid-1960s. "Frequently, I would be up at 2 or 3 in the morning, or all night long doing my work because this is the time of the action." She began by painting watercolors on location, but that proved frustrating with the fast pace of the market. "I remember taking my watercolors and finding a great little halibut with the tail flopped out of the box, and halfway through the watercolor it was sold and gone." She soon switched to sketching at the market, using a camera for backup detail, and then finishing the work in her studio.

Naima began painting the fish market full-time in 1983, then, from 1984 to 1997, she had a studio above one of the vendors. Since they only worked nights, a vendor allowed her to use his stand as an art gallery by day. "I called it 'art in the afternoon, fish in the morning,'" says Naima.

She put her work in the space, people came in to buy it during the day, and then at 6 PM every night she took it all down so the space could spend the night as a fish market. The relationship was an amiable one. "I even worked there during Christmas," says Naima. "It was a smoked fish company and they'd get very busy at Christmas. I would write out orders and take money for them as they got busy." She smiles and says, "I thought it would only be a two or three week show, and it lasted fourteen years. Until the building was sold and the fish company had to leave and I had to leave."

Now Naima makes the trip north to Hunts Point once a week, driving from the Lower East Side in Manhattan. The transition to the new location, says Naima, has been very difficult for her personally. "I know the guys have had their adjustments, but I've had a lot of adjustments." She explains that when the market was in its original location, she'd either forgo sleep or wake in the middle of the night to go to the market. But the commute north makes a late-night visit for inspiration more than a little arduous. "This is psychologically very difficult," says Naima. "I have to bundle up, go to my car, figure out all my gear because I'm leaving my studio, drive up the FDR drive, hope that there's not a crash in the middle of the night that closed the drive. I go through this desolate neighborhood and finally get here. So there's a psychological barrier as well as the physical inconvenience. I used to be a twenty-minute walk from the Seaport. That sweet little commute makes this seem like a very disagreeable affair."

Despite these obstacles, she's trying to get back into a regular routine coming to the new market, looking for inspiration. "I'm trying to get more enthused about the scene here," she says. For the move to the new sterile environment has not dampened her love for the market, and there are enough reminders of the past: the men with their hooks, the boxes of fish and, especially, the smell. "Your clothes pick it up, your hair picks it up, and especially the schmutz on your shoes. Now that I'm not in the atmosphere every day, I put on special clothes, because it is kind of offensive to other people when you go around during the day and you smell of fish." She says it all with a glint in her eye, the pungent smell of fish is a badge of honor, a mark of membership.

Naima is confident that she will regain her enthusiasm as an artist, but she is less optimistic about Lower Manhattan and the end of the Fulton Fish Market. "Not only is downtown a shadow of its former self, the life has sort of gone out of the neighborhood," she says mournfully. "Gentrification is happening; however, the fish market buildings are sitting there derelict. They never had a plan. There was nothing in place when the market was moved. Giuliani really wanted to get them out. The city's been wanting to get them out for sixty years, but it didn't happen, the guys didn't want to move. But Giuliani put the screws to them and this administration didn't care to reverse that."

The vendors and their salesmen, like Naima, have little choice if they want to stay in the business. "They're here now," she says, "trying to do the best they can."

—————

On the other end of the market, Tim, a salesman, stands near a dozen cartons of cod waiting for customers. It's a slow Tuesday morning in March. At 46, Tim still has the lean, athletic build of a much younger man, all his hair, and a boyish, angular shape to his face. Though he's a fish salesman instead of a fisherman, he has that outdoorsy quality—tan, weathered, fit—that makes him look like he'd be right at home on a boat. Or a ski slope. Or coaching baseball. His tousled, sandy-blond hair completes the All-American Athlete look. He wears an oatmeal-colored sweater and jeans, no jacket, and, of course, his hook over his shoulder.

Unlike Pan, Tim prefers the cheaper hook. "Some guys have thinner ones," he says. "They'll have them stainless steel or twisted." He points to his and says, "This one I've had for twenty years. Most of the guys do. It's mine. This here is worth like $25. It depends what you're into." His words suggest room for personal choice but his tone and blank expression suggest that the $25 hook is the better choice. He points out a smaller hook used by most of the customers. "Those," says Tim, "are better for picking out stuff." He adds, "I don't generally pick out stuff. If I want to pick out stuff I pull it out with my hand."

Tim has worked at the market for twenty-eight years, he says, initially making no distinction between the two markets. But there are differences, he admits. "You don't have as much walk-on business as you did down there. People have to commute up here, first of all, then they have to pay to get in. Here it's more factorylike than anything else. Downtown just had a little bit more life to it. We used to just have strangers come by. You'd be surprised how much it adds up when you get strangers in there. Or you got somebody coming out of a bar, 'Hey, how much is this?' They might be drunk or whatever, but you'd be surprised, walk-on business was good business." Also, he adds, "We were close to Chinatown and in Chinatown they eat a lot of fish."

The move to the Bronx was touted as a boon to the wholesale fishing trade, but according to Tim, it has not worked out as well as everyone hoped. "I think a lot of owners thought it might be good for business, considering the meat market's here, the produce market is here, but I don't think it improved business as much as they thought, if at all." Tim describes how the developers allocated the amount of space a vendor could have at the new market. "They pretty much went according to the space you had down there," he explains. "If you wanted to acquire more space you could. That was up to the city and that's how they decided to build this place. There were guys that went out of business that had intentions of coming up here but just didn't make it." Also, he adds, "You've got a huge electric bill you didn't have down there."

Another, more personal difference is his commute to and from his home in Staten Island. "The move affects me," he says. "It was a lot closer when we were in Manhattan. I went from a twenty-minute ride in and a thirty-minute ride home to a forty-minute in and hour-and-ten, maybe hour and a half, going home." Still, he says of the move, "Most of us had no choice. It's our livelihood and we all have to support our families."

Also, Tim says, "I *did* like being outdoors. The new location helps our industry in a way and it hurts in others. I liked the fact that it was outdoors, but this place protects the fish at all times, especially during the summers. It's usually 40 degrees in here all year, which protects the fish for more shelf life."

Tim's shift runs roughly 10 PM to 10 AM depending on the night. Two nights a week he starts at 10 PM and three nights a week he begins work at 11 PM. "I like the hours," he says. The market is closed on weekends, so everyone has off Friday and Saturday nights, then returns Sunday night for a busy Monday morning. This is another form of continuity with the original market, which also operated Sunday to Thursday nights from midnight to 9 AM. Tim's strategy for switching back and forth between the day and night schedule is as complicated as it sounds: "What I do, personally, is I stay up all day Friday. Friday night I don't work. So, Thursday night," meaning Friday morning, he'll leave work and "stay up all day." His expression leaves no room for anyone to suggest that it's a difficult way to live. "I'm used to it," he says.

According to Tim, the nightshift is more demanding on a salesman's family than it is on the salesman. "It's very stressful on our families," he says. "If I can take a two-hour nap on Friday, I'll do that. I try to be on the same page as my wife at that time. That way I can have some sort of a life with her." Depending on traffic, Tim returns home each morning between 11 AM and noon and goes immediately to sleep. He wakes up around 6 PM, has dinner, and then might nap for another hour or so before leaving for work around 9 PM. "If there's stuff to do during the day," he says, "you just cut back on your sleep. You still want to be involved in your kids' lives, as well as have some sort of a relationship with your wife." His ex-wife was not as supportive of the life, though it was her uncle who introduced him to the trade. But his current wife is more understanding. "Thank God my wife is the way she is. If you ain't got the right woman. . . . Thank God I've got the right one now."

Tim has entertained the idea of owning his own stand but has not pursued it. "It takes a little bit of money," he says with great understatement, "and I have a big family. Money is a little hard to come by. Between me and my wife we have seven children. We put half of them through college. It's a little tough to put money aside for a business. I'm sure it takes a good sum of money just to buy one of these places."

The money may be elusive, but Tim certainly has the experience to run his own stand at the market. Tim's job, like many of the more seasoned salesmen's, involves more than setting up and selling the fish. "Part of a salesman's job," Tim stresses, "is also to produce fish." By "produce fish" Tim means just that: produce the number of fish they have available to sell. He does this through long-term relationships with fishermen, mainly from Montauk, who supply him with fluke, porgies, codfish. In his words, "A little bit of everything." His relationships, he says, started with one boat and then spread from there through social networks by word of mouth. When the fishermen are out on their boats, says Tim, they tell one another about him. "Just like we talk here, they talk there."

It works like this: "I have a relationship with a boat and he'll send me one hundred cartons, about 6,000 pounds. He'll send me 3,000 pounds of whiting, 1,000 pounds of fluke, 1,000 pounds of porgies, 1,000 pounds of butterfish." That's one day's worth of fish. "Sometimes," says Tim, "it's a lot more than that. Yesterday, we probably sold over 100,000 pounds." His boss and the other salesmen help sell what he produces. If he has a day like that, say on a Monday or Thursday, and sells out of everything, he'll pay the fishermen their share and they will set him up with more fish. They will contact him by phone from the boat at night and say "Timmy, listen, my boat's out, it'll be in tomorrow, we're going to have this . . ."

Despite his good relationships with the fishermen, some of them also sell their fish to other companies. "So we're in competition with each other here to make our boat happy. That way we get a little bit bigger share of the fish next time."

The salesmen do not work on commission, but the expectation to produce is high. "It's a straight salary," says Tim, "but you still gotta push." Tim explains that salesmen's salaries are set by the United Seafood Workers union, whose members include salesmen, wholesale vendors, and retail markets, including Shop Right, a supermarket chain. "I'm not even sure what the scale is," admits Tim. "Some guys make more; it depends on if you're a producer or not. I'll leave it at that." Tim says that beyond what you produce, you have to know the market, set fair prices, and try to compete with the other vendors. "If you merchandize your stuff the right way," he says, "you'll sell it." If he sells too cheaply, he cannot pay the fishermen what they think the fish is worth and they will respond by giving other salesmen a greater share of their catch.

To be a good salesman, Tim has learned how to merchandise his inventory to the various customers that pass through the market each night. That includes a sense of how culture intersects with taste in seafood. "Whiting," he says, "will sell very well in the black neighbor-hoods. Snapper, striped bass, black sea bass down in the white neighbor-hoods. You'll have what they call Polack or kingfish, or Spanish mackerel in the Spanish neighborhoods. Different fish, different places. Eel is all sushi, fluke and the tuna fish is all sushi quality for Japanese restaurants. Most of our traders are Asian, whether it be Korean or Chinese. That's true for everyone. I'd say 85 percent of our business is Asian. Most of them are Korean."

He also mentions that none of the owners are Asian and there is little ethnic diversity among the salesmen. "Most of the people who become salesmen start out at a lower level and you get promoted from within," he explains. "And I just think people are more comfortable with their own kind. Unfortunately, that's the way it is." Phillip Lopate, in his book *Waterfront*, noticed the same pattern in the old market down in Manhat-tan: "Fathers pass the job down to sons, with very little mobility from one generation to the next; workers stay workers, and bosses, bosses."

Father to son means the market is very much a man's world. "If there are any women," Tim says, "it's usually a bookkeeper. There are no women salesmen. What woman wants to be in this business anyway and listen to all these guys talking rough? I wouldn't talk that way in front of my mother or my sister. I wouldn't talk that way in front of any woman."

---

A loud shriek pierces the dull hum of the market, "Aaarrrgh! Honey, how are you?"

Its source is a tiny woman with frizzy hair pushing a cart through the chaotic market. She smiles broadly and calls out to passing salesmen, "Honey, hey!" One salesman keeps walking but gives her a big smile and says, "Hey, honey, how you doin'?" Apple Annie, as she calls herself, calls out to another salesman in a squawking caricature of a New York accent: "Hey! Honey!" When another passes, she squawks at him too. "Agh!," she says, "I know them all, I'm in here forty-two years." Apple Annie is rouged up for a night on the town yet wears a bedraggled knit sweater and skirt. Her skirt has giant pockets below the knee; she fills them with money from the men.

The cart holds a single black plastic trash bag full of packs of cigarettes. That's all she sells from the cart, she says, because "that's all they want." Apple Annie says, "I never smoked in my life," but she knows a niche when she sees it. "Listen," she says, "the people that work here go crazy because you're not supposed to work at night. It upsets their clock." She works this schedule, she says, because "when you're past eighty and you don't work, you're dead. You become dead. I'm alive."

Annie finishes her sentence in time to squawk at another salesman as he passes by. "Hi, Honey! Look, this is my boyfriend, all these guys." He smiles at her and approaches the cart. He reaches into the plastic bag, grabs a pack of cigarettes, and slips her $5. She bends at the hip to put it in her skirt pocket. He smiles at her again and walks away. More men approach the cart. She has not had to move for a while. As a young guy reaches into her cart, she commands him flirtatiously, "Take it out!" He smiles. "They like to smoke. Two things they like, and one of them is smoking. Take it out, honey! Put it in, take it out!"

"I got it, Annie," he says.

She asks, "What are you doin'? How much you owe me now?"

"Forty," he replies as he walks away.

She calls out after him, "Forty? When you gonna pay? Get outta here!"

"Every Friday I pay," he calls back over his shoulder.

Apple Annie knows they will pay. "I give 'em credit and they like me," she explains. "I don't remember everything; they remember. I have fun with it, I don't sell hard, I don't care. I treat them so nice, they don't cheat me."

When her audience of men leaves, Apple Annie explains that when the market is open she'll stay up all night, but on the weekends she stays on a day schedule and sleeps nights. She reiterates that she's been doing this for forty-two years, most of them at the original market. Back then, she says, she could get to work by bus in five minutes. She says she is not the only one who has experienced hardship since the market moved to the Bronx. "Some companies went out of business. They have a high rent here. They pay thousands of dollars."

The original market was a literal home to her. One of the owners let her stay in a back room of one of the offices—for twenty years. She points him out with a pale, wrinkled hand. "AGGGGHHH!" she screams, "I'm a screamer! If someone lived in my space for twenty years . . ." He never once asked why she was there. "Never came to the door and never asked for a penny rent." She adds, wistfully, "It was clean and nice and renovated."

Apple Annie will push her cigarette cart for another two hours. "Then the papers come and I sell the paper," she explains. "They deliver it to the café and I pick it up there." By the time the sun peeks over Rikers Island she will have sold out of those, and one of the men will drive her back to Manhattan.

For now, however, she is doing a brisk business. Another young man approaches, reaches into the bag, and she grabs his head, pulling it into her ample chest. "Fuckin' I love these guys! Give me a kiss!" She laughs.

"I scream," she roars, "I'm a SCREAMER."

A few more men draw near, reaching into her cart, offering her a few dollars and a smile. Apple Annie beams. The space may have changed, but the men are still loyal.

"Look at 'em come!" she screams, "Aghh! My boyfriends."

4:22 UPTOWN TRAIN AT 168TH STREET

5:05 LUCKY STOP DELI

5:13 LEVAIN BAKERY

# EIGHTEEN: HERE IS NOT MY HOME

**N**o one is normal who comes in at night."

Fatima, 33, smiles slightly and steps back from the cash register at the Cheyenne Diner, easing her small, curvy frame against the counter. She wears a uniform of a red short-sleeve shirt with an American Indian on the back, black long-sleeve t-shirt underneath, black apron at her waist, black pants, and black shoes. A tight ponytail contains her black, curly, shoulder-length hair and highlights her face. Her contagious smile reveals slightly crooked teeth and the smallest of dimples on either side of her mouth. "Anyone on the streets at 3 or 4 in the morning is not regular," she continues, her words tumbling out in a lyrical Dominican English. "They can be crazy people. That's why you have to be sweet and sour. You have to know how to manage people."

Two months later, on a slow Monday night in mid-May, Fatima takes a short break from taking orders and ringing up the occasional customer. Sipping from a Diet Pepsi, she watches Mr. Gerry at the grill and teases the much older Indian cook into a rare chuckle. It's only 2 AM but Mr. Gerry is already frying up a mountain of bacon for the breakfast rush at the end of their shift. He says he's 65, and she knows not to challenge him, but Juan, who works with them, guesses that Mr. Gerry is at least a decade older. Mr. Gerry wears gold-framed glasses over his tired brown eyes, a white chef's shirt, white apron, navy pants, and sport sandals. He speaks little and smiles less, but when he does open his mouth it's clear that he's missing several of his front teeth. His short black hair stands up on end, not unlike a porcupine's. He and Fatima have an easy rapport after nine months of working together, a credit to her boundless energy and charm.

Fatima came to the Cheyenne Diner after several other nightshift jobs in and around the city. She has lived nearly half her life on the nightshift, first in the Dominican Republic and then in New York City. She likes the hours for the freedom, despite the surveillance cameras overhead, and the money, despite the occasional slow night. At least at night she doesn't have to share the tips.

Juan, 43, is down in the basement kitchen catching up on dirty dishes and waiting for the next delivery order. He too wears a white chef's shirt, with checked chef's pants and, when he goes out on deliveries, a navy Members Only–style jacket. His short black hair stands up on end a bit too, though tonight it's slicked down with gel. Though the night is quiet, for now, they have learned to be ready for anything. Juan still remembers the "kid," as he calls him, who was high and broke through a basement door because he was convinced that his girlfriend was hiding in the kitchen. Or the street brawl right outside, which shattered a window next to one of the booths.

"The place is really not safe," Fatima explains. "At night it's just Mr. Gerry, Juan, and me, and Juan is always out with the deliveries. So here it's really not safe." She shrugs and grabs her cigarettes for a quick smoke outside. "We take a chance."

On this lonely stretch of Ninth Avenue, beyond the radiance of Penn Station and Times Square, the Cheyenne provides some welcome light and life to a darkened city. The diner is, of course, open days too, but it is squat and shabby and in the harsh light of day it gets lost among the more modern shops that surround it. At night, bathed in a garish pool of neon and fluorescent light, it is a beacon on the corner, and the contrast with its neighbors is completely reversed. Like most diners, the Cheyenne was built to be seen at night.

On the next corner of Ninth Avenue, the Skylight is also open, spilling its neon and fluorescent light onto 34th Street. Steve is there, calling orders back to the busy kitchen, and helping the hostess to seat a steady stream of customers for the two waiters on duty. It is one hundred feet closer than the Cheyenne to the 35th Precinct of the NYPD and that, apparently, makes all the difference for hungry cops. But it is also brighter, the diner decor more focused, deliberate.

Though the Cheyenne is showing its age and suffering as a consequence, it is the original of which the Skylight is a nostalgic recreation. It is one of the few remaining diners in the city that can make a legitimate claim on the glory days of mass-produced, homogenized, and wildly popular all-night diners. The Cheyenne's gleaming stainless steel "dining car" exterior has welcomed insomniacs and nightshift workers on break since the 1930s. It's what's known to diner buffs as a Paramount diner. According to Richard Gutman in his book *American Diner,* New Jersey's Patterson Vehicle Company got into the growing diner business in the 1920s by building what were known as Silk City diners. By the early 1930s, a Silk City man named Arthur Sieber opened his own company: Paramount Diners. They were one of the first to use the now ubiquitous Formica, covering every surface including the ceiling. Easy to apply, available in myriad colors, and eventually impervious to cigarette burns, Formica soon became integral to the classic diner look. Until stainless steel, that is, which Paramount introduced. The diner with a stainless steel exterior and an interior slathered in stainless steel and brightly colored Formica, Art Deco angles and touches, and interesting tile patterns is a Paramount diner—or a reproduction meant to look like one.

Inside the Cheyenne, after dark, Fatima, Mr. Gerry, and Juan replace the dayshift crew of close to ten employees, and the noisy buzz of the dayshift subsides into the quiet hum of fluorescent lights and Top 40 radio. The red vinyl booths of the long, narrow dining area are empty, as are the stools at the counter, which sags under the weight of a large television. But each seat awaits a customer with an upright, oversized menu that's easy enough to navigate for the cherry Coke, BLT, or slice of cherry pie that customers seem to crave from the moment they walk into a diner.

The Skylight may see more action at night, but it must work overtime to reproduce an experience that the Cheyenne offers effortlessly: the familiar fourteen-ounce bottle of Heinz ketchup, the cake stand on the Formica counter, the reliability that more often than not the soup of the day will be split pea. Salt and pepper shakers sit perpetually refilled on every table, silverware and white napkins are always set at every seat, and those oh-so-comforting glass sugar canisters await those who like their coffee light and sweet. On the hottest of nights, the fake palm tree near the back door sways from the night breeze, allowing people to imagine they are somewhere, anywhere but here. Swathed in this sameness of the Cheyenne, they could be in their favorite hometown diner, or the one where they took their first date, or even the one down the street. Some nights, the television blasts infomercials such as Creflo Dollar proselytizing the prosperity gospel or Victoria Principal selling a beauty product called Reclaim. Their sales pitches compete with the radio, belting out oldies such as "Shake Your Booty" and "Save the Last Dance for Me." Other nights, the soundtrack consists only of the sizzle of bacon on Mr. Gerry's grill and the clink of dishes as Fatima or Juan clears another table.

There are some things, however, that are unique to the Cheyenne. There is the North American Indian iconography, much of it curiously juxtaposed, such as the diner's logo of an Indian chief astride a longhorn steer, or the incongruously named "Sioux" burger: it comes with guacamole. One night, a man waits at the counter for his order and, in the kind of chitchat that people feel freer to engage in after midnight, asks Mr. Gerry, "Are you Native American?" Mr. Gerry gives him a gruff "No," then with uncharacteristic charity adds, "I am Asian American. I am Indian Asian." The man replies, "Oh, because you have a lot of Indian, Native American, pictures." Tersely, Mr. Gerry replies, "They've been up a long time." And if the pictures show their age, so does the diner. The bathroom, cold and damp in any month, smells like one on a long-distance bus; the smell occasionally seeps into the diner. Outside on 33rd Street, a taxi relief stand draws drivers who come in for coffee and the bathroom. Beside the relief stand where drivers often nap, there's a church with a statue of Jesus and a sign saying "Come to Me All You That Labor and I Will Give You Rest."

But the main difference at the Cheyenne is Fatima. Those Heinz bottles, salt and pepper shakers, and sugar canisters do not fill themselves. Fatima is tireless, and always ready with a smile.

The following night, a Tuesday, the streets surrounding the Cheyenne are full of kids in prom attire and sailors in for Fleet Week. Rod Stewart bellows out "Forever Young" overhead as Fatima slips in and out of Spanish to tell her story. She explains that she has worked the nightshift in and around New York City since she immigrated in 1995. She tried working the dayshift once, but found the hours and the pace too strenuous. "In the daytime, you have to take care of the people, but at this time, nobody cares. And still, the people who go around in the night, they always give good tips. I like it."

Fatima adds that she also likes the nightshift for the autonomy, or at least the perception of autonomy, that she enjoys without management on site. "Nightshift is not bad," she says. "You don't have boss under you." But then Fatima points to the surveillance cameras that dot the ceiling of the diner. "They have the camera, they follow all night long. Sometimes they're awake more than twenty-four hours, more than us, checking from home."

Fatima, like most nightshift workers, must also contend with the practical limitations of the schedule. Sleep is a constant negotiation. She explains, "You have to remember that your timing is going to be changing in your body. Everything's going to be changing." She keeps pace with those changes, doing what she can to fool her body into sleep or wakefulness when it is convenient for her schedule. "Mostly when I'm off, on Sunday, I don't sleep all night long," she says. "I sleep, like a little bit, a half hour and then 2 or 3 in the morning I don't wake like a normal time. I just don't sleep normal. It's really hard. I always use the sleeping tablets. And I try to get like four to six hours if I can get through, because sometime I wake for no reason."

These negotiations are necessary if Fatima hopes to engage the waking world at any practical level. "You lose your time," she explains. "Sometimes if I need to go to the hospital, I don't have time." Sunday night is her one night off a week, leaving Mondays for any errand-running she needs to accomplish. "I go to the bank, pay my bills, whatever I have to pay. And then Mondays, if I have to go to the hospital, I go in a hurry."

Eating habits also change, and Fatima has developed her own system for fooling her body into a night rhythm. "I try to eat whatever is healthy all through the night. I don't eat in the daytime, because if you eat in the daytime you're gonna sleep and you're gonna get lots of weight more. So you have to eat like normal, like if it's a regular day."

As with so many others who work the nightshift, the physical effects of off-hour labor are mirrored in social relationships. Fatima already contends with the geographical separation from her mother and daughters in the Dominican Republic, and her schedule exacerbates that separation, excluding her from the possibility of local surrogates for familial support. "It affects completely the whole life," she says of the nightshift. "Everything changes. You lose your friends. Completely, you're gonna lose your friends, you're gonna lose many things. Normally you don't have a social life." For Fatima, however, already thousands of miles from family, this lack of friends does not represent additional loss. As she says, "All my life is together with my family, not really with the world outside." What does represent greater loss, though, is anything that threatens her connection to her family. When she lost her mobile phone and it took a week to get a new one, her sense of disconnection increased. Technology both speeds up the global incessant economy and sustains the ties workers have to their families back home. Shaking her head, Fatima says, "I never knew a phone could make you depressed. I couldn't believe that. I was depressed for a week, because I call my family every day." A week later, armed with a new phone, she says, "I feel much better."

---

At 2:30 AM, Juan takes a break. Mr. Gerry fixes him a plate of rice and chicken (it's not on the menu), and Juan eats hungrily before he returns to the basement kitchen or out into the night for a delivery. His job here is an unremitting cycle of deliveries, dirty dishes, and piles of potatoes to wash before the morning rush. He has worked at the Cheyenne for two years, this time. Like many undocumented Mexican immigrants, Juan has moved back and forth across the border several times in his working life. With a family to support in Mexico, the United States provides a good income but it will never be home.

His first job in New York City was washing dishes in a Chinese restaurant. "They closed at 1 in the morning," he says in a clipped, rapid-fire Spanish, "and at 1 in the morning I would begin washing everything in the kitchen, cleaning and cleaning. I was only here eight months, and I went back to Mexico." The second time in New York, he found this job through his brother-in-law, who worked the dayshift. Juan worked the nightshift. "After one year and two months," says Juan, "I went back to Mexico." This is his third time working in the United States. "And this time," he says, "I've been here two years. It's hard but, you know, you have to work."

In New York, Juan has worked only nightshift jobs. As he describes it, "I don't know what the daytime is like in New York." He works seven nights a week, 364 nights a year, for $4 an hour. "It's a lot of work," he says. "I don't like to work the night, but I have to work to take care of my family." He's smiling but he has giant bags under his eyes.

The work is physically punishing and, not surprisingly, his health is suffering. "I don't feel good," he says. "Since I don't sleep very well, it hurts a lot here." He points to the back of his head and neck and continues, "It hurts a lot." He also admits that he's been hit by cars, twice, on his bicycle making deliveries. "But I never went to the hospital," he says. "Well, once I went to the hospital. In December, I was having some drinks. I stepped out of a bar, and I don't remember what happened, but when I woke up I was in a hospital. I drank too much. I fell, but I don't know what happened. I was alone." He points to a few scars on the side of his face and explains that this happened on Christmas Eve, his one night off a year. That's the only night of the year that the Cheyenne closes. "Now," he adds sheepishly, "after that, I don't go to any bars."

His break over, Juan steps behind the counter to where Mr. Gerry stands at the grill. French fries cover the black rubber mats on the floor. Juan ties up several giant black trashbags, heaves them onto his shoulders, and heads toward the trap door that leads to the basement. "It's dirty," he says in Spanish, nodding at the floor, "every night, every day, always dirty."

Like many other nightshift workers, Juan has had to adapt to the peculiar exchanges that take place on his shift, especially on his frequent deliveries. "I don't speak English, only the numbers. It's a problem, because customers ask me questions I don't understand. I've never had the time to study English. I bought a book so I could study, but I don't have time. I come home only to sleep, I get up to go to work, bathe, and go. That is my life. I am very tired, but I want to save a little more money."

Juan's experience is not unlike that of millions of other recent immigrants, especially those without legal status in the United States. The dislocation of transnational migration is an emotional burden that many like Juan bear in exchange for the promise of economic security. One of the defining characteristics of contemporary transnationalism is the ambiguity of social connections. Fatima and Juan are spread thin across continents, dividing their loyalties among family, friends, and wherever they consider home. But the intersection of transnationalism and the nightshift produces a deeper ambiguity, where one becomes spread thin over time as well as space. As Melbin points out, the night is a frontier in which new immigrants are putting down roots—further complicating their "place" in the world.

"In Mexico," says Juan, "I did not work at night, only here. In Mexico, I was working in the day. In Mexico, I only worked eight hours. Only eight hours." But in New York, he has always worked the night and has always felt disconnected from the city. "I don't have time to get to know New York," he explains. "I thought I would leave after two years, but now I am thinking I will go back in December. Forever. I am not going to come back here. Maybe I will start some business in Mexico City."

―――――――

The next night, a Wednesday, Fatima has no reaction to the man in his forties who walks in to the diner wearing a leather skirt. He and his friend, she explains, are regulars. Neither does she react when a group of boisterous 30-somethings stumble in wearing wristbands from a concert and drinking out of giant Bud Light cans in paper bags. A few minutes past 2 AM another such guy enters, using his bagged Bud Light as a microphone, scream-singing "Night Train" to anyone in earshot. He's coming from the fourth and final Guns N' Roses concert, a kickoff to the band's European tour. Tonight guitarist Izzy Stradlin joined the band and vocalist Kid Rock sang, you guessed it, "Night Train."

On another May weeknight, round about midnight, two young women stumble into the Cheyenne and pour themselves into a booth by the door. One, barely conscious, orders a cheeseburger. The other orders a mushroom quesadilla and two glasses of wine. Fatima tells her they have no wine or beer.

"Something else?" Fatima asks. "Maybe a glass of water?"

The other girl quickly cancels her quesadilla. Fatima calls out to Mr. Gerry, "No mushroom quesadilla, okay?" The other girl calls out to her friend, in Spanish, "Leila, *despierta*." One wants to leave but the other is hungry. Leila stumbles out; her friend runs after her. The cheeseburger sits waiting. From behind the counter Mr. Gerry announces, "Leila *muerte*." Leila is dead. Fatima laughs and explains, "I have lots of wine, but I told them I don't have." After dark, a fair number of Fatima's customers have had too much to drink, but she has honed her skill in dealing with them in her years on the nightshift.

Fatima displays this skill on a regular basis. With Leila and her friend, she responds sweetly, firmly, but inaccurately that they do not have wine or beer—and even dares to suggest a glass of water. On another night, it works in another direction: when a drunk customer staggers toward the door, leaving the $15 she returned from his $20 on the counter, she wordlessly picks it up, slips between him and the door, and gives it to him. She holds the upper hand in both encounters.

In each of these interactions, and a thousand more each night, Fatima is engaging in a subtle use of power that social scientists have observed among many in the service industry, from waitresses to flight attendants. It's part of something called "emotional labor," a term coined by Arlie Russell Hochschild in her classic study *The Managed Heart*. In certain occupations, such as working at a diner, employees are encouraged to manipulate their own feelings so as to produce a particular and predictable response in customers. The better they act as if they enjoy what they're doing, the more they succeed at their jobs. The danger for employees is that some are so good at the performance, they can become estranged and alienated from themselves. As such, they are in turn more easily controlled by employers.

According to the anthropologist Greta Foff Paules, however, a waitress such as Fatima can see herself as an entrepreneur, less loyal to the company than to her customers. After all, a large portion of her wage is earned from tips, not a paycheck, allowing her to control her own emotional labor. In *Dishing It Out*, Paules argues that a waitress may be submissive, aggressive, or friendly, but less because the job demands it than because she sees its utility. Fatima is in complete control of her emotions and is well aware of how they can get her what she wants. This is especially important on the nightshift when she is the only waitress on the floor and the customers can be unpredictable.

Just how Fatima employs emotional labor in her nightly interactions with customers can be surprising. As a woman, she confirms much of the research on gender and the service industry; women tend to be more adept at handling customers than men. As a Latina, she confounds conventional wisdom. "Sometimes," she admits, "I pretend I don't speak Spanish." This response is not uncommon. The sociologists Jennifer Lee and Jody Agius found that Latina cashiers were likely to be more friendly toward white customers than toward other Latinas. The reason? The Latina cashiers believed the white customers raised their own status by proxy, and therefore gave them preferential treatment.

This may be one reason Fatima occasionally pretends not to speak Spanish—even to other Dominicans. She tells a story about a customer who asked for chicken fingers. Fatima had been speaking to her in English but did not immediately respond to her request. The customer's companion said to her, in Spanish, "Go slowly. I don't think she understands what you're saying." Not only did Fatima understand her English, and her Spanish, but she shared her ethnicity. As Fatima explains, laughing, "She's Dominican! I can see by her accent she's Dominican. I'm Dominican."

---

On another Tuesday night at the Cheyenne, a young man in his midtwenties pushes through the glass door at 3:30 AM carrying several buckets and an invoice for Fatima. The two of them chat a bit, and then he sets to work with a large metal can and a spray hose.

Rick has worked the nightshift as an exterminator for seven years. Spraying sixty-seven restaurants in Manhattan every week, it is one of the few jobs that require the cover of darkness to be effective. As he explains against the backdrop of Mr. Gerry beating eggs, "It would really screw up your whole day if you went to have lunch at a really busy delicatessen and a guy was walking around with a respirator. It would kill business real quick."

Working nights, Rick shares some of the social disconnection felt by Fatima and Juan, though one defined by time rather than distance. He hardly sees his wife and child, and has no time for a social life. For Rick, this is a benefit of the nightshift: "It's like two ships passing in the night, which, believe it or not, is helpful for a marriage." A nightshift job can bring a welcome social distance from domestic problems that may seem intractable. Melbin cites family tension as a reason some choose to move out of phase from the rest of the household. However, the dislocation and alienation of the nightshift affect far more than one's marriage. Rick also admits that he has few friends. Though native-born, Rick knows the same isolation as Fatima, Juan, and Mr. Gerry, demonstrating the power of night as a kind of transgressed border that makes everyone feel out of place. For this reason, they are drawn to a community they create themselves—of those who work nights.

Asked if they miss the sun, Rick replies, "No, the exact opposite."

"I don't want to see the sun," Fatima interjects. "You get used to the nighttime and don't want to see the sun. It bothers my eyes. My curtains are completely black."

Fatima and Rick both laugh, sharing a knowing look. Then Fatima adds, "We're like vampires."

The phone rings and Fatima brightens as she answers it, putting up a bubbly front for the customers on the other end of the line. She jots down a few orders, confirms with Mr. Gerry, and hangs up the receiver.

"Delivery!" she calls into the intercom to Juan.

Mr. Gerry throws a few burgers onto the grill, and Rick says his good-byes.

At 5 AM, the day's fresh supply of bagels and juice is delivered. Though there's still a full moon hanging over the twenty-four-hour post office across the street, you can feel the city waking up. A young woman, rested, showered, and coiffed, sits on the diner's front steps sending a text message on her Palm Treo before coming inside for a toasted bagel with cream cheese.

Fatima leans back against the counter, a far-off look in her eye and a rare sag around her shoulders.

"I am always more tired after my day off," she says. "My body is more tired."

Juan appears from downstairs and takes the order from her hands. Then he is off into the night again on his battered gray and green Mongoose Basher bicycle.

Fatima finally admits, "Tonight I want to go home." But she does not mean her small, lonely apartment in the Bronx.

"Santo Domingo," she clarifies. "Here is not my home."

# EPILOGUE: DAYBREAK

I t's 2 AM in early summer and we stand at the confluence of Broadway, Seventh Avenue, and 42nd Street. There are only a few more hours before the sky begins to lighten in the east, but it was Friday night a mere two hours ago, so the wide sidewalks are still a crush of revelers. Some sailors saunter past, their crisp white, bell-bottom uniforms standing out in the crowd. They seem out of place, anachronistic, and yet so thrillingly, timelessly part of Times Square. It's also prom season, and a few dozen teenagers wobble on their high heels under the lights of Broadway, their dates disheveled and trailing behind. Some pause before a hansom cab, clumsily pet the horse, and move on. The coachman will work another hour, then guide his carriage back to the stable.

In these hours before daybreak, Times Square is still a garish explosion of electricity. The low clouds and early morning mist refract the glow of billboard-sized video screens, scrolling marquees, and the brilliant storefronts that stay lit long after closing. The air itself seems weighed down with light.

A few blocks south, and light evaporates. The nightshift city falls into its more familiar darkness, punctuated here and there by an island of light, a café or corner deli. In the dark, Broadway is just another street.

"We don't close," says John, the Korean cashier at an overlit café a bit south of Times Square. He wears a khaki uniform—pants, button-down shirt, and cap—and stands at the register from 7 PM to 7 AM seven days a week. "I'm slim but my calves are strong," he explains. "I can sleep standing."

Before coming to work in the café, John was a successful entrepreneur in wholesale fabrics. "John" is the name his clients and partners called him in his eight years in textiles. The name stuck, but the business didn't. "We grew too fast," he says, "and we collapsed too fast."

The overhead speakers slip into a Grateful Dead tune, "Touch of Grey," as John describes his life now. He sees his daughter on weekends when she is not in school, and hardly sees his wife at all. That's okay with John; as he explains, when you have only an hour together you have lots to say. He smiles and says, "I make less than 10 percent of what I used to make in my business, but somehow I feel happy. I feel blessed."

---

Most of the nightshift workers we've met can easily list the benefits of a life lived out of sync. Steve at the Skylight and Fatima at the Cheyenne enjoy the autonomy afforded by the nightshift; the owners are asleep and there is no one looking over their shoulders as they go about their work. Parents can arrange their schedules so that one parent is always at home with their children. Both Sunny in Brooklyn and Louie at the Skylight talked about the simple pleasure of bringing breakfast to children at the end of their shift. Hassan at the Lucky Stop Deli and Alam at a café in Penn Station like the slower pace at night, finding that having fewer customers makes the nightshift "easier" than the dayshift. Taxi drivers Cliff and Malik both commented on the lighter traffic at night. Nurses, taxi drivers, and Peter at JFK often earn more money from the night differential, a bonus for the hardship of working all night. And today women are not only "allowed" to work nights, they can pursue full-time careers without having to hire full-time caregivers. Esther spoke about being able to contribute to her church in a larger way by working nights than she could by working days. Friends and community are not optional, in her view. "I want to have a community life," she said. "I want to have friends. I want to help them. I want them to help me. So that depends on me, on how I deal with people."

But few choose the nightshift for any of these reasons. For many, it is the only shift available. They may have children at home and need the flexibility of an off-hour shift to manage childcare. They may be new to a profession such as nursing or mass transit where dayshifts come with seniority. Or perhaps their language skills or immigrant status force, or enable, their employers to keep them hidden on the nightshift.

Steve and Fatima may have more autonomy at night, but surveillance cameras linked to the owners' home computers watch their every move. Sunny may be able to bring his granddaughter breakfast, but he has to comfort her by telephone when she can't sleep at night. Peter had to take a semester off from school because his "cognitive functioning" decreased, his GPA suffered, he gained weight, and though he laughs about it, he falls asleep on nights out with friends. Fatima pays more for health care because she is off only on Sunday nights and does not have time to wait at the hospital. Families must choreograph their lives around the worker who must sleep while they are awake and leave for work as they prepare to sleep. It is enormously difficult for nightshift workers to make contributions to their communities, both because they are always tired and because they are often at or on the way to work when meetings or other civic activities occur. And it is bad for one's health to work nights. Digestion problems, obesity, and a host of other bodily calamities occur when the diurnal eating life is overturned to accommodate a nightshift schedule. The reasons given for why an individual chooses or ends up on the nightshift vary, but for the roughly 7 percent of the city's workforce that works some portion of the night, the difficulties can be startlingly similar.

A slender orange volume titled *Night Work: Its Effects on the Health and Welfare of the Worker* was one of the first treatises on this subject. Published in 1977 by the International Labor Organization in Geneva, the report outlines the many negative effects of nightshift labor, ultimately calling for a ban on night work or, at the very least, strict regulations. *Night Work* was a response to the consequences of an emerging global incessant economy, the offspring of worldwide industrialization. Thirty years on, that global incessant economy is in full swing, supporting a modern postindustrial distribution of production that depends on labor twenty-four hours a day, seven days a week. We cannot comprehend the texture of modern society if we fail to understand the experiences of the millions of people who work nights as part of this new economy. Not least because the nightshift is too easily overlooked as a site of exploitation—something Karl Marx understood more than a century ago. As geography has collapsed in on itself through transnationalism, time is the new measure of cultural and political economic distance. New immigrants increasingly fill the thankless, relentless nightshift jobs for wages that barely cover rent and that keep them separated from family back home.

And yet. As with most cumbersome, historically produced systems of inequality, power is applied from multiple competing sources and rather inconsistently—there is always room for individuals to exercise resistance and turn the system to their own advantage. There are indeed high costs to the health, families, and social lives of those who work nights. But nightshift workers put a premium on the autonomy their shift affords them, sense greater cohesion among coworkers at night, savor the stillness impossible by day in New York City, and often see it as a temporary way to pursue goals such as raising small children, going to school, or gaining necessary work experience. The isolation and inversion of the nightshift are damaging, but regulations limiting or banning nightshift labor would not be as productive as requiring that employers pay a night differential in either money or extended time off to compensate for the adverse health and social effects. The problems and their solutions will not be found in unilateral pronouncements based on statistical summaries. Like most phenomena in society, they are complex, requiring sustained engagement with the experiences of real people on the ground in the night doing their jobs and living their lives.

————————

Back in the café just south of Times Square, John watches a group of barely clothed women stagger past the open door. Their dates linger at the entrance, then hurry to catch up. He chuckles and says, "Crazy people are intimidated. They don't come in here. I don't know why." In the back, a crew of construction workers clad in dusty jeans and reflective vests gather up their hardhats and make for the exit. We watch them trudge through the door, back to their jobs, and we decide to follow them out.

John smiles, then waves goodbye. As we leave, Jerry Garcia sings, "I will get by . . ."

Broadway from 42nd Street to 14th Street is interrupted by squares, from Times to Union, each with its own character and history. Moving south between the gaudy glare of Times Square and the quiet, unassuming slumber of Herald Square, the sidewalks are deserted. Storefronts are locked tight behind metal gates, and even the apartment buildings look abandoned. The only light comes from the receding haze of 42nd Street behind a range of skyscrapers and the street lamps that cast a green pall over everything.

Herald Square at 34th Street is quiet as well, though there is a slight quickening of traffic, schools of yellow taxis gliding toward the clubs a few blocks south. Small cliques of young men and women emerge from the subways below. They do their little orientation dance, heads swiveling, trying to get their bearings, then move south in the direction of the taxis. On one corner, a vendor and his cart wait for the occasional late-night customer. He's from Bangladesh and has manned the cart for three years from 7 PM to 3:30 AM. He is alone in the silent square, but he is not afraid. "There are lots of police," he says, and points out cops patrolling the large intersection in pairs. A couple of bars in the immediate area provide him with all of his customers after midnight and his only bathroom at this hour.

Continuing south on Broadway, we pass more and more people, all of them Asian, departing from clubs on 32nd Street in Little Korea. Department of Sanitation trucks roar past, their nightshift crews collecting trash up and down the subdued side streets. In the distance, the Empire State Building on Fifth Avenue stands lightless in the gathering fog.

Nine blocks south is Madison Square, and in between, a half dozen nightclubs spill their music and patrons onto the streets. Each club is marked off by velvet ropes, a crowd of hopefuls waiting for burly bouncers to let them pass, and the ever-present street vendor sending his oily smoke into the air. By the time we reach the park at Madison Square, at ten minutes to 3 AM, the crowds outside the clubs pool in the streets instead of the sidewalks. The atmosphere is tense: voices are raised, a scuffle or two breaks out. It is all suddenly pierced by the wail of a siren. Two, then three, police cars race down Broadway and into the square. They pass the crowds and career into the park itself. More arrive from the other side, and cops on foot dash in after them. For a moment the leafy park is a fantastic light show of red, white, and blue.

Passing under the prow of the Flatiron building at 23rd Street, we move on toward Union Square. We pass a yellow taxi, red and blue lights flashing. It's an undercover police car disguised as a cab, known as a "6Y" medallion, and two cops are frisking three black men. Across the street, three young white men argue loudly, one throws a punch. They turn, notice the police, and hurry on. And finally, at the northern edge of Union Square, a beleaguered newsstand clerk sits a few feet away from a dozen or so shadowy figures huddled around the entrance to the small park. "They're always there," he says angrily. "They're smoking crack."

———————

In the night, nothing is what it seems. A taxi turns out to be a police car. Young women who look like sex workers turn out to be on their way back from prom. A homeless man turns out to be an outreach worker, and the dapper man in the suit turns out to be homeless. This is the city at night as many would expect, playing to the stereotype of lowered inhibitions and vice. Darkness may awaken latent fears, but it is the excitement that a border has been crossed and the normal rules of society have been suspended—at least for a few precious hours—that makes the night transgressive, dangerous, and thrilling to those who work in the day. For those who work in the night, the dayshift interlopers are like foreign tourists; they exoticize what seems utterly mundane but pay handsomely for the privilege.

There is hardly a site of nightshift labor that is not affected by these lowered inhibitions, especially when they are mixed with alcohol. Rarely does a street vendor, deli clerk, or train conductor have to manage an abusive, inebriated customer on the dayshift. At night, it is a routine part of the job. Hassan and Sunny keep baseball bats and sticks handy, while others, like Fatima, rely on psychology and the power of suggestion in handling unruly patrons. Nightshift train conductors double as bouncers, and diners double as bars. The economy of the night itself is fueled by alcohol. From the ferries to the trains, the diners to the delis, alcohol is sold and consumed throughout the nightshift city.

Nightshift workers are not immune. At a deli across from the newsstand at Union Square, eight men sit on stools in the back drinking from a case of Heineken. They are all from Mexico, and they all work at a furniture store on the block. It's 3 AM and they've been off work for a couple of hours. A few beers at the deli at the end of the Friday night shift is a burgeoning tradition for the group; they all work together but they live "all over." Others on the nightshift have found ways to reconcile the socially acceptable after-hours drink with an off-hour shift. It may be 8 AM, but they've just worked a twelve-hour shift on a fishing boat, in a hospital, or serving rowdy customers in a diner or deli. So like many others, they have a few drinks with friends after work and learn to ignore the sideways glances from morning commuters with their oversized coffees, possibly the same folks who had a few too many the night before.

In these pages, we've attempted to bring into focus people and predicaments one rarely sees no matter how late one travels into the night. The early morning after-work drink is but one example of how nightshift workers must accommodate a life out of phase with the rest of the city. Sleep is put off until daylight, if not sacrificed entirely to make time for the family, friends, and commonplace responsibilities that still run on a diurnal schedule. Breakfast, lunch, and dinner lose all meaning as meals that mark time. Jessica, a nurse on the PICU, renames her meals as prelunch lunch, lunch, postlunch lunch, and breakfast. And since most of nightshift workers' waking lives are lit with artificial light, the sun no longer heralds the day; it is an obstacle to sleep. Jessica has used blackout curtains and a sleeping mask, while her coworker Tamar sleeps with a hood over her eyes.

These sacrifices of a life out of phase make the global incessant economy possible. Whether the late-night impulse cravings supplied by diners and delis, or the more constant, democratic necessities of security, transportation, and emergency services, the dayshift city cannot exist without nightshift labor. They are the skeleton crew that keeps the city running as it slows but never stops in its nighttime slumber, and they deserve a level of respect that factors in the considerable obstacles they must overcome. If we took seriously the plight of those who toil through the night, we would recognize that they are not interchangeable but unique and skilled employees. We would provide office hours for nightshift workers to go to the doctor, dentist, union, or other routine necessities in the hours that fit their schedules. We would provide flex-time for nightshift workers with spouses and families, to choose how many hours a week they'd like to be together. We would be better friends, children, tenants, and neighbors to those who work nights, resisting the temptation to force the sleep-deprived to sleepwalk through our diurnal lives. This is a call for greater civic engagement, not necessarily government intervention. It's about respect, generosity, and kindness toward the person who's made possible whatever enjoyable experience the night has given to those of us who work days and play nights.

But the night does end.

———————

Sitting on the low-slung steps at the southern edge of Union Square at 4:30 AM, we wait for the first hint of morning light. The cement plaza here surrounds a statue of George Washington and still holds memories of twenty-four-hour vigils in the aftermath of 9/11. By midday it will be crowded with students and street performers, protestors and salesmen. For now, it is almost empty. The faint scent of bleach hangs in the air, barely masking the pungent smell of urine. Public bathrooms are hard enough to find during the day, all the more so at night. A few clubgoers cross the empty space on their way to the subway and a pair of tattooed cops head for the precinct under the plaza. Four sailors strut across 14th Street, their uniforms still crisp, still white after a night on the town. To the right, art vendors have already set up their tables to stake out their spaces, napping briefly on benches until morning. It's still dark but the birds begin to sing. It's a startling sound, reminding us of its absence for the past several hours and audible only because the rest of the city has yet to rise.

In these moments between the last bar closing and the first store opening, long before the sun crests over the far edge of Queens, there is a change in the night that anticipates daybreak. But for the birds, the city settles into a preternatural quiet. Ferries steam across the harbor with more deckhands than passengers. Empty taxis line the curbs at designated shift-change locations. The diners have all sold their last hamburgers, and the bodegas their last beers. The sidewalks, streets, subways, and buses discharge the last of the inebriated and sleepless and wait in silence for the onslaught of dayshift commuters. Everywhere nightshift workers settle into the predawn calm, waiting for their dayshift replacements and another restless day's sleep. The city's public spaces are empty, unnervingly so.

In this calm space, a liminal time that is neither day nor night, all seems full of an elastic potential energy. The city is poised to snap back to normal, throwing all those now at rest into action, and allowing nightshift workers to melt into the daylight. Deckhands on a pier in Sheepshead Bay are hosing down the decks of the *Brooklyn VI*, the sun still hiding behind the bay and the ocean beyond. Taxi drivers lean on idle cabs sipping hot chai tea and gossiping about crooked brokers and exorbitant lease rates, the last fare logged in an hour or two earlier. The night manager at a Manhattan diner leans wearily on the counter, his face blank, lost in thought, as a man who may very well have nowhere else to go chatters on endlessly, mostly to himself. A second-year resident allows himself a moment's rest on a second-hand couch in the doctors' lounge, hoping none of his patients code until he gets at least an hour of good sleep. But like most things liminal, a state of inherent instability, the quiet won't last long.

Day breaks in the subways first as dayshift workers trundle onto the trains, wordless and drowsy. Next, the momentum of the new day bubbles up from below as the streets begin to flow with dayshift taxis. Sidewalks seem to narrow in the crush of fresh-faced pedestrians. The pace quickens as trains from Long Island and New Jersey arrive at Penn Station, flooding the terminal with suits, briefcases, and quarter-folded newspapers. Diners and bodegas fill up with early risers. Caffeine slowly replaces alcohol as the drug of choice, and one can feel the city rousing itself for another day.

Somewhere in the midst of this mounting activity, the nightshift workers have quietly punched out and begun the reverse commute toward home. Billy will enter his empty apartment wind-blown and weary, pop open a beer, and unwind before bed. James will hang up his doorman's uniform and make his way to the edge of Queens, perhaps stopping at the gym before calling it a night. Malik will park his cab on a corner in Manhattan and wait for his dayshift partner before taking the subway back to Brooklyn. Raif will walk the two blocks from his subway stop in Brooklyn, soaking in his five minutes of sun, before climbing into bed and praying no one needs the super this day. Fatima will call her mother in the Dominican Republic and chat with her daughters, growing up two thousand miles away, before going to sleep alone, again. Sunny will drive over to check on his second business, a deli in Queens, before heading home to a house full of family and two energetic grandchildren. Esther will change out of her hospital scrubs and commute home to Long Island, where she will cook up a large Malayalam breakfast for herself, and then try to sleep before the first lawnmower or car horn thwarts the attempt. For those ambling toward bed while most of the city rises, there is a kind of shallow victory in passing through another night.

And each night ends the same. Daybreak brings the sting of light and renewed life to the city as celebrity. As the sun rises, so do the metal gates protecting dayshift businesses from the uncertainty of a city on a sleepless binge. The nightshift workers and their helpmate patrons are in the shadows now. But so is the nightshift city, the other New York.

# ACKNOWLEDGMENTS

Where does a book begin, precisely? This book surely originated in part when Russell's grandmother, Marion, first took him to the Avalon Diner in Houston, Texas, sparking an enduring fascination with all things diner. There is also a large debt owed to his parents, Ralph and Ginny Sharman, for always encouraging his work, and Cheryl's, as writers and scholars. Corey wishes to acknowledge his wife, Marion Hayes, for her love and support and his parents, Jack and Peggy Hayes, for their lifelong encouragement. And we all recognize that none of this would be possible without a God for whom darkness is as light.

This particular book would not exist without those whose stories fill its pages: Steve, Malik, Cliff, Peter, Rachel, Jessica, Tamar, Angela, Catherine, Dave, Esther, Hassan, Sunny, Jahi, Jill, Ahmed, Lamine, Alam, Raif, George, Will, Barry, Murray, Ricardo, James, Billy, Alanna, Ben, Chuck, Tom, Pan, Tim, Naima, Apple Annie, Fatima, Juan, Mr. Gerry, Rick, and John. There are countless more amazing nightshift laborers in New York City who took the time to talk with us and, though not in the book by name, their experiences added much to our understanding. Even beyond New York, wherever we went we encountered many people who had worked nights at some stage in their lives, who recounted in proud and wearied tones how hard it was, and each such conversation helped in some small way.

Research and writing assistance came in many forms. A friend as solid as they come, the writer Owen Egerton accompanied us on fieldwork, read drafts, and generally cheered us on. Friends and writers Jodi Egerton, Patton Dodd, Andrea Jeyaveeran, and Richard Vernon also deserve praise upon praise for reading drafts. Richard deserves an extra pint, or ten, for numerous instances of invaluable fact-finding assistance. Additional friends, students, and colleagues recommended books, articles, twenty-four-hour sites, and people who worked nights. Some of the most fruitful such tips came from the anonymous reviewers of the book proposal; from our friends Jeremy and Megan O'Grady, Mark Swanson, Ruben Austria, Tashya Leaman, Nancy Pedulla, Rebecca Fraser, Milind Sojwal, Jen Downs, Adam and Edith Barker, Shannon Haragan, and Tony Hale; Alex Vitale, Mariana Regalado, Deanna DeSilva, and Anila Thomas at Brooklyn College; anthropologist Ruth Behar; sociologist Sharon Zukin; urban planner Simone Buechler; the online reference librarians at the New York Public Library; and Association of Health Care Journalists members Diana Mason, Lynne Lamberg, Roxanne Nelson, and Abby Christopher. Thanks also to Elizabeth Bernstein and Priscilla Alexander for taking the time to enrich our understanding of the plight of sex workers. Brooklyn College provided Russell with some much-needed time off from teaching (and graciously scheduled what classes he did teach in the afternoon). Anthropologists Paul Stoller, Kirin Narayan, and Betsy Krause offered invaluable comments on the penultimate draft of the book. And special thanks to Nancy Foner and Michael Blim who, as usual, offered much-needed encouragement.

Finally, immense thanks to our editor, Stan Holwitz, for his enthusiastic support of this and all our other projects. Without an editor, an idea remains only that: an idea.

# REFERENCES AND SUGGESTED READING

## THE NIGHT

Caldwell, Mark. *New York Night: The Mystique and Its History.* New York: Scribner, 2005.

Coyne, Kevin. *A Day in the Night of America.* New York: Random House, 1992.

Gies, Martha. *Up All Night.* Corvallis: Oregon State University Press, 2004.

Jakle, John A. *City Lights: Illuminating the American Night.* Baltimore: Johns Hopkins University Press, 2001.

Melbin, Murray. *Night as Frontier: Colonizing the World after Dark.* New York: Free Press, 1987.

Schivelbusch, Wolfgang. *Disenchanted Night: The Industrialization of Light in the Nineteenth Century.* Berkeley and Los Angeles: University of California Press, 1988.

## NEW YORK CITY

Burrows, Edwin G., and Mike Wallace. *Gotham: A History of New York City to 1898.* New York: Oxford University Press, 1999.

Hamill, Pete. *Downtown: My Manhattan.* New York: Little, Brown, 2004.

Jackson, Kenneth T., ed. *The Encyclopedia of New York City.* New Haven, CT: Yale University Press, 1995.

Lopate, Phillip. *Waterfront: A Journey around Manhattan.* New York: Crown Publishers, 2004.

Mitchell, Joseph. *Up in the Old Hotel and Other Stories.* New York: Pantheon Books, 1992.

New York Civil Liberties Union. *Who's Watching: Video Camera Surveillance in New York City and the Need for Public Oversight.* Fall 2006.

Rosenblum, Constance, ed. *New York Stories: The Best of the City Section of the New York Times.* New York: New York University Press, 2005.

Sanders, James. *Celluloid Skyline: New York and the Movies.* New York: Random House, 2001.

White, E. B. *Here Is New York.* New York: Harper, 1949.

Whitehead, Colson. *The Colossus of New York: A City in Thirteen Parts.* New York: Doubleday, 2003.

## LABOR AND SHIFT WORK

Beers, Thomas M. "Flexible Schedules and Shift Work: Replacing the '9-to-5' Workday?" *Monthly Labor Review* 123 (2000): 33.

Bowe, John, Marisa Bowe, and Sabin C. Streeter. *Gig: Americans Talk about Their Jobs at the Turn of the Millennium.* New York: Crown Publishers, 2000.

Folkard, S., and T. H. Monk, eds. *Hours of Work: Temporal Factions in Work-Scheduling.* New York: John Wiley and Sons, 1985.

Granovetter, Mark S. *Getting a Job: A Study of Contacts and Careers.* Cambridge, MA: Harvard University Press, 1974.

Rosa, Roger R., and Michael J. Colligan. *Plain Language about Shiftwork.* Cincinnati: National Institute for Occupational Safety and Health, 1997.

Terkel, Studs. *Working.* New York: Pantheon Books, 1974.

U.S. Department of Labor. *Workers on Flexible and Shift Schedules in May 2004.* Washington, DC: Bureau of Labor Statistics, 2005.

## HEALTH EFFECTS

Basner, Robert C. "Shift-Work Sleep Disorder: The Glass Is More Than Half Empty." *New England Journal of Medicine* 353, no. 5 (2005): 519–521.

———. "Sleep Deprivation: Clinical Issues, Pharmacology, and Sleep Loss Effects." *New England Journal of Medicine* 352, no. 20 (2005): 2145–2146.

Campbell, Scott S., Charmane I. Eastman, Michael Terman, Alfred J. Lewy, Ziad Boulos, and Derk-Jan Dijk. "Light Treatment for Sleep Disorders: Consensus Report." *Journal of Biological Rhythms* 10, no. 2 (1995): 105–109.

Carpentier, James, and Pierre Cazamian. *Night Work: Its Effects on the Health and Welfare of the Worker.* Geneva: International Labor Organization, 1977.

Caruso, Claire C., Edward M. Hitchcock, Robert B. Dick, John M. Russo, and Jennifer M. Schmit. *Overtime and Extended Work Shifts: Recent Findings on Illnesses, Injuries, and Health Behaviors.* Cincinnati: National Institute for Occupational Safety and Health, 2004.

Chen, Honglei, Eva Schernhammer, Michael Schwarzschild, and Alberto Ascherio. "A Prospective Study of Night Shift Work, Sleep Duration, and Risk of Parkinson's Disease." *American Journal of Epidemiology* 163, no. 8 (2006): 726–730.

Czeisler, Charles A., James K. Walsh, Thomas Roth, Rod J. Hughes, Kenneth P. Wright, Lilliam Kingsbury, Sanjay Arora, Jonathan Schwartz, Gwendolyn E. Niebler, and David F. Dinges for the U.S. Modafinil in Shift Work Sleep Disorder Study Group. "Modafinil for Excessive Sleepiness Associated with Shift-Work Sleep Disorder." *New England Journal of Medicine* 353, no. 5 (2005): 476–486.

Kushida, Clete A., ed. *Sleep Deprivation: Basic Science, Physiology, and Behavior.* New York: Marcel Dekker, 2005.

Lamberg, Lynne. *Bodyrhythms: Chronobiology and Peak Performance.* New York: William Morrow and Company, 1994.

Lamberg, Lynne, and Michael Smolensky. *The Body Clock Guide to Better Health: How to Use Your Body's Natural Clock to Fight Illness and Achieve Maximum Health.* New York: Henry Holt & Company, 2000.

Ribeiro-Silva, Flaviany, Lucia Rotenberg, Renata Elisa Soares, Joseane Pessanha, Flavia Leticia Ferreira, Paula Oliveira, Aline Silva-Costa, and Ana Amelia Benedito-Silva. "Sleep on the Job Partially Compensates for Sleep Loss in Night-Shift Nurses." *Chronobiology International: The Journal of Biological and Medical Rhythm Research* 23, no. 6 (2006): 1389–1399.

Santhi, Nayantara, Jeanne F. Duffy, Todd S. Horowitz, and Charles A. Czeisler. "Scheduling of Sleep/Darkness Affects the Circadian Phase of Night Shift Workers." *Neuroscience Letters* 384 (2005): 316–320.

Straif, Kurt, Robert Baan, Yann Grosse, Béatrice Secretan, Fatiha El Ghissassi, Véronique Bouvard, Andrea Altieri, Lamia Benbrahim-Tallaa, and Vincent Cogliano. "Carcinogenicity of Shift-work, Painting, and Fire-fighting." *The Lancet Oncology* 8, no. 12 (2007): 1065–1066.

van Mark, Anke, Michael Spallok, Richard Kessel, and Elke Brinkmann. "Shift Work and Pathological Conditions." *Journal of Occupational Medicine and Toxicology* (2006): doi:10.1186/1745-6673-1-25.

Duneier, Mitchell. *Sidewalk*. New York: Farrar, Straus and Giroux, 1999.

Rossi, Peter H. *Down and Out in America: The Origins of Homelessness*. Chicago: University of Chicago Press, 1989.

Snow, David A., and Leon Anderson. *Down on Their Luck: A Study of Homeless Street People*. Berkeley and Los Angeles: University of California Press, 1993.

## SERVICE INDUSTRY

Agius, Jody A., and Jennifer Lee. "Raising the Status of the Cashier: Latina White Interactions in an Ethnic Market." *Sociological Forum* 21, no. 2 (2006): 197–218.

Bearman, Peter S. *Doormen*. Chicago: University of Chicago Press, 2005.

Bodega Association of the United States, Inc., website at www.bodegaassociation .org.

Gutman, Richard. *American Diner*. New York: Harper & Row, 1979.

Hochschild, Arlie R. *The Managed Heart: Commercialization of Human Feeling*. Berkeley and Los Angeles: University of California Press, 1983.

Paules, Greta Foff. *Dishing It Out: Power and Resistance among Waitresses in a New Jersey Restaurant*. Philadelphia: Temple University Press, 1991.

Sirianni, Carmen, and Cameron L. Macdonald. *Working in the Service Society*. Philadelphia: Temple University Press, 1996.

## HEALTH CARE INDUSTRY

Aiken, Linda H. "U.S. Nurse Labor Market Dynamics Are Key to Global Nurse Sufficiency." *Health Services Research* (2007): doi:10.1111/j.1475-6773.2007 .00714.x.

Brown, Verlia. "From the President: Happy Birthday, America." *Report: The Official Newsletter of the New York State Nurses Association*, July/August 2006. www.nysna.org/departments/communications/publications/report/2006/jul_ aug/president.htm (accessed 4/9/2007).

Center for Health Workforce Studies. "Preliminary Findings from a Survey of Hospital Registered Nurses in New York." School of Public Health, University of Albany, SUNY, December 2006.

Cunningham, Peter, and Jessica May. *Insured Americans Drive Surge in Emergency Department Visits*. Washington, DC: Center for Studying Health System Change, 2003.

Novak, R. D., and S. E. Auvil-Novak. "Focus Group Evaluation of Night Nurse Shiftwork Difficulties and Coping Strategies." *Chronobiology International* 13, no. 6 (1996): 457–463.

Webber, Nancy. "The Nurse Shortage in New York: Where We Stand Now." *New York Nurse*, January 2007. www.nysna.org/departments/communications/publications/newyorknurse/jan/shortage.htm (accessed 4/9/2007).

## TRANSPORTATION INDUSTRY

Cudahy, Brian J. *Under the Sidewalks of New York: The Story of the Greatest Subway System in the World.* New York: Stephen Greene Books, 1988.

Gambetta, Diego, and Heather Hamill. *Streetwise: How Taxi Drivers Establish Their Customers' Trustworthiness.* New York: Russell Sage, 2005.

Mathew, Biju. *Taxi! Cabs and Capitalism in New York City.* New York: New Press, 2005.

U.S. Department of Labor. *Risk Factors and Protective Measures for Taxi and Livery Drivers.* Washington, DC: Occupational Safety and Health Administration, 2000.

## FISHING INDUSTRY

Burger, J., B. B. Johnson, S. Shukla, and M. Gochfeld. "Perceptions of Recreational Fishing Boat Captains: Knowledge and Effects of Fish Consumption Advisories." *Risk Analysis: An International Journal* 23, no. 2 (2003): 369–378.

Burger, Joanna, Kerry Kirk Pflugh, Lynette Lurig, Leigh Ann Von Hagen, and Stanley Von Hagen. "Fishing in Urban New Jersey: Ethnicity Affects Information Sources, Perception, and Compliance." *Risk Analysis* 19, no. 2 (1999): 217–229.

Environmental Defense. *Sustaining America's Fisheries and Fishing Communities.* www.environmentaldefense.org/documents/6119_sustainingfisheries.pdf (accessed 3/29/2007).

Kurlansky, Mark. *Cod.* New York, Penguin, 1997.

———. *The Big Oyster.* New York: Random House, 2007.

Mid-Atlantic Fishery Management Council. *2003 Proposed and Final Federal Recreational Management Measures.* www.mafmc.org/mid-atlantic/publications/regulation/regulations-03.pdf (accessed 3/29/2007).

———. *2007 Proposed and Final Federal Recreational Management Measures.* www.mafmc.org/mid-atlantic/publications/regulation/regulations-07.pdf (accessed 3/29/2007).

New York State Department of Environmental Conservation. *Marine Recreational Fishing Laws and Regulations, June 16, 2006.* Bureau of Marine Resources. www.dec.state.ny.us/website/dfwmr/marine/finfish/fishlimits.pdf (accessed 3/29/2007).

Toth, John F., Jr., and Ralph B. Brown. "Racial and Gender Meanings of Why People Participate in Recreational Fishing." *Leisure Science* 19 (1997): 129–146.

Worm, Boris, Edward J. Barbier, Nicola Beaumont, J. Emmett Duffy, Carl Folke, Benjamin S. Halpern, Jeremy B. C. Jackson, Heike K. Lotze, Fiorenza Micheli, Stephen R. Palumbi, Enric Sala, Kimberley A. Selkoe, John J. Stachowicz, and Reg Watson. "Impacts of Biodiversity Loss on Ocean Ecosystem Services." *Science* 314 (2006): 787–790.

## SOCIAL THEORY

Anderson, Benedict. *Imagined Communities.* New York: Verso, 1991.

Bourdieu, Pierre. *Distinction.* Cambridge, MA: Harvard University Press, 1984.

Foucault, Michel. *Discipline and Punish.* New York: Pantheon, 1977.

Giddens, Anthony. *The Runaway World: How Globalization Is Shaping Our Lives.* New York: Routledge, 2000.

Gitlin, Todd. *Media Unlimited: How the Torrent of Images and Sounds Overwhelms Our Lives.* New York: Henry Holt, 2002.

Goffman, Erving. *The Presentation of Self in Everyday Life.* New York: Doubleday/Anchor, 1959.

Jacobs, Jane. *The Death and Life of Great American Cities.* New York: Random House, 1961.

Lemert, Charles. *Social Theory: The Multicultural and Classic Readings.* 3rd edition. Boulder, CO: Westview Press, 2004.

Sassen, Saskia. *The Global City: New York, London, Tokyo.* Princeton, NJ: Princeton University Press, 1991.

Sennett, Richard, and Jonathan Cobb. *The Hidden Injuries of Class.* New York: Knopf, 1973.

Turner, Victor. *Dramas, Fields, and Metaphors.* Ithaca, NY: Cornell University Press, 1974.

Zukin, Sharon. *The Cultures of Cities.* Cambridge, MA: Blackwell, 1995.

# INDEX

**Designer**
J. G. Braun
**Text**
10/14 Janson
**Display**
Robust ICG
**Compositor**
Binghamton Valley Composition, LLC
**Printer and Binder**
Thomson-Shore, Inc.